International Trade and Political Institutions

With love to:
  Angus McGillivray-Smith;
  Duncan McGillivray-Smith;
  Rosalind Jill McLean;
  Duncan John McLean;
  Julie Marie Pahre;
  Eric William Pahre;
  Hannah Louise Schonhardt Bailey;
  Samuel John Schonhardt Bailey;
and those still to come.

International Trade and Political Institutions

Instituting Trade in the Long Nineteenth Century

Fiona McGillivray

Assistant Professor of Political Science, Yale University, USA

Iain McLean

Professor of Politics, Oxford University and Fellow, Nuffield College, Oxford, UK

Robert Pahre

Associate Professor of Political Science, University of Illinois, Urbana-Champaign, USA

Cheryl Schonhardt-Bailey

Senior Lecturer in Government, London School of Economics and Political Science, UK

Edward Elgar

Cheltenham, UK • Northampton, MA, USA

Published by
Edward Elgar Publishing Limited
Glensanda House
Montpellier Parade
Cheltenham
Glos GL50 1UA
UK

Edward Elgar Publishing, Inc.
136 West Street
Suite 202
Northampton
Massachusetts 01060
USA

A catalogue record for this book
is available from the British Library

Library of Congress Cataloguing in Publication Data

International trade and political institutions : instituting trade in the long 19th
century / Fiona McGillivray . . . [et al.].
     p. cm.
   "Earlier versions of the chapters were presented at a miniconference
'Instituting trade: trade policy and 19th century political institutions' at the
Center for Political Economy, Washington University, in 1997, and at the 1998
American Political Science Association Annual Meeting, Boston" — Pref.
   Includes bibliographical references and index.
   1. Commercial policy—History—19th century.   2. Tariff—History—19th
century.   3. International trade—History—19th century.   4. Institutional
economics—History—19th century.   I. McGillivray, Fiona, 1967–
HF1411.I51845   2001
382′.3′09034–dc21   2001023780

ISBN 1 84064 690 X

Printed and bound in Great Britain by MPG Books Ltd, Bodmin, Cornwall

Contents

List of Figures

List of Tables

Preface

We come from diverse backgrounds, but have a common interest. We discovered our common interest in the political economy of trade policy at conferences at which we met and explored our varying but complementary methods and findings. Our unity and diversity are nicely symmetrical. One of us is a Scot at an American university; one a Scot at an English university; one an American at an American university; and one an American at an English university.

Our case studies cover the 'long nineteenth century' from 1778 to 1914. This was the period in which emerged both classical patterns of trade and classical modes of thinking. We have found that, in thinking about our themes, our understanding of both trade and trade theory has deepened. Although each case study, and the conclusion, are individually authored, we have each reviewed one another's work. We almost (but not entirely) agree with one another. Our case studies are designed to work as 'analytic narratives' (cf. Bates et al., 1998). Whether they work as such is for the reader to judge. We thank each other, and our families, for mutual assistance and support. We are proud to dedicate this book to our children as inadequate compensation for seeing too little of them while we were working on it. Two of them arrived while this labour was also under way, and another is due before the book is published.

Earlier versions of these chapters were presented at a miniconference 'Instituting Trade: Trade Policy and 19th Century Political Institutions' at the Center for Political Economy, Washington University, in 1997, and at the 1998 American Political Science Association Annual Meeting, Boston Marriott Copley Place. We thank the chairs and discussants at those meetings, and Norman Schofield for arranging the Washington University miniconference. We also acknowledge our individual obligations as follows.

Pahre: This research was supported by a Rackham Graduate School Faculty Fellowship. It has benefited from comments by Pradeep Chhibber, Matthew Gabel, Ann Lin, Ronald Rogowski, and Michael Ross, and participants at a seminar at the University of Illinois Department of Political Science. I would like to thank José-Raúl Perales Hernandez for outstanding research assistance in putting together the database.

McGillivray: thanks for suggestions and criticisms from Lee Epstein, Matthew Gabel, Douglass North, Norman Schofield and Alastair Smith.

McLean: Grateful thanks to the Leverhulme Trust for funding, to Valerie Cromwell and D. R. Fisher for access to data, and to Beata Rozumilowicz and Camilla Bustani for locating and coding data.

Schonhardt-Bailey: Many people have contributed their thoughts, suggestions and criticisms to my chapter and conclusion in their various forms, including Andrew Bailey, Fabio Franchino, Doug Irwin, David Lake, and Timothy McKeown. I owe special thanks to Kenneth Shepsle. I have also benefited from the feedback of several audiences including: the 1995 and 1998 American Political Science Association annual meetings; the University of Sussex; the '1846 Freedom and Trade 1996: A Commemoration of the Repeal of the Corn Laws' conference; (Manchester 1996); "Instituting Trade: Trade Policy and 19th Century Political Institutions" mini-conference and the Rational Choice Group (October 1997).

New Haven; Oxford; Urbana; London. October 2000.

1. Tariffs and modern political institutions: an introduction

THE POLITICAL ECONOMY APPROACH TO TRADE POLICY

It is widely accepted that politics plays an important role in determining international trade policy. Pinning down why, and how, politics matters is more difficult. Economic theory tells us that any two individuals can make themselves better off by engaging in trade. Even though one individual might be absolutely better than the other at making a variety of goods, if they both focus their efforts on those goods that they are relatively better at making, and then engage in trade, they are both better off. This simple interaction needs no monitoring, coordination or enforcement by the state. Prices are determined by the market, itself affected by assets, technology and the desires of individuals.

Parallel arguments have suggested since the 1700s that nations benefit from trade in much the same way as individuals (Irwin, 1996). If nations specialize in those goods that they are relatively better at making, and exchange these for goods that they produce less well, then all nations will have more of the goods they desire.

Despite these benefits of trade, the politics of free trade are fraught with controversy. Historically, few nations have wholeheartedly adopted free trade policies. Most nations today maintain some protectionist policies, including tariffs, import quotas and indirect barriers such as regulatory restrictions or subsidy assistance. When nations do engage in free trade, they typically 'manage' it through international institutions and multilateral or bilateral trade treaties (Bagwell and Staiger, 1990).

Neoclassical economics provides few reasons why governments interfere in the market for international trade. Certainly most economic officials would agree that free trade maximizes total world output, at least in principle. However, leaders are concerned not just with maximizing the size of the world's pie. Leaders are practical men and women, not scholars of international trade theory. They are interested in 'assembling and retaining political support, winning elections, and building institutional power bases' (Shepsle, 1985: 235). If this means sacrificing the overall size of the pie in

1

order to get a larger slice for their supporters, then they will make the sacrifice. Nations engage in international trade not only to maximize joint output but to distribute the wealth that trade creates.

These basic facts immediately raise the question of whose welfare matters – that of the nation as a whole, or that of individuals and groups within it? Kenneth Arrow (1951) conclusively demonstrated that there is no unique, right or appropriate way to aggregate the welfare of individuals into the welfare of the group, that is, into a single social welfare function (see also Gibbard, 1969; Satterthwaite, 1975). Even if there were a single social welfare function, politicians would have no particular reason to maximize it. Political leaders do not enact policies that enhance some mystical idea of the social good. Instead, they use policies and the resources at their disposal to enhance the welfare of those who support them in order to maximize their own political support (see Pahre, Chapter 2). Politicians formulate trade policy with a view to the political costs and benefits it affords them in the political market for trade policy (Magee, Brock and Young, 1989).

Understanding trade policy therefore requires the study of this political market. We will use an approach to this study called public choice theory. Public choice uses the tools of modern economics to analyse the workings of political institutions and the behaviour of governments (Frey, 1984; Mueller, 1989). Political leaders are self-interested actors whose choice of strategies is shaped by the institutional context in which they find themselves, and the welfare of the key individuals who enable them to keep their jobs. The political institutions and the social rules and norms of a given polity determine who these individuals are, as well as the balance of political power among trade-affected interests, and the extent to which politicians seek to appease these interests in formulating trade policy.

In this framework, differences in political institutions explain why nations adopt different trade policies even though their leaders all pursue the same basic objective. Different political rules lead to different political outcomes. Understanding the effects of these rules normally requires, then, a comparative perspective that allows us to test hypotheses about institutions in different political, cultural and ideological environments. Through such research we may improve our understanding of how ideas, material interests and institutions matter, by developing theoretical case studies of comparable past events.

These institutions vary not only from one country to another but across time in a single country. Not only comparative study but comparative historical study is appropriate.

Since policies are shaped by the rules of the game, and these policies determine the identities of the winners, it is not surprising that political competition should extend to the choice of the rules. Each individual wants to structure the rules so as to favour policies that promise redistributive benefits for him or herself. Conflict thus ensues over the choice of rules. The intensity of this conflict, and the importance of its results for all subsequent decisions, policies and hence economic and social development, are what makes the study of institutional formation essential (Calvert, 1995). Understanding these changes in rules points us towards the study of history.

Throughout these historical processes, social interaction is also governed by ideas. Ideas affect what people want, in that they may shape preferences (Schonhardt-Bailey, Chapter 5). Ideas may also shape how people think they can achieve the ends they desire. McLean's Chapter 4 provides an example of this role of ideas, documenting how beliefs possibly shaped Peel's and Wellington's choices over trade policy in 1845–6. Ideas such as liberalism also lay behind many of the institutional changes we see over time, and thus have an indirect effect on trade policy outcomes.

In sum, then, explaining trade policy requires that we begin with material interests. Yet any account based solely on material interests must be incomplete. For this reason, we then turn to institutions and/or ideas. Within this analytical framework, our approach is both historical and comparative. For convenience, we focus on the economies of the North Atlantic economy from 1783 to 1914. While Pahre's chapter provides an overview of trade cooperation in this entire region, the other chapters focus on some of the important individual states within it, especially the UK, Germany and the rising power of the USA.

Looking Backwards to see Forwards: Infusing Political Economy with History

Our comparative and historical perspective differs from most previous research on institutions within economics and political science, which has preferred to focus solely on contemporary institutions. Both non-Marxist political economy and public choice theory, for example, have been dominated by the study of postwar USA and the international organizations it created. Even when scholars have tried to detail the mechanics of institutional change, they have generally taken a more narrow perspective limited to the last half-century. For example, a literature on the changing delegation of trade policy through Reciprocal Trade Agreements Act (RTAA) and Fast Track authorization (Bailey, Goldstein and Weingast, 1997) has tended not to look back to trade policy delegation before World War I. With the partial exception of Britain, research on tariff policy in the nineteenth century using modern analytical tools is extremely rare.

This oversight is unfortunate. Historical work opens a rich database of institutional experience that has not been adequately exploited by the public choice, comparative or international relations literatures. Beyond mere data, history also highlights the importance of sequence, which now goes under the name of 'path dependence'. Understanding contemporary events requires a study of history because yesterday's events allow some choices today and preclude yet others.

What we are today reflects the past. During the historical period that we examine in this volume, the state widened its role in structuring conflict over trade policy. Interest groups, political parties, legislatures and an agenda-setting executive emerge as political institutions in Western Europe in the nineteenth century. This period also saw the birth of modern political ideologies. Liberalism became the central social movement of the nineteenth century, and provides a point of departure for its rivals such as Marxism, radicalism or nationalism. Indeed, one could argue that liberalism has provided an important part of the world-system's central ideology in the last two hundred years, along with universalist rationality, truth-seeking and a belief in assimilation through 'modernization' (Wallerstein, 1983, 1994).

International trade institutions also emerge during this period, notably frequent negotiations between countries over trade and routinized trade treaties with reciprocal most favoured nation (MFN) clauses. In Chapter 2, Pahre shows how politicians' pursuit of political support both leads them to impose tariffs and makes them willing to negotiate reciprocal reductions in these tariffs. Once in place, these institutions constrain domestic politics, which can no longer change trade policy rapidly in response to international economic change.

Besides the simple act of creation, the history of an institution affects its workings today. For example, in Chapter 3, McGillivray studies the origins of the commerce clause of the US Constitution, which centralized tariff-making authority in the federal Congress. This resulted in higher external state tariffs but helped liberalize world trade by forcing Britain to open some of its colonial markets to US products and shipping. This commerce clause then played an important role in US constitutional development by distinguishing interstate from intrastate commerce in a manner not found in most other nations.

Likewise, the history of an ideology affects its importance today. Anthony Howe (1997) has recently examined the repeated reinventions of free-trade liberalism in Britain, showing how interests and party politics regularly changed the meanings of this ideology. These changing meanings of liberalism are not evident even in a classic such as Charles Kindleberger's *Rise of Free Trade in Europe* (1975), which emphasized crossnational differences in liberalism but did not consider changes in the core of its meaning.

Free traders remain important supporters of trade liberalization through the World Trade Organization (WTO) today, but the current version of liberalism reflects changes in that history. Studying that history illuminates why free-trade liberals support the WTO while an ahistoric ideational approach would obscure the tensions in that ideology. Most nineteenth-century Liberals opposed signing the trade treaties upon which the WTO relies, preferring unilateral liberalization. The experience of the nineteenth-century regime and its breakdown between the world wars convinced most Liberals that negotiated tariff reductions, not unilateral liberalization, were most likely to lead to a world of freer trade. Only by looking at the history of the trade treaty regime and the changing ideology of free trade can we understand how free trade ideology became what it is today.

Besides affecting trade policy directly, ideologies also affect it indirectly by influencing voting behaviour. This relationship is central to Chapters 4 and 5, in which Schonhardt-Bailey and McLean examine how ideologies, religion and beliefs about the national interest shaped the vote in the UK and Germany. Schonhardt-Bailey explores the early years of a process that has become central to the right-of-centre catch-all parties in Britain, Germany and the USA. These parties build their appeal to non-members in part on the claim that their party represents the national interest in trade and other issues. Because a history of highly ideological parties makes this appeal more difficult, she argues, past institutional choices constrain ideological choices today. Such path dependence provides fertile ground for historical research.

While Schonhardt-Bailey looks at the opportunity to make new ideological appeals, McLean takes these ideologies as given. He emphasizes instead the consequences of these ideologies at the mass level and, more important, in structuring the options seen by leaders such as Peel or Wellington. He uses new archival research to show just how the institutional and ideological context of mid-century England gave Peel and Wellington room to manoeuvre in repealing the Corn Laws. McLean argues that leaders such as Peel can use ideology strategically to create free trade in a 'hostile' political environment. However, the effects of both institutions and ideologies are context-specific. Their histories matter, both theoretically and empirically.

For these reasons we believe that a comparative historical perspective can deepen our substantive understanding of the modern role of the state. Schonhardt-Bailey's Chapter 5 is the most explicitly comparative, while Pahre presents a broad overview of developments in other countries. In the other two chapters, comparisons occur across time within a single country. Such comparative historical research allows us to test hypotheses about institutions in different political, cultural and ideological environments. As a result, we may improve our understanding of how ideas, material interests and institutions matter, by developing theoretical case studies of comparable past events.

Like others, we reject a purely narrative account as practised by many traditional historians. Instead, we seek to structure our narrative theoretically, an approach that has come to be called – not surprisingly – analytical narratives (Bates et al., 1998). The common analytical theme in our historical analyses of interests, ideology and institutions is public choice theory (especially that subset of public choice theory known as endogenous tariff theory). Public choice theorists have built theories of institutions and to a lesser extent ideology (Hinich and Munger, 1994).

Through such studies, this volume seeks to broaden public choice theory in trade politics to allow for the study of ideas and institutions in a longer time horizon. We aim to deepen our substantive understanding of modern political institutions in the firm belief that where we are today is in large measure a function of the choices made by important ghosts of the past.

Existing Theories of Trade Policy

This approach is grounded not only in history but in the intellectual history of the field of international political economy (IPE). Existing theories of trade policy in both political science and economics have found themselves propelled in the direction of studying institutions and ideas. This is especially true in the literature known as endogenous tariff theory (ETT), the research tradition in IPE with the closest links to public choice theory.

There is little question that the study of institutions and ideas has received insufficient attention from the field of international political economy. Instead, material interests have been used as the main predictor of economic policy outcomes. This is most obvious in Marxist political economy, which emphasizes the material interests of classes. Yet neoclassical political economy's study of the material interests of firms, interest groups and consumer-voters shares this materialist focus. Because material interests have often provided compelling explanations for the formulation of public policy, it is not surprising that their importance often goes unchallenged by scholars.

Given this focus, theoretical debates have often raged not about whether interests matter but rather *whose* material interests matter most. For Marxists, the material interests of the class are key; for public choice theorists, the material interests of the individual consumer, firm or politician matter most; for many Realists, the material and security interests of the state determine outcomes. Scholars focusing on domestic political actors, such as the 'UCLA school of political economy', have examined whether the interests of owners of factors of production or the interests fixed to specific industries both predict trade policy outcomes (Frieden, 1991; Frieden and Rogowski, 1996; Rogowski, 1989; see also Gabel, 1998; Magee, 1972).

Despite their different emphases, all these approaches point to material interests as the primary explanation for political behaviour. Even so, recent years have seen each approach begin to include other kinds of explanation. Following Gramsci's lead, many Marxists have given ideology a more central place in their theories (Cox, 1981). Institutions such as the state also play an important role in many Marxist or Marxian theories (Skocpol, 1985). Realists find neo-Liberal theories of international institutions and social constructivist accounts of the national interest to be twin challenges demanding a response. Scholars focusing on domestic political actors increasingly acknowledge the importance of institutions in understanding endogenous tariff formation (Finger, Hall and Nelson, 1982). Other scholars have sought synthesis of several approaches built on interests and ideology (Goldstein and Keohane, 1993b).

While the exact reasons for this move vary by approach, each has faced problems such as those that Peter Gourevitch (1986: 113–19) identifies for the study of economic interest alone: while economic interest accounts for preferences it cannot explain how these preferences turn into policy, or how one group triumphs over another. These concerns have led to a focus on institutions and ideology in each approach. The following review points towards the substantive need for a better understanding of how institutions, ideology and material interests influence trade policy. Though some scholars seek a new paradigm for research based on either ideology or institutions, we believe it is rash to discard many of the insights that we have gained from an interest-based paradigm. Rather, what is needed is a selective integration of the interests, ideologies and institution literatures.

The International Level

The primary international-level explanations for variation in trade policy are realism, cooperation theory and hegemony theory. Though distinct, their intellectual histories overlap enough so that we may discuss them in tandem. All Realists assume that the state is the primary actor in international politics. Explaining trade policy therefore requires understanding the state's goals (Krasner, 1976, 1978). Some Realists emphasize national wealth as a central goal. They argue that states use market power to achieve wealth through optimal tariffs or other coercive trade policies (Conybeare, 1987; Lake, 1988). Hegemonic stability theory extends this reasoning to see how a single large state may or may not act in ways beneficial to the system as a whole (Keohane, 1984; Pahre, 1999). Other Realists argue that states must worry not about wealth but about *relative*

8

International trade and political institutions

wealth, because the anarchic international system forces them to seek positional goals such as relative power (Gowa, 1994; Grieco, 1990; Stein, 1984).

Scholars reacting against this tradition point instead to international institutions such as international organizations, regimes and other forms of international cooperation. This research has shown that even self-interested relative power-maximizing states have an incentive to cooperate, and that international institutions can play an important role in encouraging this cooperation (Keohane, 1984). Even on its own terms, then, Realism must address international institutions.

Other critics of structural Realism have shown how the theory makes ambiguous predictions (and policy recommendations) for the foreign policies of individual states. At one extreme, then, in Alexander Wendt's phrase, 'anarchy is what states make of it'. This argument has led to a renewed interest in Gramscian hegemony and the ideological constructions of international relations (Wallerstein, 1994). Even from a more traditional theoretical standpoint, a state's definition of its interests, the beliefs it holds about human nature and the institutional environment in which it finds itself shape foreign policy choices.

A state's definition of its own interests often reflects domestic political battles over those interests. Trade policy, like many other policies, has redistributive consequences, making some individuals better off at the expense of others. These redistributive consequences are masked when theoreticians discuss trade in terms of unitary countries. Contrary to theory, countries are not unitary actors but collectivities of individuals, firms and groups. Some of these players benefit from a given trade policy – whether protectionist or free trade – while others suffer. Distributional problems persist even though unrestricted trade is normally the best policy choice from the perspective of the national economy.

In sum, then, whereas scholars at the international level have traditionally looked at material interests or relative power maximization, research has increasingly been drawn to international institutions or international ideological constructions. In addition, an individual cannot neatly separate international trade policy from its domestic distributional consequences. This leads us to the domestic level of analysis.

Domestic Level

Though international-level theories have dominated the field for several decades, the end of the Cold War has increasingly pointed theorists towards the study of how domestic politics affects foreign policy (Goldstein and Keohane, 1993a; Gourevitch, 1986; Keohane and Milner, 1996; Milner, 1988; Rogowski, 1989; Schonhardt-Bailey, 1991a, 1991b, 1994). Others have explored more specifically how domestic institutions shape international relations (Barnett, 1990; Bueno de Mesquita and Lalman, 1992; Siverson, 1997; Smith and Hayes, 1997). In either case, these scholars argue, foreign policy inevitably reflects leaders' domestic political problems.

Much of the research that challenges the international level is comparative. Some authors find that differences in constitutions, such as variation between democratic and non-democratic regimes, provide a key factor in explaining differences in foreign policies. Others argue that parties and governing coalitions (Simmons, 1994), interest group lobbies (Milner, 1988; Schonhardt-Bailey, 1991a, 1991b, 1994), or quasi-constitutional changes in trade policy institutions (Finger, Hall and Nelson, 1982; Goldstein and Keohane, 1993b) are the critical variables. While this research accounts for many anomalies left by Realism, it can hardly be credited with offering a general theory of domestic politics. Even the work that uses public choice theory generally ignores supply-side political institutions such as legislatures and administrative agencies (Nelson, 1988).

Though unfamiliar to many political scientists, the leading domestic level theoretical explanation of trade policy is probably the so-called ETT. ETT is a subset of public choice theory in that it rests its analysis on the material interests of firms, consumers and politicians. Developed largely by economists, ETT seeks to equate trade policies to prices in an economy, so that the endogenous behaviour of lobbies, parties and politicians creates an endogenous political equilibrium. Such theories assume that firms face a choice between investing in economic behaviour and 'investing' in politics by lobbying officials, supporting parties or participating in campaigns with the aim of obtaining private economic rents. Looking only at economic investment choices neglects the intimate relationship between politics and economics, and the way that uncompetitive firms might compensate for their economic weaknesses through political action.

Empirically, ETT has successfully generated a large number of well-supported hypotheses. We summarize many of these in Tables 1–3, with representative but not exhaustive citations to each claim. It is unlikely that any other approach could boast a comparable number of logically interrelated testable propositions. These hypotheses offer a sharp rebuttal to the common claim that the 'democratic peace' is the only well-supported regularity in the field of international relations. Moreover, ETT's proponents agree on a large number of core assumptions and recognize many of the hypotheses described in Tables 1.1–1.3, thereby facilitating cumulative research. This stands in contrast to approaches such as Realism, whose proponents disagree even about the main assumptions and central claims of the theory (Vasquez, 1997).

As this list of hypotheses shows, ETT examines how tariffs vary in three

Table 1.1   Endogenous tariff theory: sectoral variation

Industries more likely to receive protection . . .

are in decline or growing slowly	Baldwin (1985); Lavergne (1983); Marvel and Ray (1985)
are less competitive internationally	Marvel and Ray (1985)
have relatively few firms	Baldwin (1985); Lavergne (1983)
have production concentrated in relatively few firms	Finger, Hall and Nelson (1982); Marvel and Ray (1985)
produce consumer goods	Marvel and Ray (1985)
have high labour ratios	Baldwin (1985); Lavergne (1983)
are in regions of high unemployment	Cassing, McKeown and Ochs (1986)
are textiles, apparel, footwear and chemicals	Deardorff and Stern (1983); Destler (1985); Ray (1974, 1981); Ray and Marvel (1994)
are agriculture in the developed world	Anderson (1992a); Anderson and Hayami (1986); Ray and Marvel (1994)
face inelastic demand for their goods	Nye (1991)
produce highly processed goods	Magee, Brock and Young (1989)
are highly unionized	Wallerstein (1987)
have less intra-industry trade	Marvel and Ray (1987)
produce goods farther down the chain of production	Husted and Melvin (1993); Ray (1974)
face increasing import penetration	Trefler (1993)
are larger	Finger, Hall and Nelson (1982)
are geographically dispersed	Pincus (1977); Schonhardt-Bailey (1991b)

dimensions. First, tariffs may vary by good. US tariffs on textiles and apparel, for instance, are much higher than tariffs on automobiles or computer parts (Table 1.1). Similarly, Britain protected corn much more adamantly than it did manufactured goods in the 1840s. Table 1.1 summarizes some of the hypotheses put forth to explain why some goods receive higher levels of protection than other goods.

Table 1.2   Endogenous tariff theory: crossnational variation

Nations with higher levels of protection . . .	
are less wealthy	Conybeare (1983); Magee, Brock and Young (1989).
have neither very large nor very small domestic markets	Bates, Brock and Tiefenthaler (1991); Cameron (1978); Conybeare (1983)
are less developed	Conybeare (1983)
have greater relative power	Lake (1988)
have smaller political jurisdictions	Magee, Brock and Young (1989)
have less diversified imports	Conybeare (1983)
have smaller GNPs	Conybeare (1983)
have smaller manufacturing sectors	Conybeare (1983)
lack other sources of government revenue	Conybeare (1983)
have a larger central government	Conybeare (1983)
face greater export instability	Conybeare (1983)
have less diversified exports	Conybeare (1983)
have smaller endowments in skilled and semi-skilled labour	Leamer (1984)
have smaller endowments in capital	Leamer (1984)

In the UK's case – which is central to Chapters 4 and 5 – greater protection for corn than for manufactured goods in the 1840s is easily explained by the restricted franchise, in which landowners were heavily over-represented in parliament. Both in nineteenth-century Britain and in contemporary cases, industries with production concentrated in relatively few firms tend to receive higher levels of protection because such industries can more easily overcome the free-rider problems and organize politically (Marvel and Ray, 1985; Schonhardt-Bailey, 1991b).

Second, tariffs may vary by country (Table 1.2). US tariffs, for instance, are generally much lower than Mexico's tariffs. Infant industry arguments and government revenue arguments are used by Conybeare (1983) to explain why Mexico's tariffs are higher than the USA. In the late nineteenth century, Britain maintained a policy of free trade while Germany enacted protectionism, in part because British political institutions facilitated the

Table 1.3   Endogenous tariff theory: intertemporal variation

Tariffs vary over time . . .	
with the domestic business cycle	Cassing, McKeown and Ochs (1986); McKeown (1983)
with economic growth	Magee, Brock and Young (1989)
with levels of development	Anderson and Hayami (1986); Magee, Brock and Young (1989)
with the terms of trade	Hillman (1982); Magee, Brock and Young (1989); Pahre (1998)
with capital labour ratios	Magee, Brock and Young (1989)
after creation of a free-trade area	Richardson (1993)
with global business cycles	McKeown (1983); Takacs (1981)

nationalizing of free-trade ideology while German political institutions favoured protectionists (see Schonhardt-Bailey, Chapter 5).

Third, tariffs may vary over time, as summarized in Table 1.3. For example, US tariffs rose in the 1800s but have declined over this century. Various explanations present themselves. Magee, Brock and Young (1989) argue that as economies develop, they become more capital-abundant. This makes it more likely that a capital party gets elected and free-trade policies become adopted. Anderson and Hayami (1986) maintain that as a country's economy grows (and its comparative advantage moves away from agriculture) it will tend to switch from taxing to protecting agriculture relative to other sectors. In Chapter 2, Pahre argues that in the nineteenth century tariffs fell as European countries expanded the franchise, developed more democratic political institutions and signed trade treaties with one another.

While most enjoy substantial support, the hypotheses in Tables 1.1–1.3 are not without controversy. One example is the relationship between the business cycle and the tariff, where some authors emphasize a procyclical explanation and others represent an anticyclical camp (Cassing, McKeown and Ochs, 1986; Hillman, 1982; Magee, Brock and Young, 1989; O'Donnell, 1978). A second example is the 'size of country' hypothesis, where tariffs increase with the size of country. Some maintain that large countries are more protectionist because they impose optimal tariffs, while others argue they are less protectionist because multinationals – which flourish in large countries – have the political clout to push for free trade (Conybeare, 1983; Magee, Brock and Young, 1989). In each of these examples, the particular hypothesis appears to be sensitive to the exact theoretical assumptions that an author makes about politics and markets; future models in which these assumptions are variables instead of parameters would exploit the 'rigorous flexibility' inherent in formal models (Pahre and Papayoanou, 1997) to develop more encompassing hypotheses about these relationships. On the empirical side, the evidence appears sensitive to research design in that crossnational tests, cross-sectional tests in a single country and longitudinal tests obtain different results.

The list of testable hypotheses shows that the literature on endogenous tariff theory has been most successful in explaining variation in tariffs across goods in a single country within a narrow time period. Sectoral variation, labour costs, stage of production and product cycle are all differences by industry or good within a single country at a single moment in time. ETT's greater success with interindustry variation probably reflects the research effort that US economists have given to explaining US tariffs. The overwhelming majority of ETT research focuses on the tariffs of postwar USA, thereby excluding variation over time or across countries (Marvel and Ray, 1985, but Caves, 1976; McGillivray, 1997; Pincus, 1975; Schonhardt-Bailey, 1991a, 1991b).

The heavy bias in the field towards studying the USA has imposed theoretical limitations. In particular, ETT usually has not problematized the institutional differences between the USA and other countries. For instance, widely-read articles examine the economic policy chosen under majority rule (Mayer, 1984), by a competitive two-party system (Magee, Brock and Young, 1989; see Lohmann, 1992), by governing parties concerned about pluralities in marginal constituencies (Conybeare, 1984; McGillivray and Smith, 1997), by a single support-maximizing leader (Stigler, 1971; Peltzman, 1976; Hillman, 1982; Hillman, Long and Moser, 1995), or by interest groups alone (Becker, 1983). These assumptions clearly reflect differing views of what drives political behaviour in the USA. Median voters, interest groups, parties, Congress, quasi-judicial bodies such as the ITC, and the executive are key features of US tariff-making, so the same is held to be true of other countries by extension. Yet parliamentary government, to say nothing of non-democracies, works very differently. Parliamentary coalition formation, to take one salient institution, has not been modelled in ETT.

The notion of firm expenditures on interest groups generating pressure is also peculiarly American. As Nelson (1988: 799) notes: 'A major problem with this literature is that fundamental assumptions about the nature of the political system are adopted without critical scrutiny'. Referenda, which can be important for tariffs, trade treaties and institutions such as the European Union (EU), have received attention in only a single article on

Switzerland (Weck-Hannemann, 1990). This work should be extended to cases in with *de facto* referenda on trade issues, such as Brian Mulroney standing for election on the issue of Canada's entry into the North American Free Trade Agreement (NAFTA).

A second limitation is that ETT is silent on the role of the state in trade policy formation. The literature can be searched almost in vain for the issues of state structure, state capacity, state autonomy or state interest to which many political scientists are attentive (Krasner, 1977, 1978; Skocpol and Finegold, 1982). The closest analogue is the research on 'administered protection' (Finger, Hall and Nelson, 1982) or Cowhey and McCubbins's (1995) analysis of bureaucratic control of policy in the USA and Japan. Pahre's model of a political support-maximizing state in this volume provides one way that public choice theory might move in this direction.

Table 1.2 illustrates that most crossnational studies of trade policy emphasize variance in wealth and development, not in institutional design and performance. Yet, it makes intuitive sense that institutional variation should play an important role in tariff formation, in part because the effects of interests will vary according to institutions of political representation. Indeed, some evidence suggests that many industry variables vary in both significance and direction across countries (Anderson and Baldwin, 1987). In particular, geographically-concentrated labour-intensive industries are well represented in both Europe and the USA but the effectiveness of their demands varies across political systems. McGillivray (1997) argues that crossnational differences in electoral rule and the nature of party competition explain why geographically-concentrated industries are politically powerful in some countries but politically weak in others.

Intertemporal variation has received even less attention in ETT than crossnational variation. Most empirical ETT is static, examining industrial structure and tariffs cross-sectionally rather than over time. Studies that have looked at tariff variation over time usually focus on key elections or legislative votes. For instance, most scholars of the most well-studied historical case, the Repeal of the Corn Laws in Britain, have not extended their analysis longitudinally to look at trade policy before or after repeal in 1846 (but see Schonhardt-Bailey, 1991a, 1991b, 1994). Remedying this deficiency requires that we look at institutional change over time and sometimes, most important, at the origins of an institution. Historical work such as this volume contributes to this agenda.

Longitudinal studies are also important because institutional change, by its very nature, reflects intertemporal considerations. A coalition in government today is rarely able to affect policy ten or fifteen years' hence. Nonetheless, it can restructure the institutions in which policy is made (sometimes in a single issue area, sometimes in many) and thereby hope to shape subsequent policy making. For example, US internationalists in power at the end of World War II anticipated a resurgence of isolationism. By integrating the USA into a set of international institutions, they hoped to bias the foreign policy system towards internationalist policy outcomes. Such cases are common, and help us see the importance of institutional (re)design in the transitional period of the 1990s. To obtain long-term benefits, a government may even forgo short-term interests. Indeed if one believes that Prime Minister Sir Robert Peel sacrificed his government and his party for the sake of the long-term benefits from free trade, then repeal demonstrates this strategy in the extreme.

In sum, understanding the role of institutions in ETT can usefully proceed in three directions. First, ETT might move into explicitly comparative work. Some recent research argues that electoral and legislative rules affect which interests get represented (McGillivray, 1997; Rogowski 1997). Second, ETT might examine a single country's institutions at a more finely grained level of institutional analysis. Finger, Hall and Nelson's (1982) study of the US International Trade Commission is one example; McLean's Chapter 4 another. Third, ETT might embark upon a longitudinal study of institutions and how they change. McGillivray's study of US trade policy before and after ratification of the US Constitution shows how centralizing power to regulate trade changed the structure of domestic conflict over trade policy and affected US bargaining leverage in international trade negotiations.

Like public choice theory more generally, ETT has also neglected the role of ideology in debates over tariffs. This failure is especially striking when we consider that debates over tariffs often invoke images such as nationalism or *laissez-faire* ideology, neither of which are specific to particular economic interests. Indeed, most ETT actors appear to care only about the protection afforded the particular goods they produce or consume. This narrow concern would better be captured in a policy space with an arbitrarily large number of dimensions, one for each tariff item. Yet tariff debates are usually single-dimensional, posing free trade against protection as general philosophies of trade policy.

ETT typically treats ideas as purely instrumental, chosen to maximize an actor's interests. For instance, auto companies might cite 'strategic trade policy' as a justification for protection. However, ideas influence choice in more interesting ways than this. They affect what we see as our interests, and our causal beliefs about how political or economic processes affect the world in which we find ourselves (Schonhardt-Bailey, Chapter 5). Ideas are also important heresthetic devices for manipulating outcomes given some institutional constraint (McLean, Chapter 4). They provide a focal point when there are multiple equilibria (Garrett and Weingast, 1983). They become embedded in political institutions and continue to influence outcomes even after interests change (Goldstein and Keohane, 1993b).

Material interests are also shaped by ideological concerns. In Chapter 4, McLean shows how a conservative interest in public order can change the preferences of protectionists such as the Duke of Wellington. The Duke's interest in constitutional order is ideological, while Peel's ability to exploit this interest rests on the particular political institutions of mid-century Britain. In other words, apparently objective interests are in fact contingent on both institutions and ideology.

Longitudinal change in ideologies, like institutional change, remains understudied. Research that treats ideology as a residual explanatory category finds it difficult to consider the effects of changing ideologies, for such an argument has too many degrees of freedom and must appear *ad hoc*. Looking at how an ideology is constructed or reconstructed, on the other hand, shows promise. We do not have as yet a theory that explains how ideas emerge and evolve, or when they have an independent effect on outcomes. Instead, they are most easily observed when interests and ideas diverge.

Developing a better understanding of how these ideas interact with both material interests and institutions is, then, at the core of this volume. Most of this interaction occurs in domestic politics and not at the level of the international system where most scholars have sought the causes of international relations.

Public Choice Theory, Institutions, and Trade Policy

As this review suggests, domestic level theories such as ETT need to consider institutions and ideologies. They can look for insight in a body of research known as public choice. Public choice theory studies how individuals and groups end up with one social choice (such as tariffs) instead of another choice (such as free trade). The theory begins with the assumption that actors pursue their goals rationally, though researchers increasingly relax this assumption in various ways.

One of the first lessons from a public choice perspective is the ever-present possibility that outcomes will be indeterminate (McKelvey, 1976, 1979). A game called 'Divide the Dollar' illustrates the general problem of indeterminacy in the public choice theory of redistributive policy. The game structure is simple: three people receive a dollar if they specify in advance how they will divide it. If they disagree on how to divide it, decisions are taken by majority vote until the proposed division cannot be defeated by another proposal. While obviously a contrived example, Divide the Dollar is a useful metaphor for redistributive policies. Tariff legislation, for example, divides some money from consumers among many producers.

Obviously, any theory of politics would like to predict a single outcome to such a game. Unfortunately, Divide the Dollar is indeterminate, since any proposed division can be defeated by another proposal. A three-way division of 33¢ for each can be defeated by {50¢, 50¢, 0}, which can be defeated by {0, 51¢, 49¢}, itself defeated by {50¢, 0, 50¢}, and so on. In each case, a majority of two prefer the new distribution to the old one. There is no equilibrium outcome, and thus no predicted outcome. This kind of indeterminacy follows from any game with at least two dimensions.[1]

The example of Divide the Dollar has direct implications for trade policy. Under majority rule, any tariff bill can be defeated by another distribution of costs and benefits. Tariff policy has at least as many dimensions as there are domestic industries. Each industry has an interest in redistributing national wealth to itself. Because tariffs are redistributive, trade policy is an issue where policy should be theoretically indeterminate. Thus, the outcome of tariff legislation should be indeterminate in majority rule systems.

Of course, most scholars believe that trade policy is not indeterminate. Tariff bills are often predictably biased towards producers, and towards industries with certain characteristics, while biased away from industries with certain other characteristics. This predictability stems from institutions that constrain the way majority rule works.

To see this, consider a revised game of Divide the Dollar. This game now consists of only two steps: first, player 1 proposes some division of the dollar, then player 2 counter-offers. Whichever proposal obtains a majority vote is final. Now the game has a unique equilibrium. Player 1 proposes the distribution {49¢, 0, 51¢} and player 2 counters with a winning proposal of {50¢, 50¢, 0}. Player 2 would like to propose taking the entire dollar herself. However, if she is to obtain a majority, she needs to give one of the other players more than they would have received under player 1's proposal. Knowing this, player 1 makes sure that he can be bought off more cheaply than player 3, while still obtaining as much money as possible.

While the details vary by situation (and formal model), this simple example captures some useful rules of thumb about institutions. First, setting the agenda is important. Players 1 and 2 gain by being able to make proposals, and player 3 gets shut out. In this example, players 1 and 2 have equal agenda-setting power versus each other. In other games, the exact sequence may privilege one agenda-setter over another (see *inter alia* Pahre, 1999: chapter 3). McLean shows in Chapter 4 how Peel and Wellington used their control of the agenda to pursue their ends in 1845–6.

Second, when institutions exist, policy outcomes show much more stability than the theory would otherwise expect (Hinich and Munger, 1994;

Nelson, 1988). This simple proposal rule transforms Divide the Dollar from an indeterminate bargaining game to a game with a unique solution. This kind of stability characterizes many of the institutions that we study in this volume, especially those institutions of a constitutional or quasi-constitutional nature.

Third, small changes in the institutions can have a large effect on outcomes. For instance, in the US Congress, changes in closed or open amendment rules or discharge petitions that allow bills out of a stalled committee can significantly shift the advantages from one set of actors to another. Knowing that such effects are important, neo-institutionalists are very sensitive to institutional rules, committee agenda-setting, floor amendments and congressional procedure (Denzau and Mackay, 1981; Denzau and Munger, 1986; Dion, 1998; Krehbiel, 1992; Moe, 1989; North, 1990; Ostrom, 1990; Riker, 1980; Shepsle, 1979, 1989; Shepsle and Weingast, 1984; Tsebelis, 1990). Scholars have recently begun to apply these theoretical models to comparative legislatures (Diermeier and Fedderson, 1996; Huber, 1996; Tsebelis, 1995; Tsebelis and Money, 1997) and to foreign policy problems (Pahre, 1997a; Smith and Hayes, 1997).

These institutional details are critical for understanding policy. Because institutions vary so much, we may despair at a general theory that predicts trade policy outcomes. Indeed, historians do not attempt such a theory. Public choice theory does not provide a unified theory of institutions, nor does it give scholars any single framework for understanding the formation, maintenance and evolution of institutions. However, public choice theory does provide tools that we can use to understand how institutions affect the incentives, strategies and choices that governments face. This points us towards theoretically-informed historical work, where institutions constrain politics, yet for any institutional regime, politics unfolds according to a theoretically-comprehensible pattern.

Public choice theory has also demonstrated that debates over changing institutions are critically important. Interestingly, these meta-institutional debates often reintroduce the kind of indeterminacy found in the simple game of Divide the Dollar. For instance, if player 3 had the power to propose a new institution, she would design one that gave player 1 the right to propose the distribution {51¢, 0, 49¢}, since both players 1 and 3 would prefer that to the prior institution. Other players with institutional proposal power would respond, reintroducing the instability of Divide the Dollar. When studying the origins of institutions, then, public choice theorists must sometimes resort to atheoretic narration. This problem aside, public choice theory provides a valuable research framework from which to study the role of institutions and material interests in trade policy making.

Public Choice Theory, Ideas and Trade Policy

Public choice theory also provides an important perspective on the role of ideas, pointing to interesting theoretical problems in the study of both institutions and ideology. As was true for institutions, we can see why ideology matters with the help of a simple example. Consider the problem of setting a country's general tariff. The legislation must set a particular tariff for a large number of individual line items. Most theories implicitly treat tariff bills as indefinitely malleable by looking at tariff variation by good in a single country at a single moment. For example, the theory assumes that a given bill might have high tariffs on eggs but low tariffs on denim, low tariffs on eggs but high tariffs on denim, or similarly high or low tariffs on both. In terms of spatial theory, this is a social choice problem in multidimensional space, in which each tariff line is a separate policy dimension. The outcome is indeterminate for the same reason that Divide the Dollar is indeterminate.

Now consider the possibility that a person's position on one issue is correlated with her preferences on other issues. For instance, a preference for high iron tariffs might be correlated with a preference for low rye tariffs. This would be true if there are two or three factors in an economy and if the factors that she owned abundantly (that is, labour or capital in this case) were relatively scarce in her country and used intensively in iron production. If she consumes rye, and if rye production uses intensively some factors such as land that she does not own, she will favour free trade in rye. In contrast, a worker who owns only his labour might prefer high tariffs on both iron and rye if both goods are labour-intensive and if the economy is relatively scarce in labour. In any case, we can probably find some conditions under which there is a solid economic foundation for an individual's preferences over the two goods to be correlated either positively or negatively.

Whatever the economic fundamentals, it would not surprise anyone if political players notice that their preferences on many issues are highly correlated with other actors' preferences. When the actors' preferences over many tariffs are perfectly correlated, then we lose no information by assuming a single underlying policy dimension. An individual's preferences on that dimension will perfectly predict her position on all the tariff issues. This logic helps explain the close relationship between material interests and ideas that is often found (Schonhardt-Bailey, Chapter 5).

In a real economy, any such correlations in preferences are unlikely to be perfect. German steelworkers and iron miners may favour protection in both raw iron and furnished steel, but iron miners want higher tariffs on raw iron than on the finished steel equivalent, and steelworkers want higher tariffs on finished steel. If actors' preferences are highly correlated, but not perfectly correlated, then assuming a single dimension will lead to errors. These errors may be politically costly, as was apparently true for small-farmer support of grain tariffs in Imperial Germany (Gerschenkron, 1943; Webb, 1982). However, if information is also costly, then certainly actors may prefer to live with some errors instead of investing in costly information that reduces errors. In a world in which actors have an imperfect knowledge of economic theory, ideology may be a relatively low-cost way to make decisions. Downs (1957: 98) notes that 'When voters can expertly judge every detail of every stand taken and relate it directly to their own views of the good society, they are interested only in issues, not in philosophies'. Real actors are rationally interested in both.

An ideology may also be a cheap way for political actors to convey information about their preferences, even if this information is subject to error. By knowing where politicians stand on the issue of protection or free trade, voters may have all the useful information they can obtain at reasonable cost (Lupia and McCubbins, 1998). For this reason, real tariff bills generally rest on the support of a coalition whose members have agreed on a package of high or low tariffs. For example, tariff reform in Third Republic France and in Edwardian Britain was fought as a pitched battle between a protectionist coalition on the one hand and a free trade coalition on the other (Smith, 1980). In other words, the infinitely many possible combinations of tariffs on a large number of goods do not occur. Instead, battles are fought along a simplified political dimension of free trade or protection (Hinich and Munger, 1994).

This point of view treats ideology as a brand name, which may be a form of information or misinformation. In Chapter 5, Schonhardt-Bailey distinguishes this role of ideology from other roles, such as preference formation. Using ideology merely as a brand name can often end theoretical inquiry. Instead of theorizing, scholars use it as a springboard for empirical studies that show the independent role of ideology in explaining, say, legislative behaviour. A more complete approach would problematize ideology better, explaining when political actors choose a broad ideology of protection or a more narrow ideology of, say, agricultural protection. Moreover, ideological explanations of trade policy often neglect any possible material foundation for the ideology. This is true of many analyses of protectionist ideology in Wilhelmine Germany, for example (see Webb, 1982 for critique).

However, the logic of the public choice approach can help us develop better theories of ideology. One testable implication of such a view is that an ideology of free trade should be more likely when economic factors are highly mobile, since mobile factors have interests on trade policy that approach the simplicity of the Stolper–Samuelson theorem. In such cases, the abundant factor will organize around free trade, the scarce factor around protection; as mobility decreases, however, the ideology becomes increasingly epiphenomenal. Low factor mobility makes sectoral interests more salient and therefore reduces the incentive to create an ideology.[2]

Ideologies may also play a role wholly independent of material interests, defining the good society. In other words, ideology may have a purely normative component. Quirk (1988) credits the formation of regulatory bodies to the selfless interests of bureaucrats to make good public policy.

Some scholars critique this type of approach because seemingly altruistic behaviour can often be explained by self-interest, incomplete information and bounded rationality (Calvert, 1995). Nonetheless, there are clear cases where electoral incentives do not explain politicians' actions and rational choice models provide elaborate but unsatisfactory explanations. Such is the case in 1846 when Peel and Wellington called for the Repeal of the Corn Laws. In Chapter 4, McLean uses archival research on Peel and Wellington's correspondence to gauge what motivated both men and to determine how they used ideas to structure parliamentary voting behaviour.

In summary, we argue the study of institutions and ideology within the public choice framework is a promising direction for understanding international trade policy. All scholars who see ideas or ideologies as predictor variables face difficulties in trying to explain when ideas matter (and when they do not) and how they intersect with economic interests and institutions. To understand this problem further, it is worth taking a few paragraphs to define the terms institutions and ideology that form the focus for our historical work.

Definitions and Classifications

Scholars have proposed many definitions of 'institution' in recent years (Calvert, 1995). Many of these definitions operate at a high level of abstraction as part of a theoretical project seeking an all-encompassing theory of institutions. For example, Douglass North (1990: 1) argues that 'Institutions are the rules of the game in a society or, more formally, are the humanly devised constraints that shape human interaction'. We prefer an even more general definition of an institution as any formalized (or semi-formalized) regular pattern of behaviour. However, we prefer to delineate our notion of 'institution' by categorizing those institutions that serve as the focus of our substantive chapters.

The modern political institutions that we analyse fall into several categories. First, *constitutional institutions* establish the fundamental rules of the political game. These include formal constitutions of the US kind and the less formal British constitution. Several features of the British constitution play a central role in McLean's account of the Repeal of the Corn Laws in Chapter 4.

Such institutions shape who plays the political game and how the relevant actors are organized. The lack of central tariff-making authority in the US Acts of Confederation, and the presence of such authority in the later Constitution, provides the central puzzle for McGillivray in Chapter 3. Property restrictions on voting meant that free-trade-oriented landowners were more successful than protectionist-oriented manufacturers in influencing each state's export policy for the simple reason that state legislatures over-represented the interests of farmers. As a result, conflict over tariff policy under the Articles of Confederation was not driven by a division of manufacturing/farming preferences between the north and south.

These constitutions may also define how people play the political game. In Chapter 4, McLean shows how the particular rules of the English constitution created heresthetic opportunities for Peel to obtain Repeal of the Corn Laws. His chapter best exemplifies the effect of institutions on individual behaviour, inasmuch as his focus is on individual politicians, rather than parties, groups or states. McGillivray shows why decentralized control over trade policy led US states to engage in open internal trade in the 1700s.

The last ten years have seen unprecedented change in such constitutions around the world, and in particular, in East Europe, Latin America. Without changing the entire constitution, other countries have significantly modified important aspects of their political system. Israel recently added to the powers of its president, Italy moved towards a majoritarian system, while New Zealand moved towards a Proportional Representation (PR) system. Like the contemporary period, the nineteenth century also saw dramatic changes in constitutions, especially from the revolution of 1848 until the unification of Germany in 1870.

A second category includes *quasi-constitutional* institutions, those considered part of the constitution in some countries at some times but not in other countries. For instance, countries differ as to whether the legislature must ratify trade treaties, but these rules are often set by legislation, not by constitution. Other quasi-constitutional institutions include electoral rules, the exact size of the franchise, informal norms of legislative-executive relations, and the like. In recent years, New Zealand and Britain have given their central banks political independence. US participation in the General Agreement on Tariffs and Trade (GATT) and other forms of trade liberalization has led to the creation of administrative law organs such as the International Trade Commission, expanded the role of the US Trade Representative in domestic and international economies, and transformed *de facto* the constitutional rules by which international treaties are negotiated and ratified (Bailey, Goldstein and Weingast, 1997; Hansen, 1990;

Lohmann and O'Halloran, 1994; Martin, 1993; O'Halloran, 1994). Directives of the EU require a host of harmonizing domestic reforms, reducing policy differences that act as barriers to economic exchange. Overseeing EU activity also leads to a variety of executive working groups and parliamentary oversight committees in member nations (Pahre, 1997a).

Constitutional and quasi-constitutional institutions are central to the study of political economy. These institutions have long generated debate among comparativists over which domestic political institutions best support economic growth, encourage trade, support stable monetary regimes, provide political stability or improve political representation (Freeman, 1989; Golden, 1993; Shugart and Carey, 1992; Simmons, 1994; von Mettenheim, 1997).

In Chapter 2, Pahre explores the extent to which these kinds of change led to major change in trade policy. He finds that rules on treaty-making are generally more important than the institutions affecting the autonomous tariff. He also argues that institutional constraints on the state's ability to generate tax revenue only affect a few countries such as Norway and Britain, in marked contrast to the claims of much of the literature. Finally, he shows how shifting access to the political system changes the balance of power between import-competing and export interests across countries and over time.

Non-governmental organizations that are central to the political system, such as political parties or pressure groups, make up a third kind of institution. In Chapter 5, Schonhardt-Bailey contrasts the effects of cadre parties in 1846 England with the modern mass parties of 1867 and 1884 or the ideological parties of the Wilhelmine Reich. These non-governmental institutions are often shaped by the constitutional and quasi-constitutional rules of a system. For example, electoral rules affect not only which industries organize and how they lobby, but also how the government responds to this political pressure. Governments do not mechanically respond to the demands of industry groups by giving the most protection to the most organized. And, to make things more complicated, non-governmental organizations interact with one another, thereby creating a network of institutional dependency and interaction. For example, the institutional structures of industry and labour affect labour unions' costs of organizing and pressuring politicians (Wallerstein, 1987).

A fourth type of institution is *international institutions* or *regimes*. The post-Cold War period appears to be a time of significant institutional (re)creation and reform at both the international and domestic level. In Western Europe, the European Community has become the EU through the Single European Act and Maastricht Treaty. In the Americas, NAFTA,

Mercosur in the Southern Cone, and a smattering of other potential free trade areas or extensions of existing areas, together form a new hemispheric trade regime. Asia now has its own trade institution in the form of the Asian-Pacific Economic Cooperation. Finally, coinciding with the spread of regional trading blocs we have now have a restructured multinational trading system, and at its pinnacle sits the new WTO. Pahre's Chapter 2 examines the political underpinnings of such organizations by studying the first international trading regime, the treaty network of the nineteenth century.

All these institutions fall into a wider definition of institutions as 'rules of the game'. The function of rules is, of course, to constrain the behaviour of actors. Any of our four types of institutions – alone or in combination with each other – may constrain actors' behaviour. Hence, we may find constraints on behaviour imposed by domestic institutions, in the absence of any constraints by international institutions. Or, international institutions may constrain actions in the absence of any other constraints. Or, we may find any number of combinations of constraints imposed by domestic and international institutions. Perhaps most important to note is that, a priori, the binding effect of rules imposed by domestic institutions is no greater or less than that imposed by international institutions – British parliamentary conventions in the 1800s were as binding as the GATT trading norms of the 1970s.

Ideas and Ideology

Like the term 'institution', 'ideology' has many different definitions. For example, Anthony Downs (1957: 96) defines ideology as 'a verbal image of the good society and the chief means of constructing such a society'. Among other things, ideas have been operationalized as roadmaps clarifying interests, focal points when a game has multiple equilibria, strategic behaviour given a set of institutional constraints, or an embedded feature of political institutions (Goldstein, 1989; Goldstein and Keohane, 1993b; Hall, 1989; Herrigel, 1993; Ruggie, 1983). Hinich and Munger (1994: 62) define ideology as

> An internally consistent set of propositions that make both proscriptive and prescriptive demands on human behaviour. All ideologies have implications for (a) what is ethically good; (b) how society's resources should be distributed; and (c) where power appropriately resides.

Other common definitions include a collection of ideas with normative implications for behaviour, economizing devices, or complex, dogmatic belief systems for interpreting, rationalizing and justifying behaviour and institutions (North, 1981, 1990, 1994).

These definitions reflect a concern with developing an overarching theory of ideology. Because we wish to use ideas to help us understand the politics of trade policy, a more limited notion of ideology suffices. We therefore use 'ideology' in the limited sense of 'a set of propositions about how society's resources should be distributed and/or about where power appropriately resides'. This suffices to capture both ideologies concerning trade policy and those supporting particular kinds of domestic institution.

This definition covers those ideas relevant to trade policy. For example, some politicians in our period had *laissez-faire* ideologies favouring free trade, including Richard Cobden, John Bright and other leaders of the Anti-Corn Law League. Other politicians had general ideologies in favour of domestic (or imperial) protection, including notably Joseph Chamberlain's Tariff Reform campaign at the end of our period. Still others linked trade protection to ideologies of nationalism and racism, such as the Agrarian League in Germany. Finally, some politicians had ideologies favouring protection of a particular industry, but linking it to other political issues. For example, those who favoured protection of agriculture in England in the 1840s also tended to favour strong state repression of breakaway movements in Ireland, and strong state protection for the Church of England. All these beliefs concerned the distribution of society's resources, and many included claims about whether power appropriately resided in a traditional élite, the people or the nation.

Ideologies also present a vision of the good society. As Schonhardt-Bailey argues, this vision is important for political behaviour and for political parties. It also shaped the political institutions people built in this century. While Pahre's chapter treats domestic institutional change as exogenous, social movements such as liberalism and nationalism lurk behind the reform acts in Britain and constitutional change in France. Just as surely, nationalism was a factor in both the Acts of Confederation and the Constitution, the trade consequences of which McGillivray analyses in Chapter 3. Though Pahre and McGillivray look at only part of the story, path-dependence conditions the histories of their cases.

Ideas also affect the goals and preferences of actors. While some public choice theorists have attempted to construct theories of ideology (Hinich and Munger, 1994), most simply assume that preferences and goals are exogenous. Ideas are simply 'hooks on which politicians hang their objectives and by which they further their interests' (Shepsle, 1985: 233). Little attention is paid to why some ideas catch on and others do not or why an idea matters at one point in time and not earlier or later. Analysis of the historical process tells us what goals leaders are trying to maximize, what policies are available to them and what institutions impose constraints.

Another important feature of ideas is the way that they are organized.

For example, mutually-exclusive ideologies may play a salient role in the organization of political parties. Schonhardt-Bailey examines such a case in Chapter 5. She maintains that polities in which political parties are highly ideological make it difficult for interest groups to exploit ideas and ideology, since party cleavages will likely dominate the ideological debate. For some interest groups, this limitation may mean the difference between successfully obtaining their policy objective, and failing to do so. It is also useful to note the limitations of explanations that rely solely upon interests and institutions. While McGillivray's chapter suggests that control over institutions means control over outcomes, from Schonhardt-Bailey's chapter we see that control of the British Parliament by import-competing landowners did not ensure the maintenance of agricultural protection, nor did control of the German Reichstag by similar interests prevent Caprivi from lowering agricultural protection through trade treaties. In short, neither interests nor institutions wholly determine policy outcomes.

OVERVIEW OF THE BOOK

The four chapters cover an assorted set of historical analyses. Yet, the important element of this collection is that they infuse a historical context into the public choice theory of trade politics and deepen our substantive understanding of modern political institutions.

Pahre's chapter provides an overview of trade policy in Europe over the century. He examines trade treaties in the nineteenth century, addressing questions raised by the modern increase in the use of bilateral treaties. These treaties are a self-enforcing institution that is as yet poorly understood by theories of IPE, which have not been attentive to explaining variation in cooperation across nations or over time. Pahre uses a political support model to explain these treaties. Variations in trade policy and treaties occur as leaders adjust their political support coalition in response to external change. For example, cheap imports force leaders to redistribute income towards those who face import competition; they also make it more difficult to sign trade treaties.

In Chapter 3, McGillivray explores how institutional choice at the domestic and international level affects regional economic integration. In the 1990s, many countries banded together to liberalize trade through regional free-trading areas. Though regional economic integration is in vogue, few of these trading blocs have attempted to centralize the political regulation of trade. Scholars disagree whether this will affect the success of these blocs (Garrett, 1992; Krasner, 1994). McGillivray argues that interstate trade in the USA between 1776 and 1788 provides a valuable empirical case for addressing this controversy. Political control of trade switched from decentralized state control under the Articles of Confederation to centralized political control under the 1789 Constitution. McGillivray finds that states faced a collective action problem because they could not effectively retaliate against the British under the Articles of Confederation system. After ratifying the Constitution, in contrast, the USA could credibly discriminate against British goods and shipping. Multilateral cooperation through a constitution enabled tariff retaliation where a network of equivalent bilateral contracts could not. Her findings suggest that whether regional trade blocs succeed in liberalizing trade depends on a variety of domestic factors, including the domestic institutional environment and the pattern of economic trade flows.

McLean's chapter offers the strongest statement in support of ideology as an important predictor of individual behaviour. For him, ETT simply fails to explain Britain's historic policy shift to free trade, since the median legislator in both the Commons and the Lords sat for an agricultural constituency and thereby should have supported protection for agriculture over free trade. As is true for institutions, ideology can affect outcomes either by changing how people play the political game or by deciding which people get to play in the first place. The key to McLean's story is that Peel and Wellington turned the one-dimensional nature of tariffs (with land at one end and capital at the other) into a multidimensional issue of tariffs, public order and Irish famine relief, thereby changing the voting patterns of conservatives in the House of Commons and the House of Lords.

McLean uses a specific piece of trade regulation to examine the mechanics of institutional process. The conventional wisdom is that free-trade ideology affected the votes of individual members of parliament. But this is too simplistic. In his study of nineteenth-century parliamentary politics, McLean documents how political leaders use ideas strategically to manipulate outcomes, in a way that depends on the institutional context. Tory party leaders used ideas heresthetically in the Cabinet, the Commons and the Lords to affect the final policy outcome – repeal. Introducing the Irish famine helped to shift the terms of debate away from a single free-trade protection dimension in the Cabinet, while the 'ideology' of public order and the Queen's Government shaped the votes in the Lords.

In Chapter 5, Schonhardt-Bailey looks at how political organizations use ideas to manipulate the political agenda. She challenges two fundamental assumptions of rational choice and public choice theory – that preferences are fixed and exogenous, and that interest groups pursue interests while political parties articulate and pursue broader ideological objectives – by introducing the notion of multidimensionality to the value of commodities. If commodities have value beyond simple consumption, then preferences are no longer contingent solely upon immediate consumption, but rather on some multidimensional valuation of the good. Moreover, if interest groups can be ideological and political parties can pursue narrow economic interests, an individual cannot help but begin to see these political institutions as manifestations of a dynamic interplay between ideology and interests. These insights into public choice and trade policy are just as relevant for modern public policy as they are for nineteenth-century Britain and Germany. She is interested in ideas not as heresthetic devices but as a means to persuade individuals to redefine their economic interests. Ideas are more than 'hooks' upon which to hang interest-based arguments. Ideas are devices by which interests are themselves restructured. 'Nationalizing the interest' is often an effective tactic that makes individuals support protection on the grounds of the national interest even when this runs contrary to their own material interests.

The historical cases in this book reflect how institutions and ideology may be treated exogenously, endogenously or as a mixture of the two. Some authors take institutions and ideology as given. Examples include McLean's treatment of the institutions and ideologies of the mid-nineteenth century; Schonhardt-Bailey's analysis of party systems in Britain and Germany; and Pahre's consideration of the domestic institutions behind the trade treaty regime. Or, institutions may be endogenous, as McGillivray finds in her analysis of changing trade clauses in the US Constitution, and Pahre finds as he explores the reasons behind the trade treaty regime in the nineteenth century. Finally, ideology, or at least the ability to exploit it, is endogenous for Schonhardt-Bailey when she evaluates the ability of interest groups to exploit the ideological strategy of 'nationalizing the interest'.

Each of the chapters points to how a focus on purely interest-based explanations falls short of explaining the structure of conflict over trade policy, necessitating greater study of institutions and ideas. Each of these chapters is part of a historical comparative line of research that expands our understanding of how political institutions, ideas and interests affect political behaviour. The contributions to the volume illustrate how the past can shed light on modern political behaviour.

NOTES

1. Indeterminacy also requires that preferences not be 'single peaked', a technical criterion always met in the case of tariff politics.
2. Verdier (1994) develops a different, interesting set of hypotheses concerning ideology. He argues that this reduced dimensionality of ideology depends on the political system. Where voters are mobilized around a highly salient issue, then the low dimensionality of Hinich and Munger follows. However, if trade policy is not salient and if voters are not mobilized, then rent-seekers can each pursue particularist policies. This results in a policy space of high dimensionality, since each tariff is its own policy dimension.

2.   Agreeable duties: the tariff treaty regime in the nineteenth century

Robert Pahre

The nineteenth century saw an unprecedented expansion of international trade. Railroad networks expanded dramatically, steamships grew in importance, and new sea routes through the Suez and Panama Canals reduced shipping times. As transportation and communication costs fell, trade became possible between hitherto isolated regions. For the first time, food staples such as wheat and beef were traded over long distances. Interdependence in trade also led to increased financial and monetary ties between countries.

Politicians apparently helped these changes along. States reformed their fiscal systems in ways that reduced or eliminated arbitrary restrictions on trade. Most European states lowered tariffs as part of this fiscal reform, making tariffs decreasingly important as an obstacle to trade.

Many countries also signed trade, navigation and tariff treaties intended to increase the economic ties between them. The secondary literature generally finds that these treaties increased trade significantly. For example, trade treaties led to unprecedented prosperity for French farmers in the 1860s, in part because of greater food exports to Britain (Smith, 1980: 165). By the early 1880s, 1200 items in the French tariff were covered by treaties, while only 300 were subject to the general tariff (Ashley, 1926: 317). Italy's treaties with Austria, Germany and Switzerland secured important export markets for southern agricultural produce, which prospered as a result (Coppa, 1970). Friedrich List argued that the reciprocal tariff elimination of the German Customs Union (*Zollverein*), alongside the railroad building of the period, was critical to German industrialization in the nineteenth century; modern research has tended to confirm his claim (for review, see Trebilcock, 1981: 39–40).

These treaties also achieved substantial political salience in many countries. Both protectionists and free traders mobilized around the treaties in France (Smith, 1980). Caprivi's tariff treaties were controversial in Germany (Weitowitz, 1978; Schonhardt-Bailey, 1998a). Commercial policy divided the Austrian and Hungarian halves of the Dual Monarchy after

1866 (von Bazant, 1894; Pahre, 2001a; Weitowitz, 1978: 53–5). Treaties to secure exports for southern agricultural produce helped mitigate criticism that a unified Italy sought only the interests of the more industrialized north (Coppa, 1970). Important treaties with Germany in 1906 and 1911 established new relations between the state and private industry in Sweden (Werner 1989).

These trade treaties came in three major waves. The first is the *Zollverein* wave, a German network of trade treaties that induced some non-German states to sign tariff treaties with Prussia.[1] The second wave, and probably the most well known in the field of international political economy (IPE), is the French-centred network that emerged after 1860. Germany and France led the third wave, which was characterized by a spread of the trade treaty network to more peripheral states, such as those in the Balkans.[2] This wave saw the greatest controversy over treaties as distributional conflicts sharpened in a world of negotiated liberalization.

This chapter seeks a theoretical understanding of this trade treaty regime. I begin by rejecting several possible explanations from the existing literature, most notably cooperation theory. None provide an acceptable account of the variation in the regime over time, nor can they explain why some countries participated while others did not. After this critique, I present a model of trade policy that rests on domestic political support maximization in a world of several states. States react to the outside world in a way that compensates domestic actors for change.

This logic of compensation leads to several hypotheses about the treaty system. For example, improving terms of trade can reflect either lower prices for imports or higher prices for exports. In either case, exporters gain and import-competers lose. Politicians can increase their political support by compensating importers for some of their loss from competing foreign goods, paying for this compensation by taxing exporters through a tariff. A similar logic lies behind the responses of states to one another's tariffs or to third parties signing trade agreements.

Domestic institutional arrangements affect the support maximization problem and thus also shape both tariffs and trade agreements. I will discuss two types of institutional change. The first are fiscal institutions. Several countries depended heavily on tariff revenue, making trade liberalization difficult. Though salient in many countries, my analysis suggests that fiscal constraints are less important than is usually believed.

The second type of institution is more explicitly political. Many countries made significant changes in their electoral systems, legislatures and executives in this century. These had important implications for trade policy. Any increase in the franchise, for example, strengthens the trade position of labour, which becomes better represented in the political system.[3] Because labour supported freer trade in most of Western Europe (Rogowski, 1989), these reforms made liberalization more likely. The model also predicts that low-tariff countries will be more likely to sign trade treaties than high-tariff countries.

In addition to these political variables, economic conditions also influence politicians' support maximization problem and thus affect both tariffs and tariff treaties. For example, declining terms of trade reduce tariffs and make trade treaties more likely. Increasing terms of trade have the reverse effect, raising tariffs, causing tariffs to be more volatile, and making tariff treaties less likely.

These political and economic variables generally focus on the level of the individual country. However, these countries existed within an international system. Their behaviour affected one another and shaped the regime as a whole. In particular, the model suggests that the regime fed on itself. When discriminatory trade treaties divert trade, third parties face higher effective protection. Because foreign protection makes treaties more likely, discriminatory trade treaties induce third parties to cooperate more. They may either seek treaties of their own with the discriminators, or pursue treaties with other states left outside the discriminatory tariff area. In either case, the regime spreads.

Because changes in the terms of trade and spread effects hit Western European countries at the same time, with effects working in a similar direction, the theory helps explain why changes occurred in a wave pattern. A coincidence of major domestic institutional changes in the 1860s spurred the middle of the three waves. A partial move to protection in the 1880s contributed to the wave in the next decade, reinforced by worsening terms of trade for many countries in the 1890s.

I test the argument with several kinds of evidence. Illustrative anecdotes suggest that the theory captures important causal mechanisms of the period. A graphical review of the long-term trends shows the role of domestic institutional reform. Finally, quantitative tests confirm several hypotheses about how states behave in a vacuum and how they react to one another. While the evidence for any one claim is partial, putting all these partial claims together provides a suggestive overview of the century's treaty regime.

OVERVIEW OF THE TREATY REGIME

Trade cooperation builds on the autonomous tariff of a country. A review of these tariffs therefore provides a necessary introduction to the study of these treaties. At the same time, many scholars have misconceptions about this period because information on both tariffs and trade treaties is often spotty. For this reason, it is helpful to review the pattern of trade, tariffs and treaties in this period before presenting the theory.

Figures 2.1–2.5 provide some illustrations of the changes for those countries for which I have data. In these figures, 'openness' is the share of imports in GDP and 'tariffs' the share of customs revenue in import volume. Other measures of protection are not practical for most countries because of data limitations (all data from Mitchell, 1975 unless noted otherwise; treaty data are from the Trade Agreements Database).

Figure 2.1 shows that Britain lowered tariffs steadily through the century, ultimately reaching about 5 per cent of the value of imports in the 1870s. This represents a major decrease from earlier policy, with tariffs as high as 60 per cent. Norwegian and Swedish tariffs remained fairly low for a half-century as Figure 2.2. shows. Scandinavian tariffs were higher than Britain's ultimate level, a little over 10 per cent of the value of imports, and somewhat more variable as well. In contrast to these open economies, French tariffs increased under the Third Republic from the low levels of the Second Empire (see Figure 2.3). Figure 2.4 shows that Italy raised its tariffs to French levels in the late 1880s, from low levels originally comparable to Britain and Scandinavia. Both French and Italian tariffs levelled off and then began to decline again.

Most of these tariff levels are higher than industrialized countries' tariffs today, though the prevalence of non-tariff barriers since the 1970s makes direct comparison difficult. A perhaps more comparable measure is each country's openness, which I define as import value as a share of GDP (or GNP). In this century, British and Swedish openness increased to a plateau of about 25 per cent. Norway saw a steady increase in openness, reaching even higher levels of nearly 30 per cent. French openness increased to a moderately high though more variable level in the 15–20 per cent range. Italy's openness was more modest, in the 10–15 per cent range from about 1890. Figure 2.5 shows that German openness declines precipitously from a high level in the early 1880s down to about 15 per cent. However, it recovered somewhat in the following decades, returning to nearly 20 per cent.

All these countries were at least as open as the largest trading countries of today, the United States and Japan, whose openness levels remain in the teens. However, there was a significant dip in several countries in the 1880s. Existing studies of trade policy find this dip familiar, and trace its causes to the Great Depression of 1873–96 (see *inter alia* Gourevitch, 1986; O'Rourke and Williamson, 1999; Polanyi, 1944; Rogowski, 1989).

Alongside these trends in trade and tariffs we also see an expansion of trade treaties, shown in Figures 2.6–2.8. France signed a significant and increasing number of trade treaties from the mid-century on. By the end of the period it had a treaty in effect with virtually every European country.

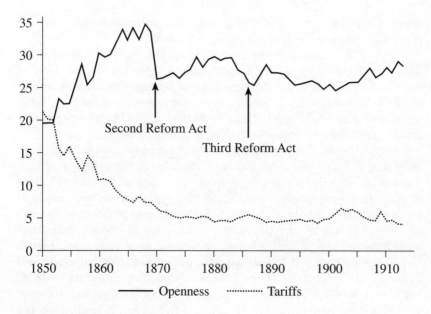

Figure 2.1   Britain, 1850–1914

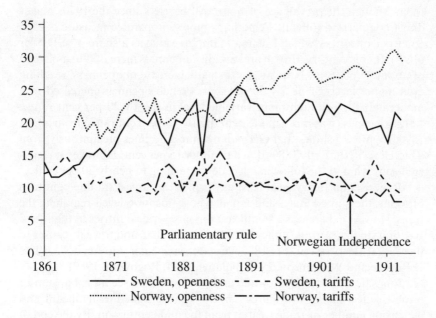

Figure 2.2   Norway and Sweden, 1861–1913

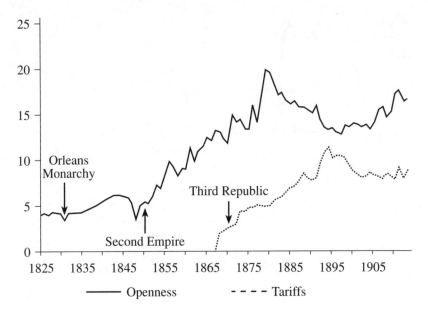

Figure 2.3   France, 1815–1914

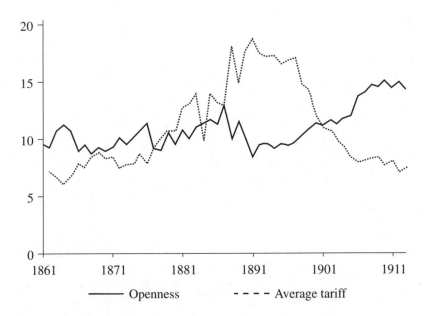

Figure 2.4   Italy, 1861–1913

Figure 2.5   Germany, 1880–1913

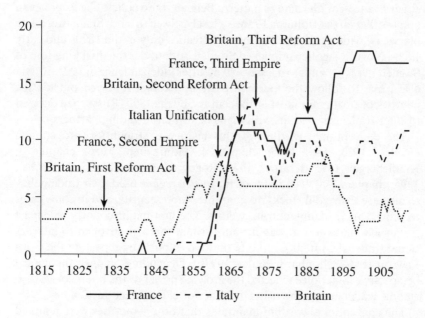

Figure 2.6   Trade treaties in effect, 1815–1913: major trading countries

Italy's treaties also surged in the 1860s, but unlike France, Italy's plateau did not include all the other countries in the region. Britain signed many fewer treaties, though it reached a moderately high plateau from the 1860s through the 1880s. However, Britain signed little more than most-favoured-nation (MFN) treaties after the 1880s (see Marsh, 1999).

Though the French treaty network is more better known, Austria–Hungary was at least as active in commercial policy (see Figure 2.7). Indeed, Austria signed more treaties than France into the 1860s, and a similar number thereafter. Because Austrian diplomacy was often oriented towards the Balkans, newly-independent states there provided attractive targets for commercial policy as the century progressed.

The pattern for Prussia (Germany) depends on whether or not we include its treaties signed with other German states through the *Zollverein* (see Figure 2.8).[4] Looking only at non-*Zollverein* treaties, Prussia was somewhat late in joining the move to trade treaties. Its acceleration comes in the 1890s, under Chancellor Leo von Caprivi's policy of trade treaties (Weitowitz, 1978). However, excluding the German treaties gives a misleading picture of Prussian commercial policy. Counting the *Zollverein*, Prussia was by far the most active signer of trade treaties, with 20 in effect before unification.

Many smaller countries, such as Belgium, Spain, and Sweden, follow either France's or Germany's pattern. Belgian trade policy, like its policy in many other areas, follows France closely. Sweden and Spain were late bloomers, with significant numbers of treaties only in the 1890s and early 1900s. Norway's policy mimicked Sweden both under the dual kingdom of Sweden–Norway and, to a lesser extent, after independence in 1905. Russia also came to follow the German pattern. Though it stayed outside the network of treaties for most of the century, by the 1890s Russia had decided to enter trade negotiations with many of its major trading partners.

The conventional wisdom of this history is straightforward enough (Ashley, 1926; Fay, 1927: chapter 4; Gourevitch, 1986: chapter 3; Kindleberger, 1975; Krasner, 1976; Rogowski, 1989: chapter 2; Verdier, 1994: chapters 7–8). The states of the *ancien regime* used their trade policy to increase their gold stocks, to guarantee food security, and in some cases to protect their manufacturing sectors. The first major country to depart from such mercantilism was Britain. Britain threw itself open to international trade when it chose to rely on food imports by repealing the Corn Laws in 1846 (Schonhardt-Bailey, 1997b). Depending on one's theoretical perspective, this choice reflected the growing power of the bourgeoisie, hegemonic leadership or the rising influence of classical economics.

The conventional wisdom maintains that other countries were tempted to follow Britain's example, but they could overcome domestic opposition

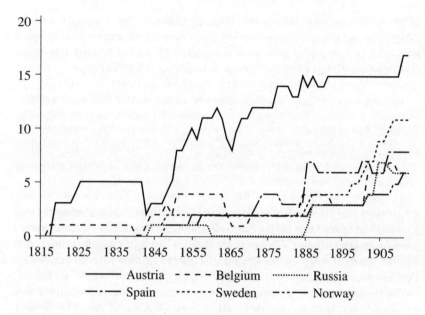

Figure 2.7   Trade treaties in effect, 1845–1913: small trading countries

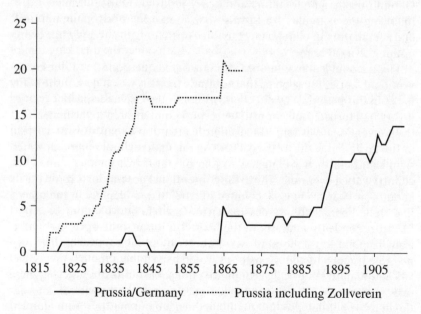

Figure 2.8   Prussian trade treaties in effect, 1815–1913

to liberalization only by signing trade agreements. For example, French Liberals in the Second Empire recognized that the best way around the protectionist legislature was to sign commercial treaties. Michel Chevalier explained to Richard Cobden (cited in Dunham, 1930: 44) that

> we shall not enter seriously and effectively on the path of free trade, however advantageous that might be for France, except through a treaty of commerce signed with a foreign power. The Corps Législatif knows very little about these matters and is led by a number of prohibitionists, who will object to everything if the question is submitted to the Chamber, and the only way to avoid submitting it is to proceed through a treaty. The constitution expressly gives this power to the Government.

When the Liberals won Louis Napoléon over, he negotiated a series of treaties that lasted into the 1880s. The first and most important of these agreements was the Cobden–Chevalier treaty of 1860, after which France and Britain brought most of Western and Central Europe into a network of trading states governed by bilateral treaties.

The conventional wisdom also maintains that the era of low tariffs was weakened, but not destroyed, by the Great Depression of 1873–96 and declining British power. Austria's autonomous tariff of 1878 launched the first attack. Bismarck's more famous marriage of iron and rye soon raised German tariffs on agriculture and heavy industry. France's Méline tariff, following the example of a Spanish law, used a logrolled minimum tariff and a retaliatory maximum tariff to force open foreign markets while giving nothing away at home.

This account leaves a number of unanswered questions. First, these conventional stories focus on tariffs, not trade treaties, which do not show any break in this period. Why did countries continue to sign reciprocity treaties if they had turned protectionist?[5] A second point, related to the first, is that the conventional wisdom has given little attention to explaining variation in the tariff and tariff treaty system. As the figures show, countries varied significantly in their willingness to join the tariff treaty system, and each country varied over time. Third, the conventional account tells us very little about how changes in each country were related to changes in the others. Did trade liberalization unleash a virtuous circle by which one country's liberalization led seamlessly to the liberalization of others? Or did politicians respond to the flood of new imports by trying to protect their own market, as many of today's theories would expect them to do?

The standard historical account does not stand alone in answering these questions poorly. The next section argues that most theories of international trade politics also fail to explain the main outlines of the nineteenth-century trade treaty regime.

COOPERATION THEORY

Trade treaties are a quintessential example of international cooperation. When they sign a trade treaty, two nations foreswear some unilateral action in favour of joint action that improves both nations' welfare. For this reason, we would expect existing theories of international cooperation to explain the tariff treaty regime we observe. Unfortunately, this is not the case.

Cooperation theory has long focused on explaining the *existence* of international cooperation in a world that lacks a central authority capable of enforcing such cooperation (Axelrod, 1984a; Oye, 1986 *inter alia*). To be specific, incomplete information, inadequately specified property rights, transactions costs and domestic political objectives are all reasons why states in an anarchic world might face problems that require international cooperation (Keohane, 1984; Milner, 1997). Many theoretical elaborations of the theory have also focused on existence, such as whether states might want to link two or more issues when cooperating, or whether multilateral cooperation makes sense (Lohmann, 1997; Pahre, 1994; Sebenius, 1983; Tollison and Willett, 1979).

Unfortunately, cooperation theory is of little use in explaining *variation* in international cooperation. Axelrod and Keohane (1986: 227) list three variables, 'mutuality of interest, the shadow of the future, and the number of players' that should explain the success or failure of cooperation. Other theories of international cooperation use a similar list (Axelrod, 1984a; Keohane, 1984; Oye, 1986).

These variables do not help us very much. First, the shadow of the future, which is central to many analyses, is almost impossible to measure. The second variable is theoretically suspect. Cooperation theory is mistaken, on its own terms, that increasing the number of players makes cooperation more difficult (Lohmann, 1997; Pahre, 1994, 1999a: Chapters 9–10). Multilateral cooperation is neither more nor less plausible than bilateral cooperation, and increasing the number of players may even make international cooperation more likely by reducing each player's incentive to cheat (Pahre, 1995). Moreover, players can construct networks of bilateral cooperation to achieve multilateral ends (Lipson, 1985).

The last variable, 'mutuality of interest', is simply another way of saying that states' preferences affect their willingness to cooperate. It is notoriously difficult to specify these preferences independently of the outcomes they are trying to explain (but see Legro, 1996). The alternative is to specify them deductively (Snidal, 1986), as I will do later in this chapter. A model of states' interests in trade policy can then predict when mutuality of interest will vary in a way that makes cooperation more likely.

In the face of such obstacles, cooperation theory is of little help in explaining why cooperation might increase or decrease over time; why some states cooperate when others do not; or why nations cooperate in one issue area but not another. The only important exception to this absence of theory is the 'relative gains' literature. Relative gains theory argues that cooperation is more difficult in security affairs than in economic affairs, and that cooperation is more difficult among two security rivals than among two allies (Gowa, 1994; Lipson, 1984; Pollins, 1989 but Pahre 1999: Chapter 7). In other words, 'mutuality of interest' might vary with security relationships, allowing a direct test of cooperation theory.

Plausible as it sounds, this last claim is apparently false in the nineteenth century. The relative gains literature claims that countries are more willing to cooperate in trade with allies than with military rivals, because an ally's gains from trade have security externalities for one's own defence (Gowa, 1994). This implies that allies should be more likely to sign trade agreements with each other than non-allies. To test this claim, Table 2.1 shows the results from cross-tabulations of alliances and trade treaties for a number of European countries.[6] For each dyad, it shows the number of years in which this pair of states had both an alliance and a trade treaty in effect, the χ^2 measure of whether the relationship between alliances and treaties differs from what the null hypothesis would expect, the statistical significance of the χ^2 measure and the direction of the relationship if it is significant. A negatively signed relationship means that having an alliance makes trade treaties less likely, while a positive relationship is consistent with relative gains theory. (Where the relationship is not significant, the sign is reported as N.A.)

The results contradict relative gains theory. The tightest form of alliance, a defensive alliance, has a strongly *negative* effect on economic cooperation. Looser entente and neutrality alliances often have a positive effect, but less frequently and at a lower level of statistical significance.

The table obviously does not show causality. The sometimes positive relationship between ententes and trade treaties may reflect a Cobdenite logic in which greater trade ties lead to a diminution of diplomatic rivalry.[7] This causal direction is more plausible for the Anglo-French dyad, where trade treaties long predated any closer diplomatic ties (see also Gowa, 1994). Whether or not this is true, it does little to help us explain the trade system itself. With this relative gains claim unsupported, cooperation theory does not help us understand the variation we observe.

Remarkably, cooperation theory does not even show us conclusively that cooperation matters. Clearly it *seems* to matter: for instance, states join international regimes such as the GATT, which has apparently liberalized trade. However, any claim that the GATT has liberalized trade must rely on a counterfactual claim that the major industrialized states would have been

Table 2.1   Alliances and trade treaties: by country and alliance type

		Years with both alliance and treaty	χ^2	Prob.	Signed
Defensive alliance					
France	Austria	0	11.65	<0.001	Negative
France	Germany	0	10.95	<0.001	Negative
France	Italy	0	0.53		N.A.
France	Portugal	0	14.74	<0.001	Negative
France	Russia	19	50.83	<0.001	Positive
France	Spain	0	15.98	<0.001	Negative
France	Britain.	0	42.31	<0.001	Negative
Britain	Austria	2	15.36	<0.001	Negative
Britain	Germany	3	3.75	<0.10	Negative
Britain	Portugal	9	35.94	<0.001	Negative
Britain	Spain	0	2.25		N.A.
Britain	Sweden	0	0.27		N.A.
Britain	Turkey	1	0.60		N.A.
Entente alliance					
France	Italy	2	3.90	<0.05	Positive
France	Russia	2	0.24		N.A.
France	Spain	9	7.30	<0.01	Positive
France	Britain	11	2.52		N.A.
Britain	Austria	9	4.95	<0.05	Positive
Britain	Italy	6	2.38		N.A.
Britain	Spain	0	1.20		N.A.
Neutrality alliance					
France	Italy	12	26.11	<0.001	Positive
France	Russia	0	1.42		N.A.
France	Britain	11	2.52		N.A.

more protectionist had the GATT not existed. If domestic support for the GATT rests on a free-trade coalition in many countries, then this free-trade coalition may have succeeded in lowering tariffs with or without the GATT. Conventional theories of tariffs, which do not distinguish between autonomous tariffs and tariff treaties, could argue little else. Only by distinguishing autonomous tariffs from trade treaties can we say that the regime itself matters. Addressing this problem requires that we develop a theory that makes clear predictions about what happens not only when states cooperate but also when they do not.

Revenue Concerns

Instead of looking at the international system, we should look inside the state. This section and the next review two common explanations for trade policy that focus on domestic institutions. This section looks at one common explanation for the nineteenth-century trade regime, the changing fiscal instruments available to the European state. The following section examines the effects of domestic political institutions on trade policy. Each kind of institution plays an important role for some countries at some times, but neither provides a general explanation of trade cooperation.

Many scholars argue that nineteenth-century liberalization reflects the development of new revenue instruments in Western Europe. Because they depended on customs revenue, a government could lower tariffs only after it had developed other sources of revenue, such as an income tax (see *inter alia* Grossman and Han, 1993; Imlah, 1958: 146–155; Long and Vousden, 1991; Nye, 1990; Stein, 1984). Common claims in the literature include the argument that Bismarck turned to tariffs to reduce the central government's dependence on contributions from the German states (see D'Lugo and Rogowski, 1993; Hallerberg, 1996), and that Italy legislated higher tariffs in 1878 to end chronic budget deficits (Smith, 1980: 144–8).

However, this argument is only sometimes consistent with the limited data available. One way to evaluate this claim is to look at the intertemporal pattern of governments' reliance on tariffs for revenue. To capture a state's dependence on tariff revenue, I have constructed a measure of tariff revenue dependence equal to customs revenue as a share of total government expenditures. Because governments developed new fiscal instruments throughout the century, the fiscal constraint should hold constant or decrease over time. Figures 2.9–2.11 show that this constraint did in fact decline for a few countries, notably Britain. The constraint remained essentially constant for Norway and Sweden, both of whom relied on tariffs for a large share of their government revenue. With somewhat higher variability, the Belgian and Italian revenue constraints also remain near a constant but low level.

In other countries, reliance on tariff revenue varies, both increasing and decreasing. Tariff reliance increases for many countries in the 1880s or 1890s, though these states had a wide range of fiscal instruments available. Austria–Hungary, France and the Netherlands all saw greater dependence on tariff revenue in the latter decades of the century despite having modern fiscal instruments available. These countries turned to tariffs for *political* reasons, not out of fiscal considerations. The revenue 'constraint' does not constrain – instead, it reflects a political choice to increase tariff protection.

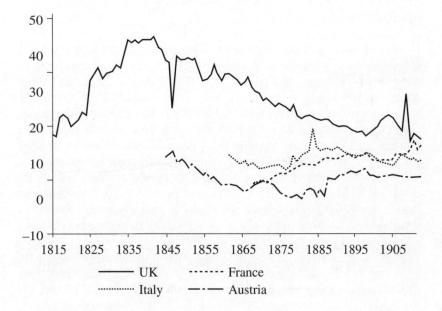

Figure 2.9   Tariffs as a share of government revenue

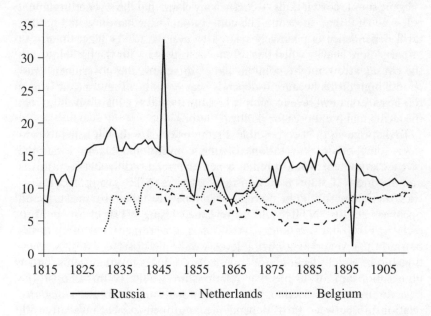

Figure 2.10   Tariffs as a share of government revenue

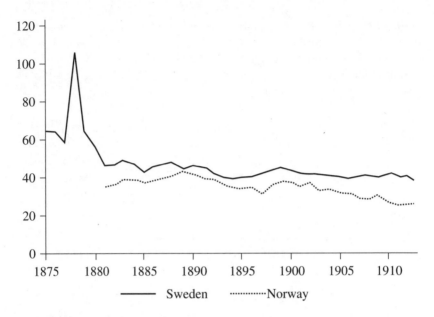

Figure 2.11   Tariffs as a share of government revenue

Some simple correlations strengthen my claim that the revenue argument is less general than it seems. The conventional expectation would be that tariff dependence is positively related to average tariffs, since states tax imports more heavily when this revenue is important for the fisc. However, the causal arrow might point in either direction: the government may choose high tariffs because it depends heavily on tariff revenue, or it may rely heavily on tariff revenue simply because it collects a lot of revenue from the tariffs that it chooses for political reasons.

To distinguish the two possible directions of causality, it helps to consider some other expectations of the conventional claim. First, the revenue argument would predict a negative relationship between tariffs and openness. If states used non-tariff barriers (NTBs) to protect industries, then there should be no relationship between the tariff measure and openness because NTBs yield no revenue.[8] Using NTBs clearly contradicts any revenue argument. Also, if a government imposed tariffs beyond the revenue-maximizing level, we should observe a positive relationship in which declining openness also reduces revenue. Thus, either no relationship or a positive relationship would count against the revenue argument. Second, the conventional story expects a negative relationship between tariff dependence and openness because, after all, the lack of alternative fiscal instruments is supposed to make a difference for trade policy outcomes. A positive relationship would suggest that states rely more heavily on tariffs for revenue as international trade increases. This increasing openness might stem from exogenous economic change such as transport costs or from a political decision to favour exporting industries.

Table 2.2   Openness, average tariffs and government tariff reliance

	Openness – tariffs	Openness – tariff reliance	Tariffs – tariff reliance
Conventional	–	–	+
Alternative	??	0/+	+
France	−0.070	0.248	0.893
Italy	−0.347	0.097	0.605
Norway	−0.479	−0.585	0.197
Sweden	−0.206	0.569	0.573
Britain	−0.886	−0.619	0.656
	Imports – tariffs	Imports – tariff reliance	Tariffs – tariff reliance
Austria	0.302	−0.073	0.846
Belgium	−0.593	−0.187	0.703
Russia	0.460	−0.265	0.744
Switzerland	−0.135	0.363	0.699

Notes: This table shows the correlation coefficient between openness (imports/GDP), reliance on tariff revenue (tariff revenue/government revenue), and the average tariff (tariff revenue/import value). Years covered vary by country depending on data availability.

Table 2.2 reports some simple correlations that call the revenue argument into question. (I use imports in place of openness for countries lacking GDP or GNP data.) A glance at the table shows that both the conventional wisdom and the alternative do well only where they agree, in the positive relationship between tariffs and tariff reliance. The conventional wisdom performs better in the relationship between openness and tariffs, where it seems that tariffs do reduce openness. However, this is not inconsistent with a political explanation in which the revenue constraint follows endogenously from a politically motivated tariff

The conventional wisdom does not account for the observed relationships betwen openness and tariff reliance. Indeed, if we use a plausible cutoff for 'no relationship' such as 0.30, then seven of nine countries yield correlations consistent with the alternative political theory and inconsistent with the conventional revenue dependence argument.

Two important countries display opposite patterns in Table 2.2, illustrating the substantive import of these findings. France follows the alternative theory, which sees tariff reliance as stemming from a political choice to impose tariffs for distributional reasons. French average tariffs and revenue concerns are highly correlated. The evidence suggests that changing openness led to a changed dependence on tariff revenue, a causal relationship that runs contrary to the conventional claim. First, average French tariffs are nearly unrelated to openness. Tariffs and openness are presumably unrelated in this way because France often used nontariff protection such as import quotas and prohibitions, which are irrelevant to the revenue concerns argument. Most important, French openness is weakly positively correlated with government reliance on tariffs. This finding suggests that increasing international trade represents an attractive revenue source for governments. Greater openness encouraged France to skim some taxes off the top, thereby reaping revenue that would be paid partly by foreign producers. In short, it is not true that an absence of other revenue sources inhibited liberalization, at least for France.

The conventional wisdom better reflects the British case, where openness and dependence on tariff revenue were indeed negatively correlated. One difference is that openness and average tariffs were also negatively related in Britain. Whereas many states had such high tariffs that lowering tariffs could increase both openness and tariff revenue, this was less the case in Britain (but see Irwin, 1988). In other words, the data are consistent with the contemporary claim that Britain only imposed revenue tariffs, and did so in a way to maximize tariff revenue. The fact that some important tariffs were imposed on demand-inelastic goods without significant domestic production – such as sugar, coffee and tea – adds force to this claim and makes political explanations less persuasive.[9]

The evidence from other countries is mixed, as Table 2.2 shows. These data suggest that revenue concerns might be important for a few countries such as Norway, Britain, and perhaps Belgium. However, the conventional argument lacks support for other countries, most notably France, where political concerns drive both trade policy and tariff revenue dependence.

This conclusion still leaves us with the question why international trade increased so dramatically, and whether states facilitated such trade. The following sections propose a political theory of tariffs in which both internal and external concerns interact to produce a country's foreign economic policy. This theory points towards some explanations for the history we observe.

DOMESTIC POLITICAL INSTITUTIONS AND TRADE POLICY

This section shows how some countries' tariff and trade treaty policies seem to have changed as the result of major changes in domestic political institutions. I focus especially on changes in constitutions and quasi-constitutional institutions (see Chapter 1), institutions that play a more direct role in the other chapters of this book. Here, I paint with a broad brush in assessing the effects of these institutions on trade policy.

Institutional changes may have one of three effects. First, domestic institutions might affect tariffs indirectly by making trade treaties either easier or harder to sign and ratify.[10] A country's legislature may have the ability to veto trade treaties.[11] When treaties require legislative ratification, executives will find it harder to liberalize tariffs through international agreement. A growing literature argues that such domestic ratification institutions, combined with differences between executive and legislative preferences, explain both the tariffs chosen by the legislature and the trade agreements negotiated by the executive (Milner and Rosendorff, 1997; but Pahre, 2001). This factor limited the commercial policies of Norway and Sweden, where a constitutional monarch appointed prime ministers independent of parliamentary majorities, yet majorities were needed to ratify treaties.[12] Legislatures might also limit the concessions an executive can make (Milner, 1997). Institutions might also change the way that politicians value the future, which would make them more or less likely to cooperate.[13]

Second, treaty institutions affect future treaties, so having already signed treaties will shape a country's tariff indirectly. Because treaties constrain states' ability to change their tariffs autonomously, a strong international tariff treaty regime will limit the direct effect of domestic institutional change on tariffs (see Hypothesis 4 below). This section suggests that these indirect effects are more important in this period – changing the rules for tariff treaties affects tariffs more strongly than changing the institutions that determine a country's autonomous tariff.

Finally, domestic institutions might strengthen either free traders or protectionists in domestic political battles over the autonomous tariff. The causal mechanisms behind such changes are familiar to endogenous tariff theory and other domestic level explanations of trade policy (see Chapter 1). For example, the political systems of most US states favoured landowners over labour and industry (McGillivray, Chapter 3). To see these effects, we must observe changes in political power. Such observations are difficult but not impossible, as a growing body of work on the nineteenth century shows (Irwin, 1989; McKeown, 1983; McLean, 1998 and Chapter 4; Schonhardt-Bailey, 1991a, 1991b, 1994, 1998a, 1998b and Chapter 5).

However, these studies necessarily limit their attention to a single country and at most a few parliamentary votes. Using this method is not practical for understanding the broad sweep of an international treaty network over a century, nor can it examine the effects of changes in one country on another country.

My approach looks at major institutional change, since changing the rules of the game is likely to lead to major shifts in political power.[14] The reform acts in Britain, parliamentary rule in Scandinavia and the Austro-Hungarian *Ausgleich* of 1867 are examples of quasi-constitutional changes within a given constitutional regime. Constitutional changes, as from the French Second Empire to the Third Republic, presumably shifted political power dramatically. For example, the steadily increasing franchise in Britain and the generally increasing franchises in most other European countries changed politicians' valuation of support from labour. While labour support was previously desired only as a way to avoid unrest, labour eventually came to play a role in electing politicians.

To see how these institutional reforms changed political power, I use a simple inductive method. That is, I look at the data from before and after an institutional change to see if the change had any apparent effect.

Consider first the effects of institutional changes on average tariffs and openness in Britain and France. As Figures 2.1 and 2.3 show, only the creation of the Second Empire in France seems to have some effect, leading to a rapid increase in openness. This is consistent with the secondary literature's focus on a reformist Louis Napoléon (Smith, 1980; Thompson, 1983). Though Louis Napoléon had initially sought administrative reform within a protectionist system, by the late 1850s he had become a more serious reformer who believed that moderate liberalization would enhance the welfare of his subjects (Thompson, 1983: 278–83). He began a flurry of trade reforms, issuing liberalizing decrees in November 1853, August and October 1855 and January 1856.

In contrast, other regime changes in France and Britain had no apparent effect on tariff policy. The Third Reform Act, creation of the Orléans monarchy, and the start of the Third Republic do not seem to have any appreciable effects.[15] Norwegian independence, which reflected in part the interests of the shipping sector in a more liberal commercial policy (Lindgren, 1959), seems to have increased openness without lowering tariffs.

Though surprising, this finding that institutions are only intermittently important is consistent with the often puzzled conclusions of the secondary literature. For example, Daniel Verdier (1994: 92) argues that the Third Republic 'presents a paradox – a protectionist team of politicians, Thiers and Poyer-Quertier, without a change in outcomes'. Ashley (1926:

282) finds a similar anomaly a half-century earlier, which he explains as follows:

> The new monarchy set up by the Revolution of July, 1830, was not likely to make any radical changes in the now almost traditional economic policy of France. Under the influence of the reaction against the extreme Protection of the last years of the Restoration Monarchy, Louis Philippe and his advisers were themselves prepared to make some amendments to the tariff; but they had been placed in power by the middle classes, who desired, above all things, to avoid the disturbance likely to be caused to trade and commerce by the more drastic political changes advocated by the republicans.

Widening the franchise simply strengthened the political and economic status quo represented by the commercial middle class (Marx, 1895/1964).

When we turn from tariffs to tariff treaties, domestic institutions may again play an important role. Quasi-constitutional changes sometimes have dramatic effects. For example, Britain did not renew many trade treaties from the 1880s (see Figure 2.6), notably failing to renew the Cobden–Chevalier treaty in 1882 (though it reached a long-awaited treaty with Spain in 1885). This roughly coincides with developments surrounding the Third Reform Act, though the causal mechanism is not clear. Verdier (1994: 92) attributes this to a rise of party politics, which is inimical to the pragmatism necessary for trade negotiations with foreigners. However, contemporary Germany also had an ideological party system (Schonhardt-Bailey, Chapter 5) but continued to negotiate treaties. Another explanation might see non-renewal as the manifestation of increasing protectionism among many newly enfranchised citizens, which narrowly failed to change the autonomous tariff in Joseph Chamberlain's later campaign for Tariff Reform (Sykes, 1979; Schonhardt-Bailey, Chapter 5).

As it did in tariff policy, the Second Empire had a dramatic effect on the number of French trade treaties. During the Restoration (1815–30) and Orléans (1830–48) monarchies, commercial negotiations often proved elusive, as the sorry history of failed talks with the United Kingdom before 1860 illustrates (Ratcliffe, 1978). However, tariffs declined and trade treaties became more common not long after the establishment of the Second Empire. Interestingly, the formal rules of treaty-making were unchanged, for the Second Empire (1851–70) followed royal precedent in giving the executive sole control over these treaties (Thompson, 1983). However, the political coalitions governing the country changed dramatically. Especially after the elections of 1857 and 1860, Louis Napoléon viewed trade treaties as a way to circumvent an increasingly protectionist legislature.

In contrast, the Third Republic required legislative ratification of trade treaties. Curiously, this did not limit the executive's ability to sign treaties in practice, though it did affect the content of some treaties signed. Figure

2.6 shows that the Third Republic successfully renewed the Second Empire's treaties as they expired in the 1890s, and the number of treaties in effect remained fairly constant.

Changing political regimes in other countries also affected their willingness to sign tariff treaties. Unification gave Cavour the opportunity to extend Piedmont–Sardinia's liberal trade policy to all of Italy (Coppa, 1970). One result was a dramatic increase in trade treaties (see Figure 2.6). Parliamentary government, in which executives with majority support reflect the will of the legislature, also removes the major obstacle to treaty ratification. This encourages treaty-signing.

In contrast to Italy, German unification seems not to have affected its willingness to sign trade treaties (see Figure 2.8).[16] However, a different kind of regime change did make a significant difference. Though labour remained excluded from the national government, the end of the *Sozialistengesetz* in 1890 created a more congenial environment for labour influence. Reflecting this change, the new Chancellor Leo von Caprivi pursued trade treaties in part to reintegrate labour into the Wilhelmine Reich (Weitowitz, 1978).

Earlier in the century, institutional reform also played a major role in Germany. Under the rules of the German Confederation, each sovereign was to give his realm a written constitution. Though implementation varied, Saxe-Weimar, Bavaria, Württemberg, Baden and Hesse-Darmstadt all had constitutions by 1820. The revolution of 1830 further strengthened reformers in many German states (Church, 1983). These political developments provided part of the background for the *Zollverein*, which spread across Germany in the 1830s and 1840s.

Institutional reform also encouraged cooperation in the largest German state. After the *Ausgleich* of 1867 created the Dual Monarchy of Austria–Hungary, trade treaties proved to be an effective way to square the divergent interests of Austrian industrialists and Hungarian agriculture (Weitowitz, 1978: 53–5). Losing the war with Prussia also freed Austro-Hungarian tariff policy from its overwhelming concern with policy towards Germany (von Bazant, 1894: 9–10; Vomáková, 1963). Figure 2.7 shows a significant increase in the number of Austro-Hungarian trade treaties under the new regime. The first such treaty, with France in December 1866, came on the heels of the Austro-Prussian War.

While domestic institutional change had a dramatic effect on larger states' participation in the trade treaty regime, it appears that smaller countries' participation was affected more by external events than their own institutional capabilities. Figure 2.7 shows that Belgium followed France in the 1860s, and Sweden followed Germany in the 1890s. Neither increase in treaties reflected any obvious domestic institutional change. Russia stayed almost entirely out of the treaty regime until the 1890s, when the government of Count von Witte changed Russian economic policy across the board.

In summary, some reforms of domestic institutions help explain some important changes in the policy of individual countries, but other reforms have no appreciable affect. Perhaps surprisingly, these institutions produce greater changes in the trade treaties than their direct effects on tariffs. These treaties then shaped each country's tariff levels over the medium and long term.

While it may be useful over the decades, looking at domestic institutional reforms cannot explain trade policy changes between reforms. In such cases, a more detailed look at the consequences of particular institutions, such as those in the other three chapters of this book, will be necessary.

In addition, any single country explanation is inherently unable to explain a network of trade and tariff treaties because no country can sign a treaty with itself. Since it binds each country's tariffs, the international network of treaties limits the effect of domestic institutional change – except for those institutions that affect a country's ability to sign trade treaties. These changes in domestic institutions are an important class of exogenous change that affects the trade treaty system as a whole.

POLITICAL SUPPORT AND DOMESTIC INSTITUTIONS

As a prelude to a model of several countries, this section and the next develop a political support theory of tariff making in a single country. The theory's main assumption stems from the Stigler–Peltzman theory of political support (Peltzman, 1976; Stigler, 1971), which Arye L. Hillman (1982; see also Grossman and Helpman, 1995; Hillman, Long and Moser, 1995; Bagwell and Staiger, 1999) first applied to tariffs. These models examine tariffs in a single country, which I extend to two countries. I exclude revenue concerns because of the analysis earlier in this chapter.[17]

Political support models assume that a single policy-maker in each country seeks to maximize 'political support,' such as votes and campaign contributions. To do this, policy-makers redistribute income from exporters to import-competers (or vice versa) until the import-competers' marginal gratitude exceeds the exporters' marginal resentment.[18] The major advantage of a political support model over lobbying and party politics models (Magee, Brock and Young, 1989) is its analytic simplicity. A political support assumption also has the advantage of allowing for countries with different political systems because I abstract from whether the support-maximizer is a monarch, prime minister or president. In addition, the political support assumption is useful for modelling trade policy between the kinds of major institutional changes discussed in the preceding section, especially when – as in the case of trade treaties – one must analyse two or more countries at once.

Of course, such simplifications have a cost. This assumption differs from most two-level theory, for example, which assumes than an executive makes choices subject to legislative ratification. Unfortunately, the two-level framework in its present state of theoretical development is of limited usefulness for explaining crossnational differences because it assumes that the executive and legislature have different preferences. This focus is misleading for those countries in which the legislature and executive do not have systematically different preferences because one branch of government chooses the other (Pahre, 1997a). In a pure parliamentary system, for example, the legislature chooses the executive, presumably selecting an executive with preferences near its own. In many dictatorships and monarchies, the executive chooses the legislature, if one exists. For these reasons, making any assumptions at all about the divergent preferences of an executive and legislature is likely to do violence to many cases, and to be irrelevant for many others.

Yet, whatever the roles of the legislature and executive, most systems have some actor seeking to maximize political support at the national level. This actor could be a prime minister maximizing his party's seats in the legislature, a president seeking popular election or the support of public opinion, or a dictator trying to maintain backing for his position among many different groups. To maximize support, this leader must balance the support from one group against the possible support from another. Assuming that a unitary support-maximizer chooses policy abstracts from these differences, while capturing the central problem that all these leaders face.

To see how political support captures several different kinds of domestic institutions, and how it differs from a two-level approach, consider three important mid-nineteenth century examples. They differ both in the role that political support played in the policy-making process, and in whether commercial treaties required ratification by a legislature independent of the executive who negotiated them. In the French Second Empire, Napoléon III sought a 'direct relation' with the people of France, and professed a concern with the welfare of each social class (Marx, 1895/1964). While he did not have to contest elections personally after being elected Emperor, he did seek political support from all classes to maintain himself in power. In short, these Second Empire institutions are well captured by the political support assumption. Two-level issues were usually irrelevant because pro-government deputies dominated the *Corps législatif*.

The institutions of the French Third Republic are more distant from the political support assumption here. Local constituencies, and not national level parties, dominated electoral considerations (Verdier, 1994). Most prime ministers were chosen by a coalition of legislative parties, and trade treaties required legislative assent. Here, the political support model captures the electoral concerns of the government of the day, but not the important coalition formation and ratification processes in the legislature. The two-level framework would model the government's need to maintain the confidence of the National Assembly when it negotiates a treaty, though the standard version of two-level theory does not examine the coalition formation problem.

Britain before the Reform Act of 1832 falls between these two French cases (Beer, 1966; Le May, 1979). Weak parties contested elections at the national level, but constituency concerns were also very important. Prime ministers sought not 51 per cent of the Commons but supermajorities that would be resistant to losses in by-elections.[19] Trade treaties required legislative ratification, but this did not pose real obstacles later in the century when the prime minister's party controlled a disciplined majority. The two-level framework is irrelevant, while the political support assumption provides a reasonable approximation of the prime minister's problem.

As this review suggests, institutions vary considerably in the countries examined. However, the political support assumption approximates political systems in which national leaders explicitly maximize popular support, or maximize the probability of election. Besides being very useful crossnationally, this assumption proves to be convenient intertemporally, allowing the study of policy changes between major institutional reforms.

The political support assumption differs from the common claim that domestic politics is largely distributive, with parties or groups trying to assemble a winning coalition to distribute income away from a rival coalition. Instead of politicians balancing interests against one another, as I assume, this alternative approach suggests that an executive is likely to side with one interest or the other, with the winner taking all (Gourevitch, 1986; Riker, 1962; Rogowski, 1989). To the extent that the balancing model is consistent with the evidence, however, the coalitional argument is less plausible.

A SINGLE-COUNTRY POLITICAL SUPPORT THEORY OF TARIFFS

This section explains the political support model that I develop formally in the Appendix. Unlike some other political support models, I begin with the conflict between two groups of producers. This lets the model concentrate on the interrelationship of tariffs in two (or more) countries. Consumer interests in lower prices affect producers' incomes, so I do not model consumers separately from their role as producers (contrast Hillman, 1982). For simplicity, I assume that each individual either gains or loses from foreign trade, and that politicians can identify the members of each group. For convenience, I call these groups 'exporters' and 'import-competers', respectively.

I use a reduced-form approach that sets aside production functions, demand and other economic variables to focus on the political problem. This reduced form uses as inputs a simplified version of the kinds of result that models of interest group behaviour (Austen-Smith, 1981; Becker, 1983, 1985) produce as outputs. I look only at material interests, in contrast to the ideological components of preferences that Schonhardt-Bailey examines in Chapter 5.

Each group provides political support out of its assets, and politicians can receive support from either or both groups.[20] The greater a group's income, the more political support it provides, as a reward for past service or an inducement for better performance in the future. Politicians balance support from one group against support from another, in an environment where not everyone can be fully satisfied simultaneously.

By allowing politicians to value political support from different groups differently, this set-up can capture the position of politicians who look first to a particular coalition (see Remark 1 in Appendix). For example, Otto von Bismarck's valuation of a given amount of political support from the Junkers was much greater than his valuation of equivalent political support from labour. Still, at the margin, he traded support from one group off against the other. Other chancellors did likewise. One contemporary British observer traced the differences between Chancellors von Caprivi and von Bülow to a different weighting of agricultural support by the two politicians, both of whom sought a balance between industry and agriculture, with cheap food for the working class where possible (Dawson, 1904: 147). These trade-offs force politicians to balance groups against one another, and this process is central to the political support assumption used here.

This feature of the model also lets it incorporate changing political or institutional conditions into the theory. Any institutional change affects a politician's valuation of political support from domestic groups. Repeal of the *Sozialistengesetz*, for example, raised the marginal valuation of labour to national politicians, even those who opposed labour's demands. While it does not predict how particular institutions affect trade policy, the model is logically consistent with the inductive analysis of this relationship in the previous section.

Whatever group they value most, politicians use the tariff to strengthen their political support.[21] Ideology plays no role in my analysis, unlike

McLean's and Schonhardt-Bailey's chapters. The model also does not explore strategic considerations such as those of strategic trade theory (Irwin, 1996; Krugman, 1986) or threats of tariff retaliation (McGillivray, Chapter 3).

Tariffs make domestic prices diverge from world prices, which I assume are exogenous. If the world prices of imported goods increase, the policy-maker will reduce tariffs. Increasing world prices for imports disturb the prior equilibrium, increasing import-competers' income and decreasing the income of exporters. The politician reduces the harm to exporters by skimming some of this windfall gain away from import-competers. The reverse is also true, of course: if the price of their products on world markets falls, import-competers will receive compensatory protection. In other words:

Hypothesis 1 Decreasing world prices for import-competing goods (that is, increasing terms of trade) lead to increased protection, and increasing world prices for import-competing goods (decreasing terms of trade) lead to decreased protection.

This hypothesis captures the well-known tendency for industries in recession, and not those benefiting from price increases, to receive protection.

Hypothesis 1 rests on the balancing logic of a political support model. Politicians balance the added support they receive from those who benefit from any given change against the support they might gain by redistributing income towards those harmed by that same change. When improving terms of trade harm import-competers, politicians use tariffs to redirect some of exporters' gains towards the import-competing sector.

Testing this hypothesis is difficult because terms of trade data are lacking for most European countries in this period. However, grain prices often provide a good proxy because grain was a major import of many advanced European countries. After the Napoleonic wars, falling grain prices led to protection in grain-importing countries such as Britain, which imposed the famous Corn Law in 1815. Grain-exporting Prussia liberalized moderately a few years later, thereby compensating its exporters for unfavourable external prices. Later in the century, grain prices fell again, especially in the late 1870s and early 1880s.[22] This reflected a dramatic change in transatlantic transportation costs, including a loss of comparative advantage for some Eastern agricultural regions. As is well known, this led to pressures for protecting agriculture in many countries (Gourevitch, 1986). Clive Trebilcock (1981: 83) notes that France, Germany, Italy and the USA all 'were reacting to a common international problem – the sustained decline in primary product prices as new transport systems opened up the world's cheapest sources of supply from the 1870s'.

This balancing logic of this theory also helps explain the role of fiscal concerns in tariffs discussed above. As openness increases, the government raises tariffs to shift some gains away from the export sector towards the import-competing sector. This causal direction, in which increasing openness leads to an increased use of tariffs for revenue, is consistent with the evidence presented earlier that most politicians chose to rely on tariff revenue and were not constrained by a lack of fiscal instruments.

Hypothesis 1 has several other implications. The response of tariffs to world prices depends on both the tariff level and world prices. With *ad valorem* tariffs, the effect of world prices on domestic prices is magnified as the tariff increases. This means that the effect of world prices on domestic incomes is also magnified as the tariff increases, so that any given disturbance of a prior equilibrium will call for a larger policy change to balance the political support of the various groups. As a result:

Hypothesis 2 Higher tariffs are more volatile than lower tariffs.

To the best of my knowledge, this volatility result does not follow from other types of endogenous tariff theory models. A theory based on winner-takes-all politics would have to argue that a strongly protectionist coalition, such as Bismarck's marriage of iron and rye, would be more unstable than a more liberal coalition. It is hard to see why this would be true.

These two hypotheses provide a simple foundation for testing the balancing logic of a political support model below. They also contribute another piece of the nineteenth-century puzzle: understanding the trade regime requires looking not only at domestic institutions but also at changing terms of trade.

TARIFFS IN TWO COUNTRIES

The next piece of the puzzle is the way in which one country's trade policy may depend on another's. In a two-country setting, exporter income in A is also a function of tariffs in B.[23] The higher B's tariff is, the lower the income A's exporters receive for their exports. This means that the government in A loses exporter support as foreign tariffs increase.

Because of this dependence on foreign openness, any increase in B's tariff will be met with a *decrease* in A's tariff. The theory is symmetrical for both countries and for tariff increases and decreases, so:

Hypothesis 3 Increasing protection in one country reduces protection in the other country, and vice versa.

This result will surprise those who think in terms of tariff wars and automatically reciprocated tariff concessions,[24] but the balancing logic is straightforward. Raising B's tariff hurts A's exporters, which disturbs the political equilibrium in A. In the initial equilibrium, the marginal political support from both domestic groups was equal. Now that A's exporters have less income, they give less support. Politicians in A can gain more support at the margin by lowering A's tariff until the increased political support from exporters equals the cost in lost political support from import-competers. Thus, A responds to B's protectionism by liberalizing.

This negatively sloped reaction function lay behind the response of many countries to Britain's unilateral liberalization in the first half of the nineteenth century. William Huskisson's reforms of the 1820s were followed by protection in many countries, including Austria, France and the Netherlands (Pahre, 1997b). British liberalization not only increased British imports but also spurred competitive sectors to export more. British iron exports threatened French manufacturers in the 1820s, for example, and they successfully demanded increases in French iron tariffs (Ashley, 1926: 276). Other examples abound, as countries from Sweden to Sicily raised tariffs on iron and cotton textiles in the 1830s and 1840s (see Williams, 1972 for examples). When Robert Peel introduced his motion to repeal the Corn Laws in 1846, he noted that 'other countries have not followed our example [of liberalization], and have levied higher duties in some cases upon our goods' (cited in Schonhardt-Bailey, 1997b: 82).

These are examples in which liberalization in one country bred protectionism in others. The reverse relationship also occurred, with home protectionism leading to foreign liberalization. As mentioned earlier, grain-exporting Prussia liberalized after Britain imposed the Corn Law of 1815. Later in the century, Chancellor Leo von Caprivi decided not to respond to other countries' protective tariffs with a protective German tariff in the 1890s because the German export industry would be hurt still further by retaliation. Moreover, higher tariffs would preclude solution of the outstanding 'social question' of how to integrate labour into the Wilhelmine Reich. Most of his government agreed that the best response to Russian protectionism was a central European customs union that would effectively lower Prussian tariffs (Weitowitz, 1978: 47–8, 56–9). This would address domestic political problems while denying any commercial advantage to Russia from German liberalization (a feature outside my model).

Such responses muted the European descent to protectionism in the 1880s and 1890s that we would otherwise expect from the declining prices for import-competing goods. All the countries of Western Europe faced similar problems, most notably the large increase in grain imports from outside Europe. As some responded with protection, others tried to keep their export markets open. Thus protectionism spread unevenly as Figures 2.1–2.6 show. The desire to keep export markets open also played an important role in the renewal and even strengthening of the trade treaty regime, which I discuss in the next section. This treaty network also muted the effects of strong demands for the protection of many sectors.

RECIPROCAL TARIFF LIBERALIZATION

The previous section examined the single-play Nash equilibrium, in which each player chooses her best response to the other's strategy.[25] The default reactions of each country to the other reduce change: liberalization breeds protection, and vice versa. Despite this, A and B can benefit from mutual tariff reductions if they select their tariffs together.

Neither A nor B will agree to any outcome other than the Nash unless they can guarantee themselves at least the same level of political support. It is also necessary that the discounted benefits from cooperation be greater than the one-time benefits from cheating plus the discounted utility from the non-cooperative outcome after the other country retaliates. For the following analyses, I will assume Grim Trigger enforcement, by which any deviation from the cooperation equilibrium is punished by permanent reversion to the single-play Nash equilibrium. Reciprocal tariff reductions are always possible:

> *Remark 2* If discount rates are sufficiently high, two countries can always sign a reciprocity treaty reducing tariffs, but not one increasing tariffs.

The logic behind this result is the usual folk theorem claim that any individually rational agreement is possible if discount rates are sufficiently high (Fudenberg and Maskin, 1986). This result also plays an important role in cooperation theory, where the 'shadow of the future' explains much variation in cooperation (Axelrod, 1984a).

Reciprocity treaties rest on the fact that tariffs impose political externalities on other countries, but no state considers these externalities when making trade policy unilaterally. In contrast, making trade policy jointly through a trade treaty allows states to take these externalities into account, which leads to lower tariffs. Each country's concessions bequeath an economic gain to the other government. This economic gain has concrete beneficiaries, and therefore also a political gain that unilateral tariff reductions alone cannot yield. Indeed, the exporters who benefit from a trade agreement are a concentrated interest and therefore have an incentive to lobby for such treaties (Gilligan, 1997; Oye, 1992).[26] This gain more than offsets the lost support from import-competers. In this way, these treaties allow the executive to take advantage of the economic gains from trade.

Again, history suggests that the model captures some important causal processes. Prime Minister Giovanni Giolitti used exactly this logic when he announced his policy of renewing Italy's trade treaties in 1903: 'In these negotiations, we will above all aim to facilitate the exportation of agrarian products and to that end we are prepared to diminish the protection granted to industry, insofar as it does not endanger its existence' (cited in Coppa, 1970: 754, 757). An 'Organization for the Safeguarding of Southern Interests in the Renewal of the Commercial Treaties' was formed to support this policy. It received a surprising ally in Piedmontese cotton manufacturers, who were willing to countenance a reduction in their own duties in order to help agriculture abroad.[27]

The political gains from reciprocity also make it a useful policy tool in the hands of politicians trying to broaden their political base. This was one reason Caprivi made commercial agreements a centrepiece of his economic policy, though many of his supporters were protectionists. One of Caprivi's goals as Chancellor was to reintegrate labour into the Wilhelmine Reich, since Bismarck's *Sozialistengesetz* clearly had not stemmed the growth of trade unions or the proscribed Socialist Party. In the first Reichstag debates over his trade policy, Caprivi stressed 'the sociopolitical function of commercial treaties with respect to unresolved social questions: "We dare not give up the hope of winning these people back"' (cited in Weitowitz, 1978: 149). Lowering grain tariffs might regain worker loyalty by reducing the cost of living for the typical worker. Moreover, the increased support from capital and labour would outweigh the opposition from the Junkers, a political effect not found in any purely domestic tariff legislation. Caprivi's treaties also benefited from the fact that both of the iron and rye parties, the National Liberals and the Conservatives, had lost ground in the election of 1890, at the expense of the Social Democrats, Progressives and Centre. Agreements with Austria–Hungary and Italy passed the Reichstag with ease in 1891.

Important as these political externalities are, the historiography normally examines trade treaties as stemming from the same domestic pressures as regular tariff bills. For example, Michael Stephen Smith (1980) treats the political choice between trade treaties or lower unilateral tariffs as no different than the choice between tariffs and quotas. As a result, he does not deem it curious that a large majority of French chambers of commerce in the 1870s supported trade treaties but also favoured unilateral protectionism (Smith, 1980: chapter 1). Similarly, farmer groups in the centre and south of France called for both higher tariffs and trade treaties (Smith, 1980: 168).

Some studies find this difference in interest in voting behaviour, with some districts supporting both unilateral protection and reciprocal liberalization. Schonhardt-Bailey (1998a) has found that some German regions voted to lower tariffs by treaty in 1893 and 1894 even though they vote to raise autonomous tariffs in 1879 and 1902. Such cases make it important to distinguish the politics of trade treaties from the politics of autonomous tariffs.

In these latter cases interest groups internalize some of the externalities of trade policy, by considering the effects of each firm's maximum tariff demand on other firms (Kiyono, Okuno-Fujiwara and Ueda, 1991). Politicians responded accordingly, using treaties to bring exporters gains that outweighed any losses to import-competers. The theory here makes a clear distinction between tariffs and trade treaties and shows how a support-maximizing politician might favour both.

Just as they change the politics of trade policy, treaties also transform the reaction of one state to another. Reciprocal liberalization affects the validity of Hypothesis 2, which states that any two countries' tariffs will be negatively correlated in the absence of a trade treaty. A tariff agreement can counteract tariff increases stemming from terms of trade effects or from changes in the other country's level of protection. In particular:

> *Hypothesis 4* When two countries sign a tariff agreement, changes in their tariffs will be positively correlated. (Thus, Hypothesis 2 does not apply.)

Because each country makes tariff concessions to the other, changes in tariffs will be positively correlated. The same positive correlation occurs when the treaty is no longer in effect, since both countries will reject the reciprocitarian tariff and return to their higher single-play Nash tariffs. These mutual increases in tariffs will also be positively correlated with one another.

Because of the mechanics of real trade treaties, I also expect a positive correlation in the period between the signing and denouncing of a treaty. First, many treaties make tariff concessions over time, so signatories' tariffs will be positively correlated during the phase-in period. Even after the phase-in, the MFN clauses in these treaties require future reductions as the result of new treaties signed with outsiders. As signatories negotiate these third-party treaties, continual tariff reductions will ensure that the signatories' tariffs remain positively correlated.

A positive correlation also occurs when two countries denounce a trade treaty, as each raises its tariff to the Nash equilibrium level. Figure 2.12 shows the effects of two dramatic cases of such denunciation, the Franco-Italian and Franco-Swiss tariff wars of 1888–93. In each case, the end of the trade treaty produces a sudden decrease in bilateral trade. Indeed the trade effects of these denunciations provide a convenient measure of the treaty regime's importance for trade. The Franco-Italian tariff war reduced bilateral trade by more than half, the Franco-Swiss war by a smaller fraction. Other tariff wars, such as the German-Russian and Austro-Serbian, also had significant effects on bilateral trade (Conybeare, 1987; Palairet, 1997). The Austro-Romanian tariff war, for example, reduced Romanian

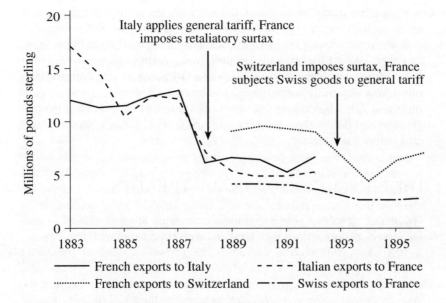

Figure 2.12   Trade effects of treaty denunciation

exports to Austria–Hungary from 40 to 4 million gulden in 1885–87 (Láng, 1906: 291–2).

These effects of trade treaties also shape the relationship between treaties and underlying changes in the international economy. When not denounced, a trade treaty insulates countries against tariff fluctuations stemming from changes in terms of trade. By binding tariffs, treaties prevent the tariff volatility that Hypothesis 1 and Remark 1 would otherwise predict. This proved to be important in the 1880s in France and other countries. As Daniel Verdier (1994: 103) notes, 'The reason why slumps did not trigger protectionist legislation is that they occurred at times when the conventional tariff [set by treaties] was not up for renewal'. Countries were constrained from changing their tariffs in response to external price developments.

This logic helps account for some of the institutional findings above. First, it shows how treaty-making rules play an important role in the trade regime by binding states against changes in their tariff in response to economic downturns. Second, it shows how treaties, once made, might also constrain the use of the revenue constraint. In these ways, a system based on reciprocal treaties differs from a non-treaty system by limiting the scope of domestic political factors in the making of trade policy. Once made, treaties also limit the effects of domestic institutional change on trade policy.

In a treaty system, signatories' tariffs will be positively related at the time they sign the treaty, throughout the term of the treaty, and when they denounce the treaty. In contrast, their tariffs will be negatively correlated in the absence of a treaty (for an empirical examination of these hypotheses, see Pahre, 1998). Like other institutions, trade treaties also constrain behaviour. In this case, treaties constrain states' response to international economic change and domestic political change. These effects will play an important role when the spread effects of trade treaties are examined in a later section. Before that, however, the next section will ask what explains variation in trade treaties.

THE LIKELIHOOD OF TRADE TREATIES

The preceding section shows that tariff treaties are always politically rational. However, they are not inevitable. To see what makes tariff treaties more or less likely, this section examines the stability condition indicating whether or not a given treaty can be enforced. Intuitively, there are two possibilities. Higher tariffs might make tariff treaties more likely because the gains from such a treaty are greater; as a result states will be loath to lose these benefits. This is the intuition in most of the political science literature, which argues that increasing the rewards from cooperation makes cooperation more likely (see *inter alia* Keohane, 1984; Oye, 1986).[28] Alternatively, lower tariffs might make tariff treaties more likely because the incentive to cheat is smaller. Moreover, with lower tariffs on both sides, any threats to return to the single-play reversion point are more credible because they are less costly to the sanctioner.

This second intuition turns out to be correct in the model here:[29]

> *Hypothesis 5* Tariff treaties are less likely for high-tariff countries than for low-tariff countries.

For this reason, we should expect a trade treaty regime to begin with the low-tariff countries. High-tariff countries may even stay outside the regime entirely, as did Russia until the 1890s (Ashley, 1926: 69–70).

This hypothesis helps account for the relationship found earlier between domestic institutional change, tariffs and trade treaties. Changes in domestic institutions may be responsible for a country having low tariffs. When this occurs, this low-tariff country will also pursue trade treaties. Again, Figure 2.6 suggests that France's increased willingness to sign trade treaties at mid-century may stem from the nature of the Second Empire, and an increase in the valuation of pro-liberalizing groups. Piedmontese leadership of unified Italy had a similar effect, making trade treaties more likely even as it lowered the general Italian tariff.

Changing domestic institutions also encouraged growth of a treaty network in Germany after the Napoleonic wars. Many German states consolidated their Napoleonic institutional reforms in peacetime. For example, Prussia had eliminated urban guilds from 1807 to 1811 and emancipated the peasants from 1807 to 1821. Many German states also reduced the privileges of traditional dignitaries and liberalized commerce (Trebilcock, 1981: 33–5). These trends tended to strengthen the commercial bourgeoisie, who had a natural interest in trade, and export-oriented landowners. The consequent reductions in the autonomous tariff made the German states more likely to sign trade treaties. The German *Zollverein* was the ultimate result.

This hypothesis also has implications for the revenue constraint. In an earlier section, I argued that revenue considerations only constrained a few countries such as Norway and Britain. We should therefore expect these countries to cooperate less than others. Figure 2.6 shows that British cooperation is indeed low compared to other large countries, especially once the network expands from the 1860s onwards. Figure 2.7 illustrates a similarly low level of cooperation for Norway, consistently among the lowest of the small states. Low levels of Norwegian cooperation persist after independence in 1905, while Swedish cooperation increases significantly. These countries' fiscal constraints made them less likely to cooperate.

The international economic variables analysed earlier also affect a country's initial tariff. A country with increasing terms of trade will turn protectionist, while a country with decreasing terms of trade will liberalize. Falling prices for imports lead to increasing terms of trade but also harm import-competers, who receive compensatory protection. Conversely, rising prices for imports harm exporters so politicians will lower tariffs when the country's terms of trade decline. Combining Hypotheses 1 and 5, then, we have:

> *Hypothesis 6* Tariff treaties are more likely among countries with decreasing terms of trade than for countries with increasing terms of trade.

This hypothesis captures one factor behind the wave of trade treaties in the 1890s. As grain prices increased again, grain-importing countries found their terms of trade decreasing. With reduced pressure for agricultural protection, these governments found trade treaties easier to negotiate (Ashley, 1926: 64–5). Germany began this wave, followed by Austria–Hungary's treaties with its Balkan hinterland. After tariff wars with Italy and Switzerland, France renewed its trade treaty network in the 1890s. For reasons I will discuss in the next section, this treaty regime then spread even to grain exporters such as Russia.

Germany had begun the first wave of treaties as well, when Prussia was a grain exporter facing lower grain prices abroad. International grain prices fell precipitously with the end of wartime demand in 1815, a price fall made worse by the English Corn Laws. This deterioration in its terms of trade harmed Prussian exports, leading to a policy in the exporters' interest: freer trade and trade treaties. It is noteworthy that the *Zollverein* began among the grain exporters of the North, spreading last to the industrial and mercantile regions of Germany.

Not only a country's own policy but also foreigners' policies affect the likelihood of cooperation. Because it increases the size of foreign concessions, larger gains from cooperation make treaties more likely:

> *Hypothesis 7* Tariff treaties are more likely when foreign tariffs begin high than when foreign tariffs begin low.

High foreign tariffs raise the gains from a trade agreement to domestic exporters without affecting the costs at all. By the same logic, low foreign tariffs reduce the benefits of trade treaties without changing their domestic political costs.

Hypothesis 7 captures an important part of the third wave of treaties in the 1890s. The preceding decade had seen increasing pressure for protectionism in France, Italy and Germany. This pressure had led to tariff increases in some cases, threats of protectionism elsewhere. These foreign tariffs made trade treaties more likely for others, especially as the existing treaties were due to expire in the early 1890s. The secondary literature identifies a move to protectionism in France's Méline tariff of 1892 and liberalization in Caprivi's *Neue Kurs*. Interestingly, both policies took the form of trade treaties, not unilateral tariff changes.

As this suggests, it is hard to say what the net effect of all these changes on the overall treaty regime should be because it takes two countries to sign a treaty. For any single country we can hold foreign willingness to negotiate constant, and we should observe changes in its treaty frequency in the directions that Hypotheses 5–8 predict.

The best way to think about the net effects on more than one country is to look at the spread effect of treaties. A treaty between any two countries will affect all third parties similarly. I turn to this in the next section.

SPREAD EFFECTS

As mentioned at the beginning of this paper, the century saw three waves of trade treaties. The clustering of treaties in three periods may stem from concurrent institutional changes, as is likely for the second wave in the 1860s. Alternatively, a treaty wave could result from changes in the terms of trade, as argued in previous sections. This effect encouraged grain-exporters of North Germany to form the *Zollverein* at the start of the century. While these factors doubtless played a role, the nineteenth-century trade treaty regime was not simply a matter of dyads choosing whether or not to lower tariffs reciprocally, in isolation from other dyads. Instead, states decided whether to sign trade treaties based in part on third parties' choices about their own foreign economic policy.

If two foreign countries sign a trade treaty, the theory suggests that each third-party country should respond in one of two ways depending on the existence of MFN treaties.[30] If the foreign countries are linked to the home country through an MFN clause, then home exporters will benefit from tariff reductions. This creates a latent demand for equilibrating redistribution towards import-competers. This protection will not occur in those sectors where the home country's tariffs are bound by MFN treaties, but it should act as a brake on the deepening of liberalization. Moreover, the foreign treaty does not create any new incentive for negotiating further tariff treaties.

A good example of such a country is Britain. Once locked into the MFN network of France and Germany, Britain did not lower tariffs further as other continental countries signed treaties.[31] Moreover, Britain tended not to negotiate treaties with these third parties as they signed treaties with France or Germany though it often agreed to mutual MFN treatment with others. Britain's 'splendid isolation' is captured by this aspect of the model.

The outcome is different without an MFN clause. In this case, the home country faces greater effective protectionism as the treaty countries' trade is diverted towards one another. This foreign protection leads to home liberalization, by Hypothesis 2. Because lower-tariff countries are more likely to sign trade treaties, the higher foreign tariffs also make home treaties more likely by Hypothesis 7. As a result, being shut out of a discriminatory area should make third parties more likely to negotiate treaties, either with each other or with the discriminatory area:

Hypothesis 8 When two countries make tariff concessions to each other that are not covered by MFN, this agreement makes third parties more likely to sign trade treaties.

In other words, trade discrimination leads to spread of the trade treaty system. This factor was decisive for bringing Russia into the trade treaty regime in the 1890s. Russian corn, for example, had paid a duty in Germany 43 per cent higher than MFN countries paid (Ashley, 1926: 69–70). After a brief tariff war beginning in August 1893, Germany and Russia came to terms in February 1894.

The second wave, in which France signed treaties with Belgium, Italy, Holland, Switzerland, Sweden and Norway, provides an excellent example of Hypothesis 8 at work. Ashley (1926: 31) argues that the Cobden–Chevalier treaty arose fears among others that did not have MFN treatment in France: 'Most of the nations which entered into the system were influenced partly by the desire not to let Great Britain secure greater advantages in France than they themselves enjoyed'. This was also the pattern for Britain herself, which tended to sign treaties defensively after the French had reached agreement with a third party (Marsh, 1999).

In the same way, the German *Zollverein* had, throughout much of the century, forced outsiders to sign treaties of their own. The customs union began in 1819–23, when the states of Schwarzburg and Anhalt gradually adopted the Prussian tariff schedule by treaty. Schwarzburg and Anhalt were joined by the Grand Duchy of Hesse in 1828, Hesse-Cassel in 1831, Bavaria and Hohenzollern in 1833, Hesse-Homburg, Baden and Nassau in 1835, Frankfurt in 1836, Weldeck in 1838, Brunswick, Lippe and Luxemburg in 1842, Hanover in 1851 and Oldenburg in 1852 (Henderson, 1939).

Each accession put pressure on neighbours to sign a treaty with Prussia lest they lose preferential access to the growing German market. For example, Britain feared that internal free trade in Germany might lead to higher tariffs against outsiders, notably British manufactures. When its quiet efforts to keep German states out of the *Zollverein* failed (Kennedy, 1980: 43), Britain had to negotiate with Prussia. Britain and Prussia signed a minor treaty in 1841, and a more important one in 1862 that was applied to the *Zollverein* as a whole (Davis, 1997).

Other states followed suit. Belgium sought a treaty with France because it 'believed that the newly formed Zollverein might close Germany against it' (Ashley, 1926: 287). Negotiations were difficult, and no such treaty was reached until 1842, and not ratified for several years thereafter. In 1853, Prussia and a reluctant Austria agreed not to levy corn duties on each other. Most important, Prussia and France signed a trade treaty in 1862 that was applied to the entire *Zollverein* in 1865 (Henderson, 1939: 273–86). In this way, the *Zollverein* may have been a catalyst for the entire trade regime. Though its motives were only partly economic, it created facts on the ground that induced third parties to sign treaties both with Prussia and with each other.

In sum, trade treaties had some spread effects on third parties. With MFN clauses, foreign treaties lead to more generalized reductions in tariffs but put pressure on governments to redistribute income towards import-competers. Without such clauses, third parties will either liberalize or scramble to sign treaties with a discriminatory trading area.

QUANTITATIVE TESTS OF THE HYPOTHESES

In this section, I provide several quantitative tests of the model.[32] First, I show that higher tariffs are more volatile than low tariffs. Second, I show that declining terms of trade make trade treaties more likely. Third, I show that trade treaties spread when countries do not grant each other MFN. Taken together, the results of these tests provide systematic evidence that the model captures important features of the trade treaty regime.

I begin with the single-country hypotheses. These test the balancing logic of the theory, which argues that politicians equilibrate the political support that they can receive from export- or import-competing interests. One way to test this is to see if governments use tariffs to counteract changes in a country's terms of trade (see Hypothesis 1). While good terms of trade data are rare, I can test the hypothesis indirectly by looking at whether we observe the tariff volatility the model predicts. Hypothesis 2 predicts that countries with higher tariffs will have more volatile tariffs than those with lower tariffs. To test this, I examine the coefficient of variation for each country's tariff.

The available data allow two possible measures of protection. The first measure is the 'average tariff', defined as customs revenue as a percentage of import volume; the second measure is 'openness', import volume as a percentage of GDP (or GNP, or NNP, depending on available country data). Openness is only an indirect measure of protection because many economic variables will affect it, such as transportation costs or a country's marginal propensity to import. However, openness weights prohibitions and import quotas fairly, since it depends on both actual imports and non-imports. In addition, this openness measure generally decreases when a country passes a tariff that historians describe as protective, and increases when a country passes a 'liberal' tariff.

The average tariff, while seemingly a more direct measure, is a very poor measure when real protection is sufficiently high. For a sufficiently high tariff on a good, the customs revenue collected will be small because very little of the good will enter. Indeed, prohibitive tariffs will appear to have an average tariff of zero. For some range of non-prohibitive tariffs, increases in the actual tariff will lower the average tariff measure. Domestic producers receive protection, affecting the openness measure, but tariff increases reduce revenue.[33] This results in an inverse-U relationship between tariffs and openness. Moreover, the average tariff measure does not capture non-tariff barriers because they entailed no customs revenue. However, import quotas and prohibitions were important for many countries in this period.

Though openness should provide a better measure of tariffs in this period, I will test the volatility hypothesis (Hypothesis 2) against both tariffs and openness. Because openness is inversely related to tariffs, Hypothesis 2 predicts that the coefficient of variation for openness is *negatively* related to the mean.

Openness data are available for five countries (France, Germany, Italy, Sweden and Britain) for some part of 1815–1913 (Tables 2.3–2.4). Average

Table 2.3 Openness volatility

	N	Years	Mean	St. dev.	Coeff. of var.
Britain	84	1830–1913	24.5	5.6	0.23
Sweden	53	1861–1913	19.7	3.7	0.19
Germany	34	1880–1913	19.5	4.0	0.21
France	89	1825–1913	11.2	4.9	0.44
Italy	53	1861–1913	10.9	1.8	0.17
Britain	53	1861–1913	27.9	2.5	0.09
France	53	1861–1913	14.8	2.1	0.14

Note: These data are the summary statistics for the openness variable. The coefficient of variation is the standard deviation divided by the mean.

Table 2.4   Average tariffs

	N	Years	Mean	St. dev.	Coeff. of var.
Belgium	67	1846–1912	2.25	1.22	0.54
Austria–Hungary	69	1845–1913	3.88	2.41	0.62
Switzerland	29	1885–1913	4.15	0.66	0.16
France	46	1868–1913	7.38	2.46	0.33
Sweden	53	1861–1913	10.71	1.50	0.14
Italy	52	1862–1913	10.92	3.75	0.34
Britain	99	1815–1913	14.61	10.75	0.74
Belgium	28	1885–1912	1.67	0.18	0.11
Switzerland	29	1885–1913	4.15	0.66	0.16
Britain	29	1885–1913	5.17	0.63	0.12
Austria–Hungary	29	1885–1913	5.35	2.01	0.38
France	29	1885–1913	9.00	1.14	0.13
Sweden	29	1885–1913	10.35	1.00	0.10
Italy	29	1885–1913	12.53	4.00	0.32

Note: These data are the summary statistics for the average tariff variable. The coefficient of variation is the standard deviation divided by the mean.

tariffs are available for seven countries. Because volatility may vary across all five countries by decade for exogenous reasons, I also test the hypothesis against a set of countries for the same periods (1861–1913 for openness, 1885–1913 for tariffs). The resulting regressions are shown in Table 2.5 (standard errors in parentheses).

Table 2.5   The volatility hypothesis

	Average tariffs		Openness	
	Various periods	Same period	Various periods	Same period
Constant	37.3	13.8	36.7	21.8
	(19.6)	(9.9)	(17.8)	(5.8)
Mean	0.492	0.700	−0.708	−0.390
	(2.238)	(1.280)	(0.991)	(0.300)
N	7	7	5	4
R^2	0.01	0.06	0.15	0.46
F	0.05	0.30	0.51	1.69
Dates	Various	1885–1913	Various	1861–1913

Note: These regressions test for the relationship between the mean and the coefficient of variation for the statistics reported in Tables 2.3 and 2.4.

All four estimates are correctly signed, though none are statistically significant at conventional levels. As expected, using openness yields better results than using average tariffs. The coefficient on openness in test (4) is significant at better than the 0.15 level (one-tailed), that in test (3) significant at just over the 0.25 level. The probability of getting all four coefficients rightly signed by chance, even at insignificant levels, is only 6.67 per cent. These tests provide weak support for Remark 2, adding to the plausibility of the political support model.

Another test of the theory is whether terms of trade affect a country's willingness to cooperate with others. I have found a long series of terms of trade data only for Britain. To test the hypothesis, I ask whether the number of treaties that Britain signs is negatively related to its terms of trade.[34] Because treaties stay in effect for a long period, I also use the lagged number of trade treaties as a control variable.

Table 2.6 shows the results of a Poisson regression testing this hypothesis. The estimates are rightly signed and statistically significant at the 0.05 level. However, the substantive importance of terms of trade effects seem to be small. A 30-point change in a country's terms of trade only produces

Table 2.6   Trade treaties and terms of trade: Britain

	Predict	Number of treaties in effect
Constant		1.34
		(0.544)
Net terms of trade	–	−0.00885
		(0.0048)
Lagged number of treaties		0.921
		(0.036)
N		83
F		343.12
Adjusted R^2		0.893

Notes: The theory makes predictions only for the sign of the net terms of trade, which is significant at the .05 level (one-tailed). Lagged treaties is significant at the .01 level (two-tailed) and the constant is significant at the .05 level (two-tailed).

a 0.25 increase in the number of treaties. On the other hand, one-fourth of a treaty is a tolerably large share of the British total in this period, which remained in single digits.

In summary, the single country hypotheses are consistent with the data but at low levels of statistical and substantive significance. Taken as a whole, of course, a group of individually insignificant estimates that are all rightly-signed is unlikely to occur by chance.

One reason for the weak results may be that the two-country hypotheses and spread hypotheses better capture the world than a one-country model. The spread hypotheses are central to these two-country hypotheses. As I showed above, signing non-discriminatory treaties should have little or no effect on a third party's own willingness to sign trade treaties, while discriminatory treaties make foreign treaties more likely. For example, if Prussia and the Netherlands have not granted each other MFN status, any treaties that Prussia sign with Saxony or Austria will discriminate against the Netherlands, making the Dutch more likely to sign treaties of their own. In this case, Prussian and Dutch treaties will be positively correlated. Once they grant each other MFN, then Dutch exporters benefit from any Prussian concessions to Austria, so the Netherlands is no more likely to sign further treaties.

To test this, I first count the number of treaties in effect for each country. Then I correlate this count with the counts for other countries before and after each dyad granted one another MFN status. I consider any correla-

Table 2.7   European trade treaties in effect before and after MFN: simple correlations

Dyad	Date of MFN	Before MFN	After MFN
Prussia–Britain	1824	1.00	−0.004
Sweden–Britain	1826 (1813)	–	−0.067
Netherlands–Britain	1837	–	0.131
Netherlands–Prussia	1841	0.545	−0.077
Portugal–Britain	1842	0.767	0.053
France–Russia	1846	–	0.633
France–Britain	1860	0.406	−0.774
Italy–Ottomans	1861	−0.117	0.404
Netherlands–Ottomans	1862	0.657	0.076
Netherlands–Switzerland	1862	0.442	0.661
France–Italy	1863	0.837	−0.090
Belgium–Italy	1863	0.719	−0.163
Italy–Britain	1863	0.690	0.014
Italy–Russia	1863	0.748	0.148
Italy–Netherlands	1863	0.743	0.204
Austria–Britain	1864	0.558	−0.526
Denmark–Italy	1864	0.647	0.155
France–Netherlands	1865	0.812	0.673
Italy–Prussia	1865	0.488	−0.061
Austria–France	1866	0.421	0.827
Austria–Belgium	1867	0.701	0.470
Austria–Netherlands	1867	0.535	0.610
Austria–Italy	1867	0.581	−0.144
Italy–Spain	1870	0.855	0.078
Austria–Spain	1870	0.693	0.866
Austria–Portugal	1872	0.685	0.273
Austria–Sweden	1873	0.187	0.674
Greece–Italy	1872	0.712	−0.021
Italy–Switzerland	1879	0.824	−0.161

Notes: These data are the correlation coefficients between the annual treaties in effect variables for each pair of countries.

tions of 0.40 or greater as the positive correlation that we should expect without MFN. With MFN, I expect no systematic relationship, which I will operationalize as any 'non-positive' correlation. I will operationalize this non-positive correlation as any negative correlation or a positive correlation less than 0.40.[35]

Table 2.7 presents the results, which are strongly consistent with the theory. Twenty-four of the 26 dyads with data show the expected positive correlation before MFN, while 20 of the 29 dyads show a non-positive correlation after MFN. The theory also gets both of a dyad's coefficients right in 18 of 26 cases. These results are strikingly accurate.

By looking at the spread of cooperation, these results help push cooperation theory in new directions. Cooperation theory argues that increasing the number of states makes cooperation harder. The theory has given less attention to the question of how the number of states may be chosen endogenously (but see Downs, Rocke and Barsoom, 1998). The theory here suggests that how a regime spreads to encompass new actors will depend in part on the principles of that regime: a non-discriminatory regime such as MFN clauses will not spread, while discriminatory cooperation will lead outsiders to join.

In summary, the evidence in this section is regularly consistent with the hypotheses of the model. While each single-country test obtains statistically weak evidence, all of the tests are rightly-signed – which is unlikely to occur by chance. The tests of the spread hypotheses are both statistically and substantively strong. Just as the theory predicts, trade treaties will spread among countries without an MFN treaty in effect. Because the theory shows how treaties constrain behaviour, we would expect the treaty-related hypotheses to receive stronger support than the single-country hypotheses. The evidence also bears out this expectation.

CONCLUSIONS

This chapter has developed a domestic political model of tariffs and the nineteenth-century trade regime. The logic of a political support model drives the results in which politicians change economic policy to compensate those harmed by external change.

External economic conditions provide a major source of variation. Countries facing decreasing terms of trade have lower tariffs, less volatile tariffs and are more likely to sign reciprocal trade treaties. Countries facing increasing terms of trade will be likely to have high and volatile tariffs, and are less likely to join a system of reciprocal trade treaties. As a result, liberal Prussia's leadership of the *Zollverein* as grain prices fell in the 1820s and 1830s sparked the first wave of treaties.

Large changes in the marginal valuation of domestic groups, which result from domestic institutional reform, play an occasional role in tariff policy. The most important example is the French Second Empire, whose greater valuation of commercial export interests led to lower tariffs.

Domestic institutions have an even greater effect on trade treaties. As a result, domestic institutional reform at mid-century spurred expansion of the treaty system. The start of the French Second Empire, Piedmont's unification of Italy, the Austro-Hungarian *Ausgleich* and perhaps the Second Reform Act in Britain all preceded the greatest increase in treaties. These make up the second wave of trade treaties.

Finally, the existence of trade treaties has spread effects on third parties. The discriminatory network of the German *Zollverein* exerted an important inducement to other countries, as did Austro-German discrimination in the 1890s. These were central to the first and third waves of treaties. Nondiscriminatory treaties have less clear effects, and may induce no change at all in foreign tariffs.

This focus on France and especially Germany stands in marked contrast to the existing literature's emphasis on British leadership. The theory also helps explain the limits of British liberalization from the standpoint of the system as a whole. Britain lowered tariffs in the first half of the century but could not induce others to follow suit; many raised tariffs in response to increased British competition. Significant *mutual* tariff reductions therefore required reciprocity treaties. A world without reciprocity treaties could not constrain tariff increases, while a world with such agreements could.

APPENDIX A POLITICAL SUPPORT MODEL OF RECIPROCITY

Single country model

I use a reduced-form model of the economy, with export prices p_1, import prices p_2, and relative prices $p \equiv p_2/p_1$. Setting aside both the demand-side (consumer preferences) and supply-side (production functions), income is simply a function of these prices: exporters' incomes $Y_1(p)$ and import-competers' incomes $Y_2(p)$, with $\partial Y_1/\partial p < 0$ and $\partial Y_2/\partial p > 0$ by the definition of exporters and import-competers. National income is $Y = Y_1 + Y_2$, which is at a maximum when $\partial Y_1/\partial p + \partial Y_2/\partial p = 0$. This represents free trade for a price-taker.

Politics are also reduced-form, with actors giving politician support as an increasing function of their incomes. Thus, the politician maximizes political support $M(Y_1, Y_2)$, with $\partial M/\partial Y_1 > 0$, $\partial M/\partial Y_2 > 0$, subject to diminishing returns $\partial^2 M/\partial Y_1^2 < 0$, $\partial^2 M/\partial Y_2^2 < 0$. The support-maximizing equilibrium is $(\partial M/\partial Y_1)(\partial Y_1/\partial p) + (\partial M/\partial Y_2)(\partial Y_2/\partial p) = 0$, which differs from the income-maximization equilibrium when $\partial M/\partial Y_1 \neq \partial M/\partial Y_2$.

To look at tariffs, we need to distinguish domestic prices in the two sectors (p_{d1}, p_{d2}) from the world prices (p_{w1}, p_{w2}). These define domestic and international price levels $p_d \equiv p_{d2}/p_{d1}$ and $p_w \equiv p_{w2}/p_{w1}$. An *ad valorem tariff* (t) on imports raises domestic prices above world prices, with $p_d = p_w(1+t)$.

Now producer incomes are $Y_1(p_d)$ and $Y_2(p_d)$, with $\partial Y_1/\partial p_d < 0$ and $\partial Y_2/\partial p_d > 0$. Political support is still a function of producer incomes, with $M[Y_1(p_d), Y_2(p_d)]$. The political support equilibrium is at $(\partial M/\partial Y_1)(\partial Y_1/\partial p_d) + (\partial M/\partial Y_2)(\partial Y_2/\partial p_d) = 0$.

The terms $\partial M/\partial Y_i$, which express the marginal political valuation of support from a given group, capture variation in the domestic political importance of different groups. Like other models of domestic politics, it yields the following intuitive result:

> Remark 1   Any systematic change in the political importance of export or import-competing groups will affect the tariff to that group's advantage.

Now use the implicit function rule to find how the tariff changes in response to world prices:

$$\frac{dt}{dp_w} = -\frac{1+t}{p_w} = -\frac{(1+t)^2}{p_d} < 0 \qquad (2.A.1)$$

This yields the following hypothesis:

> Hypothesis 1   Decreasing world prices (that is, increasing terms of trade) lead to increased protection, and increasing world prices (decreasing terms of trade) lead to decreased protection.

The result parallels Hillman (1982) with a minor change. Hillman's approach requires the assumption that industries care not only about their final domestic price but also care whether that price comes through global market change or political intervention. Thus, actors must determine whether domestic price changes have external economic causes or internal political causes. I think this unlikely, and assume that firms are motivated by profits from whatever source.

Because higher t raises the absolute value of this derivative, it is also true that:

> Hypothesis 2   Higher tariffs are more volatile than lower tariffs.

Two-country model

With two countries, we must distinguish incomes in country A, $Y_{1A}(p_{dA}, t_B)$ and $Y_{2A}(p_{dA})$, from those in B, $Y_{1B}(p_{dB}, t_A)$ and $Y_{2B}(p_{dB})$. Here, the foreign tariff affects exporters in the home country, perhaps because of market imperfections or optimal tariff concerns. The politicians in each country continue to maximize their own political support functions, $M_A = M_A[Y_{1A}(p_{dA}, t_B); Y_{2A}(p_{dA})]$ and $M_B = M_B[Y_{1B}(p_{dB}, t_A); Y_{2B}(p_{dB})]$. The political support equilibrium now occurs where $(\partial M_A/\partial Y_{1A})(\partial Y_{1A}/\partial p_{dA}) + (\partial M_A/\partial Y_{2A})(\partial Y_{2A}/\partial p_{dA}) = 0$ and $(\partial M_B/\partial Y_{1B})(\partial Y_{1B}/\partial p_{dB}) + (\partial M_B/\partial Y_{2B})(\partial Y_{2B}/\partial p_{dB}) = 0$.

To find how A's tariff depends on changes in B's tariff, I use the implicit function rule:

$$\frac{dt_A}{dt_B} = \frac{\dfrac{\partial M_A}{\partial Y_{1A}}\dfrac{\partial^2 Y_{1A}}{\partial p_{dA}\partial t_B} + \dfrac{\partial Y_{1A}}{\partial p_{dA}}\dfrac{\partial^2 M_A}{\partial Y_{1A}^2}\dfrac{\partial Y_{1A}}{\partial t_B} + \dfrac{\partial Y_{2A}}{\partial p_{dA}}\dfrac{\partial^2 M_A}{\partial Y_{1A}\partial Y_{2A}}\dfrac{\partial Y_{1A}}{\partial t_B}}{p_w\left[\dfrac{\partial M_A}{\partial Y_{1A}}\dfrac{\partial^2 Y_{1A}}{\partial p_{dA}^2} + \left(\dfrac{\partial Y_{1A}}{\partial p_{dA}}\right)^2\dfrac{\partial^2 M_A}{\partial Y_{1A}^2} + 2\dfrac{\partial Y_{1A}}{\partial p_{dA}}\dfrac{\partial^2 M_A}{\partial Y_{1A}\partial Y_{2A}}\dfrac{\partial Y_{2A}}{\partial p_{dA}} + \dfrac{\partial M_A}{\partial Y_{2A}}\dfrac{\partial^2 Y_{2A}}{\partial p_{dA}^2} + \left(\dfrac{\partial Y_{2A}}{\partial p_{dA}}\right)^2\dfrac{\partial^2 M_A}{\partial Y_{2A}^2}\right]} < 0$$

(2.A.2)

With additional assumptions over some cross-partials in this term, it is unambiguously negative. I make the standard assumption that $\partial^2 M_A/\partial Y_{1A}\partial Y_{2A} = \partial^2 M_A/\partial Y_{2A}\partial Y_{1A} > 0$, that $\partial^2 Y_{1A}/\partial p_{dA}^2$, $\partial^2 Y_{2A}/\partial p_{dA}^2 < 0$ (price changes have a diminishing marginal effect on incomes), and that $\partial^2 Y_{1A}/\partial p_{dA}\partial t_B = \partial^2 Y_{1A}/\partial t_B\partial p_{dA} < 0$. This last assumption is the most problematic, and implies that as p_{dA} increases, domestic goods become more expensive for exporters, reducing the effects of foreign tariffs on their real incomes.

Even without these assumptions, the derivative will often be negative. That is, the assumptions are sufficient but not necessary to yield the following hypothesis:

Hypothesis 3 Increasing protection in one country reduces protection in the other country, and vice versa (that is, trade policies will be negatively correlated).

Reciprocal tariff liberalization

There are joint gains to *A* and *B* from reducing tariffs jointly because of the externalities that each country's tariffs imposes on the exporters of the other. To prove that mutual tariff reductions are politically rational, I first determine that *A* can maintain its equilibrium level of political support (t^*_A) if $dM_A|_{dpw=0} = (\partial M_A/\partial Y_{1A})(\partial Y_{1A}/\partial p_{dA})dp_{dA} + (\partial M_A/\partial Y_{1A})(\partial Y_{1A}/\partial t_A)dt_B + (\partial M_A/\partial Y_{2A})(\partial Y_{2A}/\partial p_{dA})dp_{dA}$. Both *A* and *B* can lower their tariffs while maintaining at least this level of support for *A* under the following condition:

$$\left.\frac{dt_A}{dt_B}\right|_{M_A=M_A, dp_w=0} = \frac{-\dfrac{\partial M_A}{\partial Y_{1A}}\dfrac{\partial Y_{1A}}{\partial t_B}}{p_w\left(\dfrac{\partial M_A}{\partial Y_{1A}}\dfrac{\partial Y_{1A}}{\partial p_{dA}} + \dfrac{\partial M_A}{\partial Y_{2A}}\dfrac{\partial Y_{2A}}{\partial p_{dA}}\right)}$$

(2.A.3)

Reciprocal liberalization requires that $dt_A/dt_B > 0$, which is true if $(\partial M_A/\partial Y_{1A})(\partial Y_{1A}/\partial t_A) + (\partial M_A/\partial Y_{2A})(\partial Y_{2A}/\partial t_A) > 0$. This condition holds when $t_A < t^*_A$, that is when *A* and *B* agree to reduce tariffs below their equilibrium level. In short:

Remark 2 If discount rates are sufficiently high, two countries can always sign a reciprocity treaty reducing tariffs, but not one increasing tariffs.

This follows because, for a sufficiently high discount rate, the loss of future discounted benefits from non-cooperation exceed the discounted gains from jointly reducing tariffs (by any amount).

Remark 2 implies in turn:

Hypothesis 4   When two countries sign a tariff agreement, their tariffs will be positively correlated. (Thus, Hypothesis 3 does not apply.)

Enforcement of Trade Treaties in Repeated Play

Once they have signed a tariff treaty, politicians face the decision whether or not to adhere to it. In each round of a repeated play game, they may defect from the agreement or continue to adhere to it.

With discount factors δ_A, δ_B, A's pay-off from continued adherence to a treaty with tariffs $\{t_A, t_B\}$ is $(1 - \delta_A)^{-1} M_A[Y_{1A}(p_{dA}(t_A), t_B); Y_{2A}(p_{dA}(t_A))]$. If A defects from the treaty today, returning to the single play tariff t^*_A,[36] B will return to its single-play tariff t^*_B in subsequent rounds, yielding the pay-off $\delta_A M_A[Y_{1A}(p_{dA}(t^*_A), t_B); Y_{2A}(p_{dA}(t_A))] + (1 - \delta_A)^{-1} \delta_A M_A[Y_{1A}(p_{dA}(t^*_A), t^*_B); Y_{2A}(p_{dA}(t^*_A))]$.

It is easy to show that A will continue to adhere to the treaty if

$$\delta_A \geq \frac{M_A[Y_{1A}(p_{dA}(t^*_A), t_B); Y_{2A}(p_{dA}(t^*_A))] - M_A[Y_{1A}(p_{dA}(t_A), t_B); Y_{2A}(p_{dA}(t_A))]}{M_A[Y_{1A}(p_{dA}(t^*_A), t_B); Y_{2A}(p_{dA}(t^*_A))] - M_A[YSUBIA(p_{dA}(t^*_A), t^*_B); Y_{2A}(p_{dA}(t^*_A))]}$$

$$(2.A.4)$$

It is trivially true that:

Remark 3   Variations in discount factors explain variations in trade agreements.

Less trivial are changes in the right-hand side of equation (2.A.4). To find out how the pre-agreement tariff levels affect the probability of a tariff treaty, take the partial derivative of the RHS with respect to t^*_A. The denominator is always greater than zero, so the sign of the derivative depends on the sign of $\{M_A[t^*_A, t_B] - M_A[t^*_A, t^*_B]\}(\delta M_A/\delta Y_{1A})(\delta Y_{1A}/\delta p_{dA})(\delta p_{dA}/dt^*_A) + \{M_A[t^*_A, t_B] - M_A [t_A, t_B]\}(\delta M_A/\delta Y_{2A})(\delta Y_{2A}/\delta p_{dA})(\delta p_{dA}/dt^*_A)$. This term is positive if $M_A[t^*_A, t_B][(\delta M_A/\delta Y_{1A})(\delta Y_{1A}/\delta p_{dA})) + (\delta M_A/\delta Y_{2A})(\delta Y_{2A}/\delta p_{dA})] > M_A[t_A, t_B](\delta M_A/\delta Y_{2A})(\delta Y_{2A}/\delta p_{dA}) + M_A[t^*_A, t^*_B] (\delta M_A/\delta Y_{1A})(\delta Y_{1A}/\delta p_{dA})$.

In the trade treaty equilibrium, a given price increase will yield a greater marginal increase in political support from import-competers than its marginal loss from exporters, so $|(\delta M_A/\delta Y_{1A})(\delta Y_{1A}/\delta p_{dA})| < |(\delta M_A/\delta Y_{2A})(\delta Y_{2A}/\delta p_{dA})|$. Because $(\delta M_A/\delta Y_{1A})(\delta Y_{1A}/\delta p_{dA}) < 0 < (\delta M_A/\delta Y_{2A})(\delta Y_{2A}/\delta p_{dA})$, the above term is greater than zero, so the numerator of the derivative above is positive. This means that increases in the single-play tariff t^*_A increase the RHS of the stability condition, making cooperation less likely:

Hypothesis 5   Tariff treaties are less likely for high-tariff countries than for low-tariff countries.

As a corollary of Hypotheses 1 and 5:

Hypothesis 6   Tariff treaties are more likely among countries with decreasing terms of trade than for countries with increasing terms of trade.

A similar analysis is possible to see how foreign tariffs affect the home likelihood of cooperation. If we assume for simplicity that the cooperative tariff t_B is independent of the single-play tariff t^*_B,[37] then it is easy to show that:

Hypothesis 7   Tariff treaties are more likely when foreign tariffs begin high than when foreign tariffs begin low.

Proof follows easily from equation (2.A.4).

NOTES

1   At the same time, William Huskisson at the British Board of Trade negotiated a series of reciprocity treaties in navigation, a subject not covered here.
2. This chapter is limited to the European treaty network. For a preliminary discussion of the Latin American treaties, see Pahre's unpublished manuscript.
3. The details vary, of course. Some previously-enfranchised workers lost the vote by the £10 property qualification of the Reform Act of 1832, though the Act generally expanded the franchise. See discussion of this Act in Schonhardt-Bailey, Chapter 5.
4. Prussian treaties with Austria(–Hungary), Denmark (through Holsten), Luxemburg, the Netherlands (which was at times the sovereign of Luxemburg), and Britain (through Hannover) are counted as extra-German, though these states were also members of the German Confederation at various times. Aside from the USA and Mexico, non-Prussian tariff treaties with the minor German states are rare but not unheard of.
5. It is possible that they signed less liberal treaties after turning protectionist than they had before. For a possible explanation, see Pahre (2001b).
6. Those shown are all European dyads that include either France or Great Britain in which either an alliance or a trade treaty was in effect in at least one year from 1815 to 1913. Data on alliances and ententes follow the Correlates of War project that is standard in the discipline of Political Science.
7. For a modern treatment of this relationship, see Papayoanou (1999).
8. Though they are NTBs, auction quotas would be an exception to this claim. While occasionally used today, I am not aware of any auction quotas in the nineteenth century.
9. Coffee and tea had partial substitutes in beer, which was produced domestically. While a desire to protect beer did affect the wine tariff (Nye, 1991), the link to coffee and tea is more tenuous.
10. It is worth noting that in all these countries the ratification constraint was rarely binding, with a rejection rate of 1 or 2 per cent over the century. The British and German legislatures never failed to ratify a treaty, while the French and Italian legislatures rejected only one treaty each. Anticipating possible non-ratification may still affect the substance of a trade treaty (Milner and Rosendorff, 1997), even when all treaties are ratified.

11. This is especially important with incomplete information, where the government must make concessions to try to satisfy the ratifier. Because it does not know the ratifier's preferences perfectly, it will sometimes misjudge the necessary concessions and ratification failure will occur (Milner and Rosendorff, 1997).
12. In the USA and Mexico, presidential independence from Congress has a similar effect inhibiting treaties.
13. A third possibility is that institutions might strengthen the pro-trade lobby, but such an account leaves unexplained why that lobby might succeed in obtaining trade treaties but fail to simply reduce tariffs as shown above.
14. This will exclude important within-regime changes, such as a move towards partisan politics, for example (see Verdier, 1994).
15. The apparent change at the time of the Second Reform Act reflects a change in the method of calculating British GNP. After a delay of five to ten years, the end of the *Socialistengesetz* in 1890 seems to have halted or even reversed the move to protectionism in Germany (see Figure 2.5).
16. Before 1860, the figure shows Piedmont–Sardinia's treaties with non-Italian states. It shows Prussian treaties with non-German states until 1870.
17. For an endogenous theory of tariffs in two countries that includes revenue concerns, see Long and Vousden (1991). The effects of revenue are intuitive.
18. As Schonhardt-Bailey shows in Chapter 5, 'nationalizing the interest' is another way that political actors can increase their political support.
19. If politicians seek an electoral majority, and no more, the results here would not necessarily follow for any politician already guaranteed such a majority. However, with multiple issues, it is reasonable to assume that politicians maximize political support (or the probability of election) when making policy on a single issue such as trade policy. See Magee, Brock and Young (1989) and Mayer and Li (1994) for a fuller discussion.
20. This assumption contrasts with Magee, Brock and Young's (1989) specialization theorems but is empirically more accurate (Austen-Smith, 1991). My reduced-form equations do not explicitly model each interest group's decision problem; for the general rent-seeking problem, see Becker (1985).
21. I set aside the question why politicians use tariffs as opposed to other policy instruments.
22. The prices of many other goods also fell during this period but agricultural prices generally fell faster.
23. This assumes that international markets are not perfectly competitive for there is implicitly some effect on exporters of restricted access to a given country's market. Exporters do not find new buyers costlessly. McGillivray provides some examples in Chapter 3, showing how disrupted trade relationships may harm exporters even in competitive primary products markets.
24. McGillivray's Chapter 3 discusses one such trade war in which some states attempted but failed to respond to British protectionism with protection of their own before 1789. One could code failed attempts at retaliatory trade policies as anomalies for Hypothesis 3. Alternatively, one could also code such cases as confirmations of Hypothesis 3, showing how politicians are forced away from non-equilibrium choices and towards the equilibrium discussed here.
25. The Nash equilibrium is the standard solution concept in game theory; most other solution concepts are refinements of the Nash (see Morrow, 1994 for introduction). The Nash equilibrium is a set of player strategies such that no player would be better off changing her strategy if no one else changes theirs. Any game will have at least one Nash equilibrium, though it may have more.
26. It is further possible that a scarce factor of production would favour a trade agreement with a country in which its factor was even more scarce (Trefler, 1993).
27. This was not entirely selfless, since the industrialists expected that increased agrarian incomes would raise the demand for their own products.
28. This also seems to be the intuition among policy-makers. Many French politicians believed that the two-tiered Méline tariff of 1892 could use its high maximum levels to force other countries into making concessions if they were to receive the lower minimum

tier tariffs. Many Austrians believed likewise, as does Johann von Bazant (1894: 5): 'Without the double-tariff system, the MFN clause has neither rhyme nor reason'. ('Ohne Doppeltarif hat die Meistbegünstigungsklausel keinen Sinn und Wert'.)

29. Which intuition is correct depends on the exact relationship between the pay-offs for cooperation, non-cooperation and the temptation to defect. In a model of public goods provision, for example, either may be correct depending on an actor's share of the total contributions to the public good (Pahre, 1999a: chapter 7). Here each state's concessions are relatively large, so the problem of defection drives the result.

30. For a theory of multilateral institutions that suggests why MFN clauses may be rational, see Pahre (1994).

31. Britain had relatively few tariffs that it could agree to reduce, though its reliance on lower wine tariffs left some room for bargaining, in principle if not in practice (Marsh, 1999; Nye, 1991).

32. Another set of hypotheses, the positive correlation between countries who have signed a trade treaty and the negative correlation between countries who have not signed a trade treaty, has been tested elsewhere (Pahre, 1998).

33. This argument was important in British debates at mid-century (Irwin, 1989).

34. Number of treaties in effect is a better dependent variable than treaties signed, for two reasons. First, treaties vary in length for idiosyncratic country-specific reasons. The Turks signed seven-year treaties, the Sardinians preferred 12-year durations, while British navigation treaties expired after ten years. Counting treaty signatures would give Turkish treaties half again as much weight as most others. Second, the number of treaties in effect changes when an existing treaty lapses, which is an important form of non-event missed by a treaty initiation variable.

35. I chose the 0.40 cut-off because of the way the data are distributed. There are no correlation coefficients between 0.30 and 0.40, and only two of the 45 coefficients are between 0.20 and 0.30. My claims are therefore not sensitive to the choice of threshold within a wide range.

36. An alternative assumption would be that A defects by choosing the tariff $t^{**}_A > t^*_A$ that maximizes M_A when B's tariff is $t_B < t^*_B$, reverting to t^*_A when B retaliates with t^*_B. This assumption complicates the notation but does not change the analysis with respect to changes in t^*_A.

37. If we relax this assumption, then the sign of the derivative depends on the sign of $[(\partial Y_{1A}/\partial t_B)(\partial t_B/\partial t_B^*) - \partial Y_{1A}/\partial t_B^*]$.

3. Trading free and opening markets

Fiona McGillivray

One theme of this volume is how institutions structure political conflict over trade policy. Institutions affect who makes the decisions and what motivates them. Therefore, an institutional change can lead to a radical alteration in policy. Since trade is a two-way exchange, such institutional change within one partner can affect the entire nature of trading relationships. Institutional changes in one nation can have trade policy repercussions throughout its trading partners.[1] The Reciprocal Trade Agreements Act of 1934, for example, was an institutional change that delegated authority for negotiating tariffs from Congress to the President. This legislative rule change in the USA not only helped liberalize US trade, it helped liberalize world trade (Bailey, Goldstein and Weingast, 1997).

In this chapter, I take a step further back in US history to focus on an earlier institutional change; one that also restructured conflict over trade policy within the USA and influenced foreign nations' trade policy. In 1783, at the end of the revolutionary war, the USA was a loose confederation of 13 states. When the USA switched from the Articles of Confederation to the Constitution in 1789, authority for interstate and foreign trade shifted from decentralized political control – 13, largely independent and autonomous states – to centralized political control – a Federal Congress.[2] It was anticipated that this rule change would alter the asymmetric nature of trading relationship between the US states and Britain. A common external tariff would create the bargaining leverage US states needed to force open British markets (Taussig, 1892).

This chapter focuses on two trading puzzles in the Articles of Confederation period. Contrary to constitutional lore, recent scholarship reveals that interstate trade was relatively open under the Articles of Confederation. What explains the appearance of a free-trade area and why did that free-trade area seek to shift to a customs union with a common external tariff? In the course of this chapter I make the following argument. Under the Articles of Confederation, we have a series of decentralized actors, all trying to maximize the welfare of their constituents; but the individual units are in competition with each other for the trade of one large nation (Britain). With the British having relative freedom to choose where to land their exports, the political competition was not between two nations, Britain and the USA, but between the individual states vying for the lion's share of trade with Britain. Because they dominated the sea lanes, British merchants landed their goods in the ports of those states offering the most favourable terms. States did attempt to place restrictions on re-exporting but were unable to enforce rules of origin. Unable to prevent trade deflection, states undercut each other's duties in an attempt to attract valuable foreign trade. Instead of cooperating, states competed for British tariff revenue.

The problem facing states was how to strategically coordinate to retaliate against British trade barriers. All states wanted to retaliate against the British for closing important overseas markets to US goods and shipping. Despite repeated attempts, however, the states failed to agree on a uniform external tariff. The problem was twofold – both a coordination and a collective action problem. States disagreed on how high trade restrictions should be and what should be taxed. Moreover, individually, each state had an incentive to free-ride on the retaliatory efforts of others. States that tried to retaliate unilaterally by imposing duties on British imports found they only punished themselves. They lost British trade to neighbouring states. States that tried to punish free-rider states, by taxing re-exported British goods, found it costly and ineffective; the British goods were simply re-routed to ports in other states. Instead of cooperating, states competed for British import trade. This created a state-by-state tariff structure on British goods and shipping which, from a retaliatory goal, was too low. Without the ability to create a unified retaliatory tariff, the states were forced to accept the British terms of trade. This confined the newly independent US states to a 'passive commerce' with their biggest trading partner, Britain.

If these are some of the properties of a decentralized regulatory system, what are the incentives for institutional change? The ratification of the Constitution in 1789 centralized the formation of trade policy in Congress. Why states wanted, or were able, to federate is not the issue here (but see Rakove, 1996). Rather, the question is, given the states enacted a constitution, what effect did this have on trade policy? This change in institutional design not only altered the US's internal and external tariff policy, it also altered the entire nature of the US–British trading relationship. The previous British tactic of diverting trade to the ports of the state with the lowest tariffs no longer worked since the common external tariff meant that British goods were subject to the same tariff wherever they were unloaded. Congress was now able to credibly restrict Britain's access to its largest export market. This empowered Congress to negotiate with the British after 1789.

Given the focus on the role of interests and institutions, this chapter parallels that of Pahre (see Chapter 2 this volume). However, unlike Pahre, it analyses how institutions affect problems of strategic coordination between nations. It is also true that ideas played an important role in the decision to retaliate with a common external tariff. It is probable that states wanted to employ restrictive tariffs because mercantilism was a widespread and popular idea in the 1780s (Nettels, 1962). Nonetheless, the constancy of these ideas cannot explain why interstate trade in goods and shipping was relatively open prior to 1789. Or why tariffs on British goods were, on average, lower under the Articles of Confederation than under the Constitution. I argue that political institutions and the strategic trading environment are the keys to understanding US interstate and foreign trade under the Articles of Confederation and the subsequent Federal period.

Not surprisingly, the chapter concludes that different political institutions lead to different trade policies. This does not imply, however, that one type of institution is 'superior' to another. Even with the same domestic interests, the strategic nature of the trading environment affects which trade policies are chosen. Thus, under some circumstances, one set of rules might generate the most preferable policies. As trading relations change, however, these same institutional rules might produce less desirable policies. Under the Articles of Confederation, centralized authority was not necessary to create open interstate trade. Open interstate trade occurs when decentralized political institutions are dominated by exporters. And, all else equal, decentralized political control can lead to lower external tariff barriers than a centralized system would. However, under a decentralized system, nations must take the trading environment as given: they engage in a passive commerce. This inability to retaliate ensures open markets stay open. Yet, when overseas markets are closed, a decentralized system means that states, or nations, are powerless to force markets open. In these circumstances protectionism survives unchecked.

The chapter is organized as follows. The first part examines interstate trading relationships under the Articles of Confederation. What explains the appearance of a free-trade area under the Articles of Confederation? State institutions, state economic interests and pre-revolutionary trade flows are used to predict the pattern of interstate trade, and the extent of discriminatory regulation among the 13 states. State tariff schedules for New York, Massachusetts, South Carolina and Virginia are used as empirical evidence.[3] The second part of the chapter focuses on foreign tariff barriers under the Articles of Confederation. Why did that free-trade area seek to shift to a customs union with a common external tariff? The same three variables, state institutions, state economic actors and foreign trade flows, are used to explain the coordination and collective action problems hindering cooperation between the states. The last part of the chapter explores the incentives for institutional change. I argue that centralized authority was not necessary to create open interstate trade in the USA. However, states were frustrated in their attempts to create a uniform retaliatory tariff until political authority for trade policy was concentrated in Congress.

INTERSTATE TRADE UNDER THE ARTICLES OF CONFEDERATION

The Constitutional Lore

It is part of constitutional lore that the 13 years under the Articles of Confederation were fraught with interstate trade disputes. States were short of revenue, and if there was an opportunity to profit from their neighbours, states took it. States used import duties, export duties, tonnage fees, pilot fees and wharfage duties to discriminate against one another. Jensen (1950: 337) argues, 'No idea is more firmly planted in American history than the idea that one of the most difficult problems during the Confederation was that of barriers to trade between state and state'. Epstein and Walker's (1995: 4) textbook on US judicial politics is typical when it claims:

> Because the government lacked any coercive power over the states, mutual coop-
> eration among them quickly dissipated. They engaged in trading practices that
> hurt one another economically. In short, the states acted more like 13 separate
> countries than a union or even a confederation.

The *Federalist Papers* are the source of the 'beggar-thy-neighbour' charac-
terizations of interstate trade under the Articles of Confederation. This was one of many arguments put forth by the framers to persuade Americans that they needed a federal constitution. In No. 22, Hamilton declares that if there is one thing we all agree on, it is that if states are not constrained, they will erect barriers to trade. As such, the power to regulate interstate trade must be centralized in Congress.

> The interfering and unneighborly regulations of some States, contrary to the
> true spirit of the Union, have in different instances given just cause of umbrage
> and complaint to others; and it is to be feared that examples of this nature, if not
> restrained by national control, would be multiplied and extended till they
> became not less serious sources of animosity and discord, than injurious imped-
> iments to the intercourse between the different parts of the Confederacy
> (Hamilton, Madison and Jay, 1787: 104).

Placing tariffs on imports from other states would be a politically inexpen-
sive way of raising state revenue. Under the beggar-thy-neighbour scenario,[4] each state had a dominant strategy to place tariffs on imports from

other states. Placing tariffs on goods from Connecticut and Rhode Island would increase revenue for New York while protecting New York's infant industries. However, the other 12 states also faced the same set of incentives. As each state unilaterally moved towards protection, cooperation ceased, reducing economic activity and retarding growth.

There are only a few examples in the *Federalist Papers*, however, of interstate trade disputes. Although the theoretical argument is credible – states needed revenue and quickly[5] – it is not the only possible scenario under the Articles of Confederation. Whether or not New York placed duties on interstate trade with Connecticut and New Jersey depends on who made the decisions in New York and what motivated them. The 13 states had different political institutions, different trading patterns and different political leaders. While discriminatory trade regulation might have boosted state revenues, it also had redistributive effects. Generally, the benefits from import duties and navigation laws were concentrated in the protected industry while the costs of protection were more widely spread over all consumers – who ended up paying higher prices. Regulating interstate trade might have increased state revenues. Yet, if it harmed the interests of political élites, it is unlikely such policies would be adopted. It is more likely that trade regulation reflected the interests of political élites, those who could influence policy making. In a decentralized regulatory setting, the important actors are the states. To understand interstate trade policy we need to focus on who made the decisions in each state, and what motivated them. The first step is to specify the interests of the different state economic actors. This will depend, in part, on the structure of interstate and foreign trade. The second step is examining how state political institutions shaped which economic interests won representation. How does representation effect the openness of interstate trade? The third step is to examine the empirical evidence. Trade regulation in New York, Massachusetts, South Carolina and Virginia are used to determine the 'openness' of interstate trade.

State Economics and Politics

In 1775, the USA had a small, thinly dispersed domestic market (McCusker and Menard, 1991). The manufacturing sector was poorly developed, in part because, during the colonial period the British had prevented the growth of a colonial manufacturing industry. For example, the production of textiles and finished iron products was restricted under British rule. In 1775, agriculture employed approximately 85 per cent of the workforce (Atack and Passell, 1979). During the colonial period most output from farms was consumed on the farm. However, the British encouraged states to send exports in primary products to Britain and its colonies. US states exported raw materials (lumber, naval supplies, salted fish, rice, tobacco, indigo, cotton and so on) to Britain and the British West Indies and imported manufactured British goods. British goods travelled by ship to US states, where many goods were re-exported between states through the coastal trade (Walton and Shepherd, 1979).

The USA did have a thriving shipbuilding industry in 1775. The US shipping industry had prospered under the British Navigation Laws (Shepherd and Walton, 1972). This shipbuilding industry was located largely in the north and dominated the coastal trade and the West Indies trade routes. Banking and insurance were the only other large industries in 1775. The embargo on British imports during the revolutionary war allowed manufacturing industries to develop, particularly in the north (Atack and Passell, 1979; Nettels, 1962). Nonetheless, agriculture was still the major US industry in all 13 states after the revolutionary war.

Unfortunately, we do not have figures on interstate trade under the Articles of Confederation or, for that matter, the colonial period. But we do have data on foreign exports during the colonial period (Shepherd and Walton, 1972). It is possible to extrapolate from these figures about the type of interstate trade taking place under the Articles of Confederation. In part, this is because interstate trade was influenced in important ways by the export sector.

Table 3.1 reveals that by the end of the colonial era different regions were specializing in the export of different products. The Middle Colonies[6] were known as the 'breadbasket' of the USA because of their high grain exports. New England[7] exported large quantities of fish, beef, pork and lumber. The Upper South[8] exported tobacco and the Lower South[9] concentrated on rice and indigo. In 1783, these were still the major trading industries in the four different regions (McCusker and Menard, 1991).

By the late part of the colonial period a lively interstate trade had developed. This had a value of about a quarter that of overseas trade. Interstate trade served two functions (Walton and Shepherd, 1979). First, it distributed US products for local consumption. As Table 3.1 shows, different regions specialized in different staple products and there was some interstate trade in these products. For example, grain moved from the Middle Colonies to be consumed in New England. There was some interstate trade in manufactured goods among the Northern states. The US manufacturing industry did grow in size during the revolutionary war; however, it was still relatively small and scattered. Most manufactured goods were imported from Britain.

The second function of interstate trade was the re-exportation of US and British goods. Re-exported goods are foreign or US goods brought into the port of one state but ultimately destined for another state. Part of

*Table 3.1   Average annual value and destinations of selected commodity
exports from four regions, 1768–1772 (pounds sterling)*

New England	Britain	Southern Europe	West Indies	Total
Fish	206	57195	94754	152155
Beef, pork	374	461	89118	89953
Wood products	5983	1352	57769	65271
Whale products	40443	804	20416	62103
Potash	22390	0	0	22399
Total products	76975	65603	278068	439101

Upper South	Britain	S. Europe	West Indies	Total
Tobacco	756128	0	0	756128
Grain products	10206	97523	68794	199485
Iron	28314	0	461	29191
Wood products	9060	2115	10195	22484
Total products	827052	99163	91818	1046883

Middle Colonies	Britain	S. Europe	West Indies	Total
Grain products	15453	175280	178961	379380
Flaxseed	771	0	0	35956
Wood products	2635	3053	18845	29348
Iron	24053	0	2921	27669
Beef, pork	2142	1199	16692	20033
Total products	68369	181759	223610	526545

Lower South	Britain	S. Europe	West Indies	Total
Rice	198590	50982	55961	305533
Indigo	111864	0	0	111864
Deerskins	37093	0	0	37093
Naval stores	31709	0	0	31709
Wood products	2520	1396	21620	25764
Total products	394030	54169	102110	551949

Notes:
The Middle Colonies are New York, New Jersey, Pennsylvania and Delaware.
New England is Massachusetts, New Hampshire, Connecticut and Rhode Island.
The Upper South is Maryland and Virginia.
The Lower South is North Carolina, South Carolina and Georgia.

Source: Shepherd and Walton (1972); McCusker and Menard (1991).

the re-export trade was collecting US goods for export to overseas markets. North Carolina tobacco was reportedly exported to Virginia before going on to Britain. Some commodities in New Jersey were re-exported through New York and Philadelphia (McCusker and Menard, 1991). The other part of the re-export trade was distributing imported British goods via costal routes. For example, British clocks landed in New York and were re-exported to New Jersey and Connecticut ports. Most of this interstate trade took place on US vessels.

So which domestic actors benefited and which lost from restricted interstate trade? The most vocal demanders of trade protection were manufacturers (Jensen, 1950). They faced import competition from industries in Northern states and in Britain. Their business would improve if they could restrict the flow of competing imports. Manufacturers, however, were not the only group who wanted to restrict trade. Navigation laws enabled shippers to carry a larger proportion of interstate trade. Shipowners and shipbuilders wanted to restrict which ships could transport interstate trade.

Not all groups, however, had an interest in restricting interstate trade. Farmers should have been relatively uninterested in levying duties on US manufactured goods or shipping. Protecting manufactured goods was costly to them, because they paid more for their imports. Navigation laws also increased the cost of re-exporting their products. The benefits to farmers from protecting their primary products was low. For many primary products (that is, tobacco, lumber and indigo), there was little or no interstate trade; all goods were directly exported to foreign markets. Where there was interstate trade in primary products, it was typically non-competitive. For example, although grain was exported from the Middle Colonies to the North East, the grain industry in the North East was small and undeveloped (McCusker and Menard, 1991).

Most historians agree that during this period, manufacturers and shippers wanted trade restrictions and that farmers were indifferent or supportive of open interstate trade (McCusker and Menard, 1991). The more controversial issue is which of these economic actors had political clout? And did this vary by state? Many historians point to manufactures as the important political actors (Jensen, 1950; Nevins, 1927; Zornow, 1954a, 1954b, 1955, 1956). Manufacturers were extremely vocal in demanding protection after 1783 when British goods began flooding the US market.

Several of the states attempted to overcome the hardships of 1780s by enacting defensive or remedial laws. The depression . . . gave birth to the American movement for protective tariffs. In 1785 manufacturers, artisans, and mechanics of New York, Philadelphia, and Boston held meetings at which they besought their state governments to impose duties for the purpose of curbing importations, stopping the outflow of specie, and aiding domestic producers (Nettels, 1962: 69).

However, while manufacturers protested loudly, they had little political voice. Farming interests, not manufacturers, were over-represented in all state legislatures. When the USA announced its independence from the British, most states reformed their colonial political institutions by eradicating the royal prerogative and empowering state legislatures (Beard, 1935). States typically chose bicameral legislatures with weak governors (Pennsylvania, Georgia and Vermont were unicameral). Only in Massachusetts did the governor have a veto (Douglass, 1955). In all 13 states, legislatures were more representative than in colonial times. Wood (1991: 250) argues:

> The state legislatures were greatly democratized by the Revolution – by both the increase in the number of members in each assembly and the broadening of their electorates. Men of even more humble and rural origins and less education than had sat in the colonial assemblies were now elected as representatives. In New Hampshire, for example, the colonial house of representatives in 1765 had contained only thirty-four members, almost all well-to-do gentlemen from the coastal region around Portsmouth. By 1786 the state's house of representatives numbered eighty-eighty members, of whom most were ordinary farmers or men of moderate wealth and many were from western areas of the state'.

The voting franchise was extended in all 13 states, yet all states retained property restrictions on who could vote and who could hold office. These varied across states but in all 13 states the property restrictions over-represented landowners, even in the more democratic North.[10] This was particularly true in the upper houses which were often indirectly elected and had higher property restrictions on office-holding. Monaghan (1935: 97) describes the New York state constitution of 1777 as 'A victory for the minority of stability and privilege'.[11] That said, manufactures and shippers did have more political representation in the North than the South. This example from New Jersey reveals the policy differences between the two groups in the state legislature.

> In 1783 the New Jersey legislature declared its ports open and free to all merchants. New Jersey merchants were not satisfied with this. They demanded import duties on foreign goods brought in by way of other states, but each new legislature refused until June 1787 when a tax was levied on imported articles, except on those were the growth or manufacture of the US. The popular protest was immediate and violent; in October 1787 the legislature suspended the law. The legislature, dominated by farmers, knew that New Jersey could not develop an independent overseas commerce and realized also that such a tariff would function as a tax on consumers for the benefit of ambitious local merchants.(Jensen, 1950: 338)

In this case, manufacturers were more concerned about gaining protection from British goods than from US products. The key to open interstate trade in US goods is that farmers were over-represented in legislatures and that manufacturers in the North were not as threatened by US manufacturing interests. As such, interstate trade in US goods is expected to be relatively open, even in the North.

Interstate trade in re-exported goods (both British and American) is also expected to be relatively open. Few of the 13 states were land-bound and there was a lively coastal trade. If New York raises its tariffs on re-exported goods, these goods will simply be re-routed to ports in other states. State revenues will fall as state ports lose valuable business. Given that farming interests are over-represented in all states, it is expected that interstate trade in foreign goods is relatively open. Where re-exportation duties on foreign goods exist, it will be in Northern, rather than Southern states.

In summary, rural interests were over-represented in all states. Generally, farmers did not support protectionist policies for US industry. What farmers cared about was cheap imports and access to foreign markets for their products. As such, there is little reason to suppose that states adopted beggar-thy-neighbour trade policies towards interstate goods and shipping. Rather, this analysis of state institutional structure and the preferences of economic interests within states suggests that interstate trade should be relatively open. What, then, is the empirical evidence?

Interstate Trade 1783–7

There is only one case of a US tariff dispute cited in the *Federalist Papers*. In 1787 New York placed duties on ships entering or leaving New York from New Jersey and Connecticut. It was historians, such as John Fiske (1892) and Allan Nevins (1927), who developed the empirical basis for the framers' arguments. Nevins (1927: 555) concludes of this period 'disputes over trade were the most constant and discreditable of all'. Fiske and Nevins were vastly influential and this story of trade conflict has worked its way into conventional wisdom.

However, little rigorous research has been done on economic conditions under the Articles of Confederation. Part of the problem is finding economic data on this period. The colonial period is referred to as the 'statistical dark age' of US history; however, the British did record information on overseas trade figures. The US Government began collecting this information after 1789. Unfortunately little is known about the period in between. Nonetheless, economic historians have begun to piece together a picture of trading patterns during this period (Walton and Shepherd, 1979). Evidence has also been gathered on the extent of trade regulation from state statutes. William Zornow, an economic historian, has catalogued tariff schedules from state statutes for Massachusetts, Virginia, South Carolina and New York. These were among the largest and were reputedly the most predatory of all the states. If anyone was warring, it should have been these states.

To put it bluntly – the evidence from these tariff schedules suggests that states were not involved in beggar-thy-neighbour trade wars. Zornow (1954a, 1954b, 1955, 1956) finds that US products were generally admitted duty-free into these states. He catalogues a typical example, 'Every barrel of beer or malt liquors which was imported into South Carolina paid two shillings, but American products were exempt' (ibid., 34). New York from 1784 onwards excluded all US goods from tariff duties (Zornow, 1956). In fact, all 13 states gradually adopted similar policies towards domestically grown products or manufactured goods (Jensen, 1950). Massachusetts and Virginia were the least cooperative. Massachusetts had, however, eliminated virtually all duties from US products by 1784 (Zornow, 1954a). It took Virginia until 1788, but it also followed suit (Zornow, 1954b).

Navigation laws were another instrument that could be used to discriminate against out-of-state producers and shippers. All states did pass some type of navigation laws. Higher tonnage duties on foreign ships and additional duties on imports docking in foreign ships were widespread. Even in 1783, US ships were generally taxed at far lower levels than foreign ships (Jensen, 1950). Over time US ships were gradually completely exempt from these laws. Massachusetts navigation laws were initially among the toughest of all the states, yet even Massachusetts had removed tonnage fees and double duties from US ships by 1785 (Zornow, 1954a).

On average, US goods travelled duty-free by 1788 and state navigation laws exempted US-owned ships. It appears that trade regulation in all 13 states became less, not more, discriminatory towards US goods and shipping during the Articles of Confederation period.

The greatest source of state quarrels seemed to be the duties states levied on re-exported goods. While many states complained that goods in transit were taxed, the taxed goods were products which were repackaged or held in inventory before being sold on to merchants in other states. Kitch (1981) points out this duty is similar to an *ad valorem* tax on stocked goods. Moreover, state regulations suggest that most goods passing directly through states went duty-free (Zornow, 1956). Often the good had to be kept in the same packaging and proof was required of the nationality of both the product and the ship that first brought the good to the USA. For example, Zornow (1956: 44) describes the case in New York:

> When ships landed at a New York port with goods aboard consigned to persons living in other states such goods were to be allowed to pass duty free upon the giving of a sworn statement as to their ultimate destination. There is a further statement that good must be re-exported in the same package, but there is no

specification that it must be re-exported in the same vessel which originally brought the goods.

At different times, different states did try to tax goods in transit but these duties did not last long. For example, in the one case cited in the *Federalist*, Hamilton describes New York's decision to put entrance and clearance fees on all vessels bound to or coming from Connecticut and New Jersey. This law was effectively repealed the next year. By 1789, re-exported goods generally passed through states duty-free. It appears that the loss of trade through a state's ports typically led to the repeal of these restrictions (Gorlin, 1990).

In summary, there is little empirical evidence that states were engaged in beggar-thy-neighbour trade policies. Evidence from state statutes suggests that interstate trade was relatively open in both foreign and US goods. What explains the appearance of a free-trade area under the Articles of Confederation? I argue that the over-representation of export interests in state institutions, the relatively small size of interstate trade in US goods, and the competition between states to attract British goods all contributed to the creation of a free-trade area.

The second part of the chapter examines why this free-trade area sought to shift to a customs union with a common external tariff. I focus on how the decentralized regulatory structure and competition for British trade created both a coordination and a collective action problem. Although states recognized the need for a uniform external tariff barrier, they repeatedly failed to agree to one. This resulted in a tariff structure on British goods, which, from a retaliatory goal, was too low. The states' failure to agree on a retaliatory tariff was, in part, a result of Northern manufacturers and Southern farmers' failure to agree on the level of the external tariff rate. In part, as well, there was a collective action problem that was structured by the decentralized regulatory setting and the asymmetric trading relationship between Britain and the US states. Overseas trade under the Articles of Confederation is discussed next.

OVERSEAS TRADE UNDER THE ARTICLES OF CONFEDERATION

At the end of the revolutionary war, the US economy hit a recession. In the 1780s, prices fell, causing farmers, merchants, shippers and manufacturers to suffer. Demand for tobacco, rice and other primary products stagnated. In 1783 the British reduced US access to the West Indies and Britain's North American colonies. Gorlin (1990: 56–57) argues, 'farmers, shipbuilders and merchants, as well as fisherman and whalers, all suffered serious economic dislocations from the loss of the rich triangular trade and the inaccessibility of important British colonial ports'.

During the colonial period, 56 per cent of US exports went to Britain and a further 26 per cent went to the West Indies. Following the revolutionary war, the USA lost much of its direct access to these markets (McCusker and Menard, 1991). Landowners in all states were badly hit. Tobacco was heavily dutied in Britain. Breadstuffs, whale oil, rice, fish and salted provisions either had very high duties or were prohibited in Britain. All West Indies trade had to be carried out in British ships. Since most West Indies trade had been done in US ships, this badly affected the ability of merchants and farmers to sell their goods there.[12] Table 3.1 depicts trading patterns before the British placed restrictions on US goods. Given this pattern of colonial trade flows, it is highly plausible that farming interests in the 1780s were badly hurt by British trading restrictions.

At the time, the question was how could US framers get better access to British markets? Congress sent John Adams to negotiate a commercial treaty with the British. The British, however, refused point-blank to negotiate with Adams on matters of trade (Nettels, 1962). It was widely felt that retaliation against the unfair trade policies of the British was the only way to open foreign markets (Rakove, 1996). At the time Adams argued:

> The commerce of America will have no relief at present, nor, in my opinion, ever, until the United States shall have generally passed navigation acts. If this measure is not adopted we shall be derided; the more we suffer, the more will our calamities be laughed at (To Jay, Oct 21, 1785).[13]

There is evidence that the British cared about access to the US markets: a significant part of British exports went to the USA (Nettels, 1962) and British trade to the USA grew rapidly before the revolutionary war. Over 40 per cent of exports from Britain went to the USA and Africa (McCusker and Menard, 1991). Although the economic recession following the revolutionary war reduced the demand for British goods, the US market was clearly growing. There were reasons to believe that a retaliatory tariff might have brought the British to the negotiating table.

Unfortunately the Continental Congress did not have the ability to enforce external tariffs or the jurisdiction to control interstate commerce. In 1781, Virginia proposed legislation to authorize the Continental Congress to levy a 5 per cent import duty against those nations which did not have a commercial treaty with the USA. The legislation was never enacted. Rhode Island was the first to back out of implementing the act; however, other states quickly followed.

States did try to retaliate individually, by levying tariffs on British imports and imposing tonnage duties on British ships (Jensen, 1950). Although states differed in the harshness of their restrictions, all states had duties on British imports and ships during this period. Lighter duties were levied on goods from nations that had commercial treaties with the US states. For example, in South Carolina, sugar was taxed at twice the rate when imported from Britain rather than Spain, France or the Netherlands (Zornow, 1955). These higher discriminatory duties on British goods, however, proved ineffective. The British did not lower their trade restrictions, nor did they enter into bilateral or multilateral treaties with the states. Most of these higher discriminatory duties were repealed by 1789. Zornow (1954a, 1954b, 1955, 1956) concludes the tariff schedules of Massachusetts, New York, Virginia and South Carolina were, by 1789, converging.

Why did the states find it difficult to coordinate on a uniform tariff barrier under the Articles of Confederation? In part, disagreement between Northern and Southern states over the size and the type of discriminatory duty prevented agreement Most manufacturing and shipbuilding industries were located in the North. Northern states are frequently described as more protectionist (Nevins, 1927; Nettels, 1962; Zornow, 1954a, 1956). It is important, however, not to exaggerate the extent of the North–South coordination problem. State statutes from Massachusetts, New York, Virginia and South Carolina suggest that tariffs adopted in Northern states were, on average, no more protectionist than those adopted in Southern states (Zornow, 1954a, 1954b, 1955, 1956). Indeed between 1784 and 1788, it appears that state tariff rates were converging (Zornow, 1954a, 1954b; 1955, 1956).

I argue that the key reason states could not agree on a common external tariff was because they faced a collective action problem.[14] In the next section I re-examine the evidence of 1783–9 in light of this argument.

The Collective Action Problem

Under the Articles of Confederation there were 13 states in an asymmetric trading relationship with one large nation, Britain. Although each state, individually, was only a small market, taken together the 13 US states made up an important market for British goods. There were numerous accessible ports on the eastern coast. British traffic, that is British goods carried largely by British ships, could unload at any of them. Given this, British traders unloaded at the port offering the most favourable terms. Any state wanting to attract business to its ports had an incentive to lower tariffs and other fees.

States wanted to use discriminatory legislation to retaliate against British trading restrictions. However, the decentralized political system under the Articles of Confederation made this difficult. If one state individually increased its tariffs, British merchants simply shifted their trade to a port with lower tariffs. Any state raising its tariffs lost business and revenue. Newly independent and without the British administrative machine, states found it difficult to enforce rules of origin. Where states imposed tariffs, trade diversion eroded higher prices on British goods. British trade moved to whichever port had the best terms, and this drove all states to give favourable terms. The British Government did not need to coordinate this response to tariffs. Self-interested merchants ensured that any state acting unilaterally was 'punished'. Gorlin (1990: 57) describes the sequence of events (see also Rakove, 1990):

> . . . every state but Connecticut had passed laws that imposed special tonnage duties on incoming British ships, levied special taxes on goods imported in British bottoms, or prohibited British vessels from loading American goods in its ports. The inability of all the states to adopt similar measures, however, doomed the discriminatory systems. Connecticut refused to pass any legislation, and the port of New Haven received the British ships that could not land in Massachusetts, New Hampshire, or Rhode Island. Virginia refused to pass discriminatory legislation on the basis that such legislation would be self-defeating if the barred goods could reach Virginia via Maryland and North Carolina. The inconsistency in the application of laws led Massachusetts to suspend its navigation act in July 1786, and Pennsylvania repealed most of its high duties when its neighboring states refused to match the tariff rates.

The Continental Congress's attempts to impose higher tariffs failed because the implementation of tariff policies was within the domain of the states. Therefore any uniform external tariff required the coordination and cooperation of the individual states. Since each state individually had an incentive to lower tariffs to attract goods, cooperation required that states coerce each other into maintaining high tariff barriers. In an attempt to coerce their neighbours, several states taxed interstate trade in re-exported goods. Trade deflection caused these states to remove re-export duties. What Nevins (1927) and the *Federalist Papers* cite as predatory attempts to stop interstate trade were really unilateral attempts to punish neighbouring states who did not levy additional duties on British goods or British ships.

New York, Massachusetts and South Carolina tried to punish states who did not retaliate by imposing duties on goods bound for defecting states. The popular dispute between New York, Connecticut and New Jersey discussed earlier was such a case. Zornow (1956) argues New York wanted to impose duties on goods entering and leaving New Jersey and Connecticut, because it wanted to prevent them from avoiding New York and Massachusetts restrictions on British shipping. Jensen (1950: 338) agrees, 'The irritation that sprang up between New York and New Jersey was the result of New Jersey's refusal to discriminate against British goods and ships as virtually all of the other states were doing'. New Jersey responded by taxing a lighthouse New York owned on New Jersey land. The Sandy Hook 'retaliation' tax may have prompted the repeal of New York's discriminatory law; however, Kitch (1981: 19) argues:

> New York made such an exemption because the Port's comparative advantage in handling through shipments was not very strong: the marine technology of the day did not limit unloading to only a few favoured places. And since New Jersey had extensive shore within New York Harbor, if New York raised the cost of through shipment, it would risk a lot of business.

New York, like other states, found that it was expensive to unilaterally sanction states who did not discriminate against British goods. Individually, states found they could not impose higher tariffs on re-exported goods for long. Trade was simply redirected through other ports. Instead of 'punishing' Connecticut and New Jersey, these regulations enriched them. Retaliatory duties crumbled as states moved to compete for British goods.

The framers depict big states as being predatory towards smaller states during this period. Madison comments:

> [A] source of dissatisfaction was the peculiar situation of some of the States, which having no convenient ports for foreign commerce, were subject to be taxed by their neighbours, thro whose ports, their commerce was carried on. New Jersey, placed between Philadelphia and New York, was likened to a Cask tapped at both ends: and North Carolina between Virginia. and South Carolina to a patient bleeding at both Arms (Quoted in Farrand, 1937: 542).

Ironically, it was the smaller states that were predatory! States like New Jersey and North Carolina were free-riding on the retaliatory efforts of bigger states. Their ports were less popular, and they could not resist the opportunity to attract trade to their ports!

In summary, all states realized they would be better off if they adopted a uniform tariff. However, because of the asymmetric trading relationship with Britain, and because the US states were a free-trade area without rules of origin, individually each state had an incentive to make their tariff slightly lower than its neighbours. While there is variance in their movement over time and across states, state tariffs appear to be converging under the Articles of Confederation.

TRADE AFTER RATIFICATION OF THE CONSTITUTION

If the collective action argument is correct, then the decentralized political structure under the Articles of Confederation frustrated attempts by individual states to retaliate against British trading practices. Following the ratification of the constitution, the authority to make and enforce trade policy was concentrated in the Federal Congress. This overcame the collective action problem associated with coordinating the actions of 13 autonomous states. Why states wanted, or were able, to federate is not the issue here. The free-riding over an external tariff barrier should have manifested itself in free-riding over institutions. However, the desire to retaliate against the British was only one of many different motives leading to the formation of the constitution (Beard, 1935; Rakove, 1996). Rather, the question is, given that states chose to federate, how did this affect overseas trade? The simple act of centralizing trade policy enabled the USA to effectively discriminate against British goods. Once the USA was credible in its ability to retaliate, the British entered trade negotiations.[15]

There is some empirical evidence that supports these predictions. Average tariffs on foreign imports after 1789 were, on average, higher under the constitution than under the Articles of Confederation (Zornow, 1954a). One purpose of the Tariff Act of 1789, Taussig (1892) argues, was retaliation against the British. Tonnage duties were imposed on foreign ships from countries without commercial treaties. US ships got a 10 per cent rebate on import duties, British ships did not (North, 1966). The British had refused point-blank to negotiate with the US emissary, John Adams, in 1785. Adams wrote to Jay, without a uniform tariff '. . . we shall be derided; and the more we suffer, the more will our calamities be laughed at'.[16] After the Tariff Act of 1789, however, the British were eager to negotiate a commercial treaty with Congress.

The framers were accurate in their prediction:

> (I)n a state of disunion . . . It would be the power of the maritime nations, availing themselves of our universal importance, to prescribe the conditions of our political existence; and . . . confine us to a *passive commerce* (Hamilton, Madison and Jay, 1787, italics added).

In summary, centralized authority was not necessary to create open interstate trade. Yet, without this centralization of authority, states were unable to coordinate on a uniform external barrier. They confined the US states to a passive commerce with their biggest trading partner, Britain.

CONCLUSION

To understand why leaders choose the trade policies that they do, it is important to consider how institutions affect strategic behaviour in a specific trading environment. The conventional wisdom is that, under the

Articles of Confederation, states adopted beggar-thy-neighbour tactics towards each other. States, being short of revenue, took every opportunity to profit from their neighbours. Farrand (1913: 7) summarizes the constitutional lore:

> The Americans were an agricultural and a trading people. Interference with the arteries of commerce was cutting of the very life-blood of the nation, and something had to be done.

Unfortunately, the conventional explanation is at odds with recent research by economic historians. Interstate trade grew increasingly open under the Articles of Confederation. What explains the appearance of a free-trade area under the Articles of Confederation and why did that free-trade area seek to shift to a customs union with a common external tariff? I argue that interstate trade was relatively open because farming interests dominated the state legislatures and this group was uninterested in protecting US manufacturing industries. Also, the ease with which British merchants could move to the ports of another state meant that states could not effectively tax the flow of imports or US goods in transit. Interstate trade grew increasingly open, not because states cooperated, but because states competed for British trade. The decentralized regulatory structure and the asymmetric trading environment structured this outcome. It also drove the strategic cooperation problem plaguing the creation of an external tariff barrier. Farmers wanted access to closed foreign markets. They believed the creation of a common external tariff against the British were essential for opening these markets (in other words, they sought to move from a free-trade area to a customs union). Yet, repeated attempts to create a retaliatory tariff failed. British merchants diverted trade from ports in high-tariff states, to ports in low-tariff states and cooperation crumbled as states moved to compete for British trade. States feared their neighbours would defect from voluntary agreements and no single state was willing to accept the costs of acting alone or of punishing defectors. The pattern of state duties during this period reflects the short-lived efforts of some states to retaliate against the British and to punish neighbouring states who chose not to retaliate. This failure to create a uniform external tariff confined the US states to a 'passive commerce' with its biggest trading partner, Britain. As long as political control was decentralized, and the US states were unable to enforce rules of origin, the British were able to dictate the terms of trade and had no incentive to sign multilateral or bilateral treaties with US states.

Centralizing political control of trade enabled the states to overcome the collective action problem and hence effectively negotiate with the British. The constitution changed the strategic relationship between the US states and Britain because it gave the national government power to enforce decisions made by Congress. This solved the collective action problem frustrating bilateral and multilateral attempts by the states to levy common discriminatory duties on the British. States now had their 'hands tied' on matters of trade. The British tactic of diverting trade between state ports no longer worked because the states could no longer compete for British trade. The common external tariff could be used to restrict British access to their largest export market and increase US bargaining leverage against the British.

NOTES

1. See, for example, Pahre (this volume) Bailey, Goldstein and Weingast (1997); Garrett (1992); Rogowski (1987).
2. The Articles of Confederation were passed in Congress in 1777 and ratified by all 13 states in 1781.
3. Source: Zornow (1954a), (1954b), (1955), (1956).
4. See Grieco (1988) for the realist explanation of this tactic. Axelrod (1984b) argues cooperation can still emerge in this situation, if actors value future pay-offs.
5. See Jensen (1950), Dougherty and Cain (1997).
6. The Middle Colonies are New York, New Jersey, Pennsylvania and Delaware.
7. New England is Massachusetts, New Hampshire, Connecticut and Rhode Island.
8. The Upper South is Maryland and Virginia.
9. The Lower South is North Carolina, South Carolina and Georgia.
10. Urofsky (1988: 70) points out, 'Conservative thought dominated constitution-making in Maryland and New York, where local aristocracies retained control for another generation. Maryland, although limiting the governor's power, provided for a bicameral legislature, with the upper house chosen indirectly through an electoral college . . . Officeholders and legislatures had to meet substantial property qualifications, especially in the senate, where each member had to own at least 1,000 pounds sterling in property. The governor had to be worth at least 5,000 pounds sterling including a 1,000 pounds sterling freehold estate.'
11. Quoted in Douglass (1955: 66).
12. During this period, trading relations often depended on personal contacts. The change in British policy meant that merchants, traders and shippers had to re-establish new relationships. This increased transaction costs and disrupted trade (Shepherd and Walton 1972).
13. Quoted from Kitch (1981: 17).
14. See Dougherty and Cain (1997) for an analysis of the collective action problem raising revenue for the national government under the Articles of Confederation.
15. See Rakove (1990, 1996) for a broader explanation of how the Constitution solved foreign policy problems.
16. Quoted from Jensen (1950).

4. Irish potatoes, Indian corn and British politics: interests, ideology, heresthetic and the Repeal of the Corn Laws

Iain McLean

[Sir Robert Peel] was prepared to argue that party ethics and constitutional government would best be served if public men did what they honestly thought right in the national interest . . . Few party politicians can work within such simple terms of reference. For them the approval of subsequent generations is an insubstantial reward; posterity has no votes at the ballot-box or in the lobbies. . . . [O]n the other hand . . . for a determined and self-willed man the appeal to posterity has one decided advantage; the verdict comes too late to affect his action (Gash, 1972: 541–2).

The Repeal of the Corn Laws by the UK Parliament in 1846 remains one of the most fascinating events in the history of political economy. A parliament securely controlled by the party of agriculture, which was the main beneficiary of protection, abolished protection. A huge range of explanations has been proposed:

Britain's unilateral move to free trade is said to have signified the triumph of Manchester School Liberal thinking; marked the birth of its international economic hegemony; launched a new form of British imperialism; paved the way for the disintegration of the Conservative party for a generation; been the catalyst for class conflict between the rising industrial middle class and the politically dominant landed aristocracy; given testimony to the organization, political astuteness and tenacity of the pro-repeal lobby, the Anti-Corn Law League; been an inevitable result of changes in the financial system and industrial structure; and illustrated the dramatic and abrupt change of mind of one absolutely pivotal individual – Prime minister Sir Robert Peel (Schonhardt-Bailey, 1997a, volume I: 1–2).

Even this list is not exhaustive, as it does not mention evangelical religion, which a recent heavily documented (and highly praised) study (Hilton, 1988) advances as a cause.

On the face of it, one theory that does very poorly is that of endogenous protection, as defined in Webster's *New Universal Unabridged Dictionary*:

> Endogenous protection: A description of the internal process by which the level of protection is explained by all individuals and groups in an economy and the political system acting in their self-interest (quoted by Magee, 1997: 526).

Magee (1997: 527) summarizes the 'five major ideas [that] emerge from the theory of endogenous protection':

> First, endogenous policies are economically inefficient.
> Second, endogenous policies are politically efficient.
> Third, government policies are interest group based.
> Fourth, government policies are just like prices in economic markets.
> Fifth, politicians are largely powerless, so that endogenous protection has no policy implications.

The central aim of this chapter is to see why these five ideas seem to fit our case so poorly. Only the first seems true. Even there, although nobody now tries to argue that protection of British agriculture up to 1846 was economically efficient, there is a continuing argument (reviewed in 2.6 below) as to which interest groups gained and lost from the move to free trade. Protection was probably inefficient in the Hicks–Kaldor sense that the beneficiaries of Repeal *could have* compensated the losers. But they did not, although Peel's Repeal package did contain tax concessions for landowners.

The chapter is organized as follows. Section 2 tries to explain the conversion of the executive to free trade. It is mostly narrative, giving the main actors' motivations as far as possible in their own private words. Section 3 reviews the roll-call analysis designed to explain the conversion of one house of the legislature – the House of Commons. Roll-call data are not available for the House of Lords, so the turning of the House of Lords is studied from the original papers of the Duke of Wellington, the man who did it. Section 4 considers the heresthetic of Peel and Wellington:

> *Heresthetic* is a word I have coined to refer to a political strategy. . . . [P]eople win politically because they have induced other people to join them in alliances and coalitions. But the winners induce by more than rhetorical attraction. Typically, they win because they have set up the situation in such a way that other people will want to join them – or will feel forced by circumstances to join them – even without any persuasion at all. And this is what heresthetic is about: structuring the world so you can win (Riker, 1986: ix).

Section 5 reviews Schonhardt-Bailey's list of explanations in the light of the evidence.

1. THE CORN LAWS 1815–46

The aim of this narrative section is to introduce the politicians who repealed the Corn Laws (Peel, Wellington and Graham), and the principal puzzle: how did they get it through two houses of the legislature and an executive cabinet, all three of which were dominated by the landed interest? The method of this section is to study them in their own private words. These throw a good deal of light on their ideology, and the high politics of getting Repeal approved by a Tory Cabinet. They cannot explain why any Tory MPs or peers voted for it. In later sections we will tackle the latter question by a statistical analysis of roll-call voting in the Commons of 1841–6 and by an analysis of the heresthetic of Peel and Wellington.

1.1 From the 1815 Corn Law until 13 October 1845

The Corn Law of 1815 forbade the import of grain to Britain until the domestic price was above some threshold (80s. per quarter for wheat). This tariff barrier replaced physical barriers that had operated (though not perfectly) during the Napoleonic wars. The 1815 Act was highly unsatisfactory. For instance, the price threshold was triggered in winter as the Baltic froze, which in itself restricted imports. It was replaced by a sliding scale of tariffs in 1828. The retiring Whigs tried to fight the general election of 1841 by committing themselves to freer trade in the hope that Peel, the Tory leader, would be trapped into a defence of the Corn Laws. Peel, who had probably already lost belief in them, but whose party's vested interest lay most strongly in agriculture, was too clever to be pinned down, and won the election comfortably. Two linked events of 1842 increased his freedom of manoeuvre: a general reduction of tariffs, and the reintroduction of income tax. On tariffs, Peel and his able lieutenant W. E. Gladstone were convinced by the ideological free-traders who staffed the Board of Trade that the revenue from tariffs could be increased, or at least not decreased, if prohibitive rates were reduced and consolidated (Brown, 1958 *passim*). The process of reducing tariffs exposed both politicians to rent-seeking coalitions of special interests, of which they were both utterly contemptuous. As Gladstone telegraphed to his diary:

> B of Trade and House 12 3/4 – 6 3/4 and 9 1/4 – 1 1/2. [ie 12.45 pm to 6.45 pm and 9.15 pm to 1.30 am]. Dined at Abp of Yorks. Copper, Tin, Zinc, Salmon, Timber, Oil, Saltmeat, all are to be ruined, and all in arms (Diary for 15.3.1842 in Foot and Matthew, 1974: 187).

In 1842, the public finances had been in deficit for four years running. Peel introduced a budget to put them into surplus (ignoring his Chancellor of the Exchequer, Henry Goulburn). He pointed out that tariffs were at a level which produced sharply diminishing marginal returns, and that extending consumption taxes to new areas would either be divisive (as with railway travel) or would bring in only 'driblets' from taxing 'pianofortes, umbrellas, or such articles'. Therefore 'I compare the complete failure of the taxes on consumption and the complete justification of the taxes on something analogous to property' (*Hansard*, 11.3.42; 3rd series v. 61, cols. 432–440). Peel had an acute sense of the 'elasticity' (his own word) of revenue from income tax compared to the inelasticity of tariff revenue. He suggested that income from tariffs would be actually increased by reducing rates – as was to prove correct. By reintroducing income tax, which had previously existed as an emergency measure during the Napoleonic wars, Peel solved the chronic debt problem of the British state. Even where tariffs brought in considerable revenue (which the Corn Laws did not), he was now freer to reduce them.

From Peel's day to this, it has been a constant charge that the Irish famine of 1845–9 was an excuse to repeal the Corn Laws, even that the troubles of Ireland were irrelevant to the decision:

> [T]hat Ireland has had anything to do with the grand convulsion that has over-turned the edifice that we were all so proud of having erected in 1841, I cannot concede. Ireland has had no more to do with it than Kamschatka (J. W. Croker to J. Graham, 21.2.46; Jennings, 1884, iii: 62).

The charge is repeated in almost every history of Ireland or of the Tory Party (see, for example, Blake, 1970: 53; Inglis, 1966: 137; Woodham-Smith, 1991: 50). The Irish cannot forgive the British for failing to prevent the famine; Tories cannot forgive Peel for destroying their party. Both, therefore, follow Croker for ideological reasons. There is a sense in which Croker was right. But it is also true that Peel, Graham and Wellington, the three principal actors, linked Irish policy inextricably to corn policy. We will shortly document this by means of their letters and memoranda. It is necessary first to introduce them properly to the story.

1.2   Peel, Graham, and Wellington

Sir Robert Peel (1788–1850) succeeded his father, a self-made Lancashire textile manufacturer, as 2nd baronet. His father bought a substantial estate at Drayton, near Tamworth, Staffordshire, which remained the family seat for Peel's lifetime. (It is now a theme park.) Peel became an MP at 21 and a Tory minister at 22. His first important job was as Chief Secretary for Ireland, 1812–18; he challenged the Irish Catholic leader Daniel O'Connell ('The Liberator') to a duel in 1815. He was Home Secretary from 1822 until resigning in 1827 over his opposition to emancipation (that is, civil and voting rights) for Irish Catholics. He rejoined Wellington's administration in 1828, again as Home Secretary. O'Connell stood in, and won, a by-election in Co. Clare despite being legally disqualified. This and the threat of further unrest changed Peel's mind about Emancipation, and persuaded Wellington to change his as well. He reportedly said to Wellington that 'though emancipation was a great danger, civil strife was a greater' (*Dictionary of National Biography*). Catholic Emancipation was accordingly carried in 1829. This was the first great U-turn of Peel and Wellington, which made them forever suspect to hard-line Protestants. He lost his seat at Oxford University; the slogan 'No Peel' is still to be seen burned by the tip of a hot poker into a door at Christ Church, his former college.

After the 1832 Reform Bill, he led the small bedraggled rump of the Tories, yet was described as 'incomparably the first man in the House of Commons' in 1833. When the Whig administration imploded in 1834, Peel became Prime Minister, although only from December 1834 to April 1835. He induced the able Graham and Stanley (later Lord Derby) to change sides and become Tory ministers, and encouraged the infant prodigy W. E. Gladstone. His 'Tamworth Manifesto' of 1834 is recognized as the first party manifesto, and he led the Tories (now taking on the name Conservatives) to victory in the 1841 general election. He had refused to take office after another Whig implosion in 1839, because Queen Victoria would not permit him to replace some Whig Ladies of the Bedchamber by his nominees. By 1841, however, the Queen supported him, having been brought round by Prince Albert, who approved of Peel.

His style of party management was brusque. He had disliked patronage ever since his days as Undersecretary for Ireland. He had a low opinion of many of his own supporters. Immediately after resigning, he told Gladstone that 'nothing should induce him again to take part in the formation of a Government'. He went on to list the tasks he hated, such as 'correspondence with the Queen, several times a day' and 'sitting seven or eight hours a day to listen to such trash in the House of Commons' (Foot and Matthew, 1974: 559). After his Government was defeated in 1846, he again remained 'incomparably the first man in the House of Commons' with the successor Russell administration eagerly but nervously asking his advice about policy. He was killed by a fall from his horse in 1850.

Sir James Graham (1792–1861) was a landowner in north-western England. Like Peel he entered Parliament in his twenties, but as a Whig. An improving landlord, he wrote a pamphlet in favour of free trade in 1826. He served in Whig governments from 1830 to 1834, but gradually fell out with his colleagues. Together with his friend Lord Stanley, he edged towards Peel, and crossed the floor of the House in 1837. He was

Home Secretary, and Peel's closest confidant, throughout the Peel administration. The notice of him in the *Dictionary of National Biography*, written by somebody who evidently disliked him, is full of references to his 'stiff and pompous' style, 'supercilious' manner to the Scots whose Church disestablishment crisis he handled in 1843, 'regarded as an intolerable coxcomb'. He was also deeply and gloomily evangelical in religion, prone (as we see below) to regarding a disaster like the Irish famine as God's judgement.

Arthur Wellesley, first Duke of Wellington (1769–1852) was of Irish Protestant background. He won fame as a war hero, first in India, then in Spain during the Napoleonic wars. He served as Chief Secretary for Ireland from 1807 to 1809. He commanded the British forces at Waterloo. He was in Tory cabinets as Master-General of Ordnance from 1818 to 1827. As befitted his background, he was bitterly hostile to Catholic emancipation, but Peel persuaded him that it was necessary for public order. He served, reluctantly, as Prime Minister from 1828 to 1830, and as Foreign Secretary in Peel's short 1834–5 administration. Throughout the ministry of 1841–6 he served as a Cabinet minister without portfolio, from 1842 also serving as commander-in-chief of the British Army. Peel had realized that Wellington neither could (having had three strokes in 1839–41) nor should hold an executive post, but placed him as Tory leader in the Lords to be 'the organ, not of this department or that, but of the whole Executive Government' (Peel to Wellington, 18.5.41, quoted by Thompson, 1986: 200). He was quite deaf, regarded with great reverence and some fear, retained his anti-Catholic and protectionist instincts, but was open to appeals to submerging his group interests in favour of preserving public order. In the next subsection we observe the Irish and Corn Law crisis emerging through the eyes and pens of these three colleagues. All quotations in *italics* in the next subsection are Peel's commentary, written between 1846 and 1850; the rest are the primary documents.

1.3   The Corn Law Crisis: 13 October to 20 December 1845[1]

The summer of 1845 was abnormally cool and wet. Landowners such as Peel and Graham watched its effects anxiously. In the autumn came the first reports that a disease that was already ravaging the potato crop in parts of Europe had spread to Ireland. The disease caused apparently sound tubers to rot in the ground or after picking. (No effective treatment was found until the 1880s; and the life cycle of the agent, a fungus called *Phytophthora infestans*, was not correctly described until the twentieth century – see Woodham-Smith [1962], 1991, chapter 5 and the sources cited there). The west of Ireland was densely populated by sharecropping peasants, outside the cash economy, who were kept alive by the potatoes they grew on their small private plots.

On 13 October 1845, Peel and Graham wrote each other momentous letters, which crossed. Peel wrote:

Whitehall, October 13.

The accounts of the state of the potato-crop in Ireland are becoming very alarming. [. . .] I presume that if the worst should happen which is predicted, the pressure would not be *immediate*. There is such a tendency to exaggeration and inaccuracy in Irish reports that delay in acting upon them is always desirable; but I foresee the necessity that may be imposed upon us at an early period of considering whether there is not that well-grounded apprehension of actual scarcity that justifies and compels the adoption of every means of relief which the exercise of the prerogative or legislation might afford.

I have no confidence in such remedies as the prohibition of exports, or the stoppage of the distilleries. The removal of impediments to import is the only effectual remedy.

Graham wrote:

Netherby, October 13.

[. . .] Indian corn might be obtained from the United States readily, and on cheap terms, if the people would eat it; but unfortunately it is an acquired taste; and if we opened the ports to maize duty-free, most popular and irresistible arguments present themselves why flour and oatmeal, the staple of the food of man, should not be restricted in its supply by artificial means, while Heaven has withheld from an entire people its accustomed sustenance. Could we with propriety remit duties in November by Order in Council, when Parliament might so easily be called together? Can these duties, once remitted by Act of Parliament, be ever again reimposed? Ought they to be maintained with their present stringency, if the people of Ireland be reduced to the last extremity for want of food?

Many politicians did not yet take the blight seriously. Peel and Graham correctly foresaw that it would lead to a dearth of seed potatoes, and hence of food, the following season. They also both saw that it called the Corn Laws into question. Graham's letter also shows what he thought free trade in grain had to do with the plight of subsistence farmers in Ireland who depended on potatoes and had no cash with which to buy grain. If Indian corn (maize) were imported free of duty, it would be hard to argue for more popular grains to be excluded or taxed.

The conversion of Peel and Graham indeed made the facts about famine a party question when it became publicly known. Protectionists had a motive for claiming that reports of famine were typical Irish exaggeration. The future leader of the Irish Party Isaac Butt wrote, 'To profess belief in the fact of the existence of a formidable potato blight was as sure a method of being branded as a radical as to propose to destroy the Church' (in *The Famine in the Land*, 1847, quoted by Woodham-Smith [1962] 1991: 50).

The correspondence continued:

Sir R. Peel to Sir J. Graham

Drayton Manor, October 15.

My letter on the awful question of the potato crop in Ireland will have crossed yours to me. I have written by this post to Lord Heytesbury [Lord-Lieutenant of Ireland].

Interference with the due course of the laws respecting the supply of food is so momentous and so lasting in its consequences, that we must not act without the most accurate information. I fear the worst – I have written to the Duke also.[2]

In the letter to Heytesbury, Peel wrote:

The remedy is the removal of all impediments to the import of all kinds of human food – that is, the total and absolute repeal for ever of all duties on all articles of subsistence.

Sir J. Graham to Sir R. Peel

Netherby, October 17.

. . . The suspension of the existing Corn Law on the avowed admission that its maintenance aggravates the evil of scarcity, and that its remission is the surest mode of restoring plenty, would render its re-enactment or future operation quite impracticable; yet if the evil be as urgent as I fear it will be, to this suspension we shall be driven . . .

Sir J. Graham to Sir R. Peel

Netherby, October 19.

My dear Peel,

I send you a further report respecting the potato crop in Ireland, which is not more favourable as the digging advances . . .

With our present Corn Laws, and with a free trade between Great Britain and Ireland, would it be possible to open the ports for provisions in Ireland, and to maintain the duties under the sliding scale in Great Britain? Would not opening the ports in Ireland mortally offend our agricultural supporters, while the free traders would be disgusted with the maintenance of the Corn Laws in Great Britain? and in these circumstances what would be our chance of obtaining an Act of Indemnity?

With a free trade between Ireland and Great Britain, the opening of the Irish ports would be equivalent to the opening of the British ports, save only that all foreign produce, to be admitted duty free into Great Britain, must pass through Ireland, and must be charged with the extra cost of transhipment, and of this extra voyage. I state these difficulties as they occur to me, that they may be presented to your mind.

Up to this point, Peel had confided in Graham and Heytesbury (the latter not a Cabinet member), but not yet to the Cabinet; when he did, he did not go as far as he had done in his letters to Graham and Heytesbury. *The Cabinet reassembled at my house on . . . Saturday, the 1st of November. On that occasion I read to the Cabinet the following Memorandum:*

[. . .] Inaction – the letting things take their own course – seems to me impossible.

With the documents we have in our possession, with the opinions of our own Commissioners as to the probable extent of the evil, the pressing entreaties from the Lord-Lieutenant for instructions, the possible contingency that in the course of two months the evil may prove to have been much more extensive than any one has yet contemplated, inaction and indifference might involve the country in serious danger, and the Government in the heaviest responsibility.

I recommend, therefore, that we should in the first place adopt some such measures as were adopted at former periods of much more partial scarcity – that we should authorise the Lord-Lieutenant to appoint a Commission for the purpose of considering the mode in which relief, when necessary, can be applied, through the means of employment where employment can be had.

[. . .] There will be no hope of contributions from England for the mitigation of this calamity.

Monster meetings, the ungrateful return for past kindness, the subscriptions in Ireland to repeal rent and O'Connell tribute, will have disinclined the charitable here to make any great exertions for Irish relief.

[. . .] Before the meeting of Parliament we must be prepared with the measures to be proposed and the language to be held at its meeting.

We must indeed be so prepared, not merely before the actual meeting of Parliament, but before we finally resolve on the calling of Parliament for the despatch of business.

The calling of Parliament at an unusual period on any matter connected with a scarcity of food is a most important step.

It compels an immediate decision on these questions.

Shall we maintain unaltered –
Shall we modify –
Shall we suspend – the operation of the Corn Laws?

The first vote we propose – a vote of credit, for instance, for 100,000*l*, to be placed at the disposal of the Lord-Lieutenant for the supply of food – opens the whole question.

Can we vote public money for the sustenance for any considerable portion of the people on account of actual or apprehended scarcity, and maintain in full operation the existing restrictions on the free import of grain?

I am bound to say that we cannot.

[. . .] Supposing it were granted to me, for the purpose of argument, that the suspension of the Corn Law is inevitable, the question arises, shall the suspension take place by an act of prerogative, or by legislation at the instance of the Government?

In favour of suspension by prerogative, there is the argument that it is done at once, that it is decisive for the time, that it prevents all that suspense and stagnation which will follow the notoriety of facts as to the potato crop, the meetings of the Cabinet, the notice in a few days of the summoning of Parliament.

It gives the earliest notice in foreign countries, and it gives to the proceeding the character of an act done on an urgent necessity, which no human foresight could have guarded against.

The objections to it are – that it compels instant decision by the Cabinet – that it imposes upon us by necessity of proving that there could be no delay.

It may justly be said, Parliament, after much deliberation, sanctioned an elabourate and comprehensive system of Corn Laws. The Crown has the power to summon Parliament by a notice of fourteen days. Why should the Crown, by the stroke of a pen, abrogate laws so fully considered by Parliament, instead of summoning Parliament at the earliest period, and inviting Parliament to do that which it is the proper province of Parliament to do?

There is this advantage also in doing whatever it may be necessary to do in the ordinary constitutional mode.

It gives us some further time for consideration.

It is possible for us to take this course – to separate today under the strong impression that the meeting of Parliament on some day not later than the 27th of November is inevitable – to have a meeting of the Cabinet finally to decide our course at the latter end of next week . . .

'Can we vote public money for the sustenance for any considerable portion of the people on account of actual or apprehended scarcity, and maintain in full operation the existing restrictions on the free import of grain? I am bound to say that we cannot'. This argument of Peel's has not been noticed much in the modern debate over Repeal, but it was probably crucial for Peel. Protection represented a fiscal transfer from consumers of grain to producers of grain. To spend public money on relief while protection kept prices artificially high was to waste public money. Peel, the most Gladstonian of early Victorian politicians, would not tolerate that. It would also concede the League's case, that the landlords were a privileged sectional interest, in the face of Peel's repeated statements that his administration was national, not sectional.

But a Cabinet representing the landed interest could not take such brutality from the Prime Minister. After a further meeting:

The Cabinet by a very considerable majority declined giving its assent to the proposals which I thus made to them. They were supported by only three members of the Cabinet – the Earl of Aberdeen, Sir James Graham, and Mr. Sidney Herbert. [. . .]On account of the gravity of the question, and the smallness of the minority assenting to my views, I might perhaps have been justified in at once relinquishing office; but after mature reflection, considering that the rejection of my proposals was not a peremptory one by all of those who for the present declined to adopt them, that additional information might materially abate the objections of many, and that the dissolution of a Government on account of differences on such a matter as that under consideration must cause great excitement in the public mind,

*I determined to retain office until there should be the opportunity of reconsidera-
tion of the whole subject. That opportunity would necessarily recur at the latter
end of this current month (November), when it was agreed that the Cabinet should
again assemble. In determining to retain office for the present, I determined also
not to recede from the position which I had taken, and ultimately to resign office if
I should find on the reassembling of the Cabinet that the opinions I had expressed
did not meet with general concurrence.*

Peel brought all but two of his Cabinet opponents into line in its meetings
at the end of November. He did not try to persuade Wellington to change
his mind about the Corn Laws. The argument that swayed Wellington was
quite different, as the following documents show. On 22 November, Lord
John Russell, the leader of the Whig opposition, issued his 'Edinburgh
letter', stating that he was now in favour of the complete removal of the
Corn Laws. On 26 November, Peel repeated that he could not accept the
measures of Irish relief which the Cabinet had now instituted, 'and undertake at the same time to maintain the existing Corn Law'. He told
Wellington for the first time what he was proposing and alerting him to the
renewed threat of the fall of the Government:

My dear Duke, In the inclosed memorandum are contained the Reasons which
induce me to advise the Suspension of the existing Corn Laws for a limited
period.
   I will not ask you to express any opinion on the Subject in returning me this
Paper. I only ask you to have the Kindness to read it – and to let me have the
Box by the Post of tomorrow evening. I thought it right to mention confiden-
tially to the Queen – that I feared there were serious differences in the Cabinet
as to the Measures which the present Emergency requires (Peel to Wellington
29.11.45. Wellington Papers, University of Southampton (hereafter (WP)
2/134/88).

At first sight this letter says nothing that Peel had not already said a month
earlier. But Russell's letter had changed the situation. There was now a possible Commons majority for Repeal, comprising Russell's Whigs, the Irish
members and Peel with a small number of followers. There was no majority for Repeal in the Lords. Peel was artfully playing on Wellington's known
ideology of fervent support for carrying on the Queen's government and
maintaining public order, under himself.
   Before the Cabinet meeting of 29 November:

*The danger to be apprehended was so fully admitted, and set forth in such strong
terms, that I thought it difficult to reconcile the issue of this letter* [to Heytesbury,
the Lord Lieutenant, with instructions about famine relief] *with passiveness and
inaction in respect to the means of increasing the supply of food.*

CABINET MEMORANDUM, November 29.

[. . .] Time presses, and on some definite course we must decide. Shall we undertake, without suspension, to modify the existing Corn Law? Shall we resolve to maintain the existing Corn Law? Shall we advise the suspension of that law for a limited period?

My opinion is for the last course, admitting as I do that it involves the necessity for the immediate consideration of the alterations to take effect after the period of suspension. I should rather say it involves the question of the principle and degree of protection to agriculture.

I must also admit that this question of opening the ports stands now in a very different position from that in which it did stand in the first week of November, when I first advised the measure.

Robert Peel.

THE DUKE'S MEMORANDUM, November 30.

I am one of those who think the continuance of the Corn Laws essential to the agriculture of the country in its existing state and particularly to that of Ireland, and a benefit to the whole community.

[. . .] It must be observed that the evil in Ireland is not a deficiency of food for the year, or even of the particular description of food, potatoes; but the great and supposed general deficiency of that description of food operating upon the social condition of Ireland; the habits of the great body of the people, who are producers of the food which they consume during three-fourths of the year in general, and who must consequently be in a state of destitution, and who have not the pecuniary means, and, if they had the pecuniary means, are not in the habit of purchasing their food in the markets.

[. . .] Here then comes the question which Sir Robert Peel has not discussed – I mean the Party view of it.

The only ground upon which I think that view important is one upon which he must be a better judge than any one else; that is, whether he could carry on a Government for the Queen supposing the support of the landed interest were withdrawn from him. I am afraid he must reckon upon its being withdrawn from him, unless he should be able to show clearly the necessity for the measure in question.

In respect to my own course, my only object in public life is to support Sir Robert Peel's administration of the Government for the Queen.

A good Government for the country is more important than Corn Laws or any other consideration; and as long as Sir Robert Peel possesses the confidence of the Queen and of the public, and he has strength to perform the duties, his administration of the Government must be supported.

My own judgment would lead me to maintain the Corn Laws.

Sir Robert Peel may think that his position in Parliament and in the public view requires that the course should be taken which he recommends; and if that should be the case, I earnestly recommend that the Cabinet should support him, and I for one declare that I will do so.

Wellington.

[. . .] Our discussions in the Cabinet continued from the day when the Cabinet reassembled (25th of November) until the 5th of the following month.

There was a period in the course of those discussions when I entertained the belief that some such measure as that which I suggested in the Memorandum of the 2nd of December might receive the assent of all my colleagues. These expectations, were, however, not fulfilled in the result.

Lord Stanley and the Duke of Buccleuch, after anxious reflection, each signified his inability to support a measure involving the ultimate repeal of the Corn Laws.

All the other members of the Government were prepared to support such a measure, and I felt assured of the cordial support of all, even of those who had hesitated in the first instance, from the moment that they consented to waive their objections. I could not, however, conceal from myself that the assent given by many was a reluctant one – that it was founded rather on a conviction (a perfectly pure and conscientious conviction) of the public evil that must arise from the dissolution of the Government at such a time and from such a cause, than on the deliberate approval of the particular course which I urged upon their adoption.

Under such circumstances, and considering the declared intention of the Duke of Buccleuch and Lord Stanley to retire from office, I thought it very doubtful whether I could conduct to a successful issue a proposal for the final adjustment of the Corn Law.

As I have previously observed, I thought that the public interest would be very injuriously affected by the failure of an attempt made by a Government to adjust that question. Other members of the Cabinet, without exception, I believe, concurred in this opinion; and, under these circumstances, I considered it to be my duty to tender my resignation to Her Majesty.

Russell could now have carried Repeal in the Commons with the votes of the radicals, the Irish, the Whigs, and Peel and one or two of his close followers. He would have had great difficulty in carrying it in the House of Lords. The next batch of documents shows a master heresthetician at work, blocking off all exits for both Russell and the protectionist Tories. Russell asked him for guarantees that he would support Repeal if Russell introduced it. Peel refused (Peel to the Queen, 15.12.45; same to same, 17.12.45. Peel, *Memoirs*, II, 235–41).

Sir R. Peel to the Duke of Wellington

Whitehall, December 14.

My dear Duke,

The Queen saw Lord John Russell and Lord Lansdowne [Whig leader in the Lords] together yesterday. The Queen observes . . . that Lord Lansdowne is very anxious to save the House of Lords from any humiliation and declared himself in the strongest terms against a dissolution of Parliament.

Lord John and Lord Lansdowne inquired from the Queen whether those members of the Government who had differed from Sir R. Peel on the question of Protection to Agriculture were willing or able to form a new administration, observing that they might else say at a later period that they were prepared, but they had never been asked.

The Queen undertook to write to me on the subject.

I certainly understood that it was the opinion of all the members of the Government that it was not for the public advantage that the attempt should be made to form a Government on the principle of supporting the present Corn Law, or avowedly upon a protection principle.

I have seen Lord Stanley this day, and he states that he could not undertake to form such a Government, or to advise the attempt.

Do you consider that I should be authorised in informing the Queen that no member of the present Government is prepared to form an administration on the principles above referred to?

I will see if I possibly can the Duke of Buccleuch tomorrow, although I feel very confident he would not undertake the task.

Ever &c.,

Robert Peel.

Duke of Wellington to Sir R. Peel

Strathfieldsaye, December 14, 1845.

My dear Peel,

I have just now received your letter of this day's date.

As well as I can recollect what passed at the Cabinet on Friday before you went to Osborne, I think that you are authorised in informing the Queen that no member of the existing Cabinet is prepared to undertake to form a Government on the principle of maintaining the present Corn Law . . .

Sir R. Peel to the Queen

Whitehall, December 17, 1845.

[. . .] Lord John Russell requires at the same time that Sir Robert Peel should give assurances which amount substantially to a pledge that he will support one of those measures, namely, the immediate and total repeal of the Corn Laws.

Sir Robert Peel humbly expresses to your Majesty his regret that he does not feel it to be consistent with his duty to enter upon the consideration of this important question in Parliament, being fettered by a previous engagement of the nature of that required from him.

Lord J. Russell to the Queen

Chesham Place, December 20.

Lord John Russell presents his humble duty to your Majesty, and has the honour to state that he has found it impossible to form an administration.

[. . .] In this uncertainty of obtaining a majority in the House of Commons, it was absolutely necessary that all those who were prominent in the political party to which Lord John Russell is attached should give their zealous aid and act in concert in the new administration.

Lord John Russell has in one instance been unable to obtain this concert, and he must now consider that task as hopeless which has been from the beginning hazardous. [Two prominent Whigs, Earl Grey and Lord Palmerston, detested each other; Grey refused to give Russell the assurance he wanted if Palmerston was to be in the Cabinet. We discuss below (section 4) whether this was the real reason for Russell's failure.]

Lord John Russell is deeply sensible of the embarrassment caused by the present state of public affairs. He will be ready, therefore, to do all in his power, as a member of Parliament, to promote the settlement of that question which, in present circumstances, is the source of so much danger, especially to the welfare and peace of Ireland . . .

Peel's heresthetic, linking Corn Law with the Famine, had put together a Commons coalition for Repeal that would not otherwise have existed. Passage of Repeal in the Lords depended on Wellington. That is why Peel's heresthetic also had to include references to public order and the Queen's government, Wellington's favourite themes. In a perfectly judged letter to Wellington when he heard that Russell had failed, Peel wrote:

Lord John Russell declines, after having accepted to form a Government. I am going to the Queen – I shall tell her at once, and without hesitation, that I will not abandon her – whatever may happen I shall return from Windsor as Her Minister.

It is necessary that we should have a Cabinet as soon as possible.

Will you have the goodness to attend a Cabinet in my room in Downing Street – at nine o'clock this Evening? (Peel to Wellington 20.12.45. WP 2/135/9. Underlining in original.)

Peel returned from Windsor as Her Minister and Wellington his most loyal lieutenant.

1.4 The Turning Point: Peel's Resumption of Office

While Russell was still trying to form a government, Protectionist peers were writing to Wellington to ask him to lead the protectionist party, now that it had become common knowledge that Peel had doubts. Lord Redesdale, Wellington's Tory whip in the Lords, wrote that as Russell, 'one of the most mischievous and reckless politicians' in the country, might 'lean to the *republican* party for support . . . [i]t is above all things necessary that our party in the House of Lords should be kept together'. He described the Tories as a powerful army 'whose staff and materiel have been surrendered to the enemy by their commander. . . . I am in the position of one in charge of a very large and important division of that army', which needed a leader. 'The integrity of the Church' was also at risk. Redesdale urged Wellington to put himself at the head of this army.

Despite Redesdale's military choice of metaphor, Wellington would have none of it. He replied with an equally carefully judged paean to Peel: the 'lamentable condition' of public affairs was due to the Reform Act, which tended to deprive nearly every Member of the House of Commons of his real Independance, and with very few exceptions, of whom Sir R. Peel is one, has placed nearly every Member in a state of dependance for his political existence.

This was to turn Tory rhetoric against Tories. Wellington went on to admit that the Tory Cabinet had split: 'the decision of the Question in one way, might have driven from them [ministers] the Majority of their supporters; a decision in the other might have been fatal to the Country and to the State itself' (Redesdale to Wellington, 14.12.45; reply 16.12.45. WP 2/134/130–131).

Thus already before Russell's failure, Wellington was signalling that he would stay with Peel, despite disagreeing with him on the Corn Laws. After Russell's failure, Peel moved swiftly and decisively.

> *After repeating the wish that I should resume my duties as her Minister, Her Majesty was pleased to observe that I might naturally require time for reflection and for communication with my colleagues before I gave a decisive answer to Her Majesty's proposal.*
>
> *I informed Her Majesty, with every respectful acknowledgement for her kind consideration, that I had been enabled to turn in my mind the course which I ought to pursue, should Her Majesty again require my services; that I had not indeed communicated with any one, but that my own mind was made up as to that course, provided it had Her Majesty's entire and cordial approval.*
>
> *I informed Her Majesty that, considering that Lord Stanley and those of my colleagues who had differed from me had positively declined to undertake the formation of a Government, and that Lord John Russell, having had the concurrence and support of all his political friends, with a single exception, had abandoned the attempt to form one, I should feel it my duty, if required to do so by her Majesty; to resume office.*

He fixed a Cabinet for the night of Russell's letter. He had already ensured that none of the potential alternatives – Russell, Stanley, Buccleuch or Wellington – would form a government. Peel wrote to a friend, 'However unexpected is the turn which affairs have taken, it is for the best. I resume power with greater means of rendering public service than I should have had if I had not relinquished it'. Stanley was later to write to the militant protectionist Lord George Bentinck:

> I own that I would rather accept from the present Administration a measure of which I did not wholly approve . . . than the risk of all the evils which must result from a long interregnum in the formation of an Administration or from a long continued struggle on such a subject as Corn Laws, to be finally decided by an appeal to the excited passions of a general Election (Stanley to Bentinck 14.1.46; Derby Papers Box 132/13, quoted by Blake, 1970: 63).

Wellington rallied to Peel without question. In his view, the issue had ceased to be the Corn Laws, and had become the continuance of the Queen's government. In his next letter to Redesdale he spoke of Peel's determination not to put the Queen into the 'necessity of offering the Administration to Mr Cobden [Richard Cobden, leader of the Anti-Corn Law League]'. Peel, he continued with deliberately vague gravity, 'has in contemplation certain measures which he intends to propose for the security of agriculture, and the Settlement of the Corn Question. I don't know, and cannot pretend to discover, what they are'.[3] By the time it became clear what they were, it was of course far too late to detach Wellington. In private, he reportedly complained to friends that 'rotten potatoes . . . put Peel in his d — d fright' (Strachey and Fulford, 1938, volume 282). But he also said, 'I cannot doubt that which passed under my own view and frequent observation day after day. I mean the alarms of the consequences in Ireland of the potato disease. I never witnessed in any case such agony'.[4]

In semi-public, he promised Prince Albert 'I'll do anything [to support Peel]: I am now beginning to write to them [protectionist peers] and to convince them singly of what their duty is' (both letters quoted by Thompson, 1986: 224. For the letters see, for example, W. to Marquess of Salisbury, 4.1.46, WP 2/135/109; W. to Duke of Rutland, 6.1.46; WP 2/135/119).

1.5   The Enactment of Repeal

Peel's package was presented to parliament in January 1846. As promised, it contained proposals for tax relief for landowners, to compensate for the loss of protection. Bentinck and Benjamin Disraeli, the effective head of the protectionist Tories, fiercely attacked Peel in the Commons. Despite the venom between Peel and his former colleagues, the result there was never in doubt. The crucial vote, on 15 May 1846, went in favour of Repeal by 327 to 229. The entire opposition – Whig, Radical and Irish – supported Peel, as did about one-third of the Tories. The other two-thirds under Bentinck and Disraeli voted against Repeal. Disraeli then made a pact with the Whigs and the Irish members to vote down the Government's Irish Coercion Bill, which was going through Parliament at the same time. Peel rejected appeals from Wellington and Cobden among others to call a general election. He offered his and his Cabinet's resignation, and the Peel administration came to an abrupt end.

In his parting remarks, Peel caused further, and gratuitous, offence to the Tories. He said that neither he nor Russell, but Cobden, deserved most credit for Repeal: 'one who, acting, I believe, from pure and disinterested motives, has, with untiring energy, made appeals to our reason, and has enforced those appeals with an eloquence the more to be admired because it was unaffected and unadorned'. This was remarkable on two counts. First, relations between the two had until shortly beforehand been extremely bad. Second, it was unhelpful to Wellington, who had frequently told wavering Tory peers that if they did not support Peel they would get Cobden. It is hard not to conclude that Peel, who had achieved what he most cared about, had recklessly lost interest in his former supporters. The gossip Charles Greville noted, 'Peel fell with great *éclat*, and amidst a sort of halo of popularity, but his speech . . . gave inexpressible offence. . . . Almost every part of it offended somebody; but his unnecessary panegy-rick of Cobden . . . above all deeply offended the Duke of Wellington' (4.7.46 in Strachey and Fulford, 1938, vol. 5: 330).[5] Conservative historians have never forgiven Peel for that speech.

But most chronicles neglect the almost silent drama in the House of Lords. The House of Lords held a veto, which could not at that time be overridden by the Commons. It was even more exclusively in the control of the landed interest than the Commons. It contained a higher proportion of hard-line supporters of Irish landlords and Anglican privilege. (The two were connected, hence Redesdale's warning to Wellington that Repeal of the Corn Laws might put the Church in Danger.) How on earth did Wellington pull it off? His feat is more startling, and less analysed, than Peel's.

A hint of his methods can be seen in his steering of the 1845 Maynooth Grant through the Lords. Maynooth was an Irish Catholic seminary, and the Peel Government's proposal to increase its grant from public funds infuriated hard-line Protestants. In the Lords, Wellington gave no ground to Protestant objections. His argument was purely based on public order. Ireland contained 8 million people (then about a third of the UK popula-tion), seven-eights of whom were Catholics. Their priests had to be edu-cated somewhere. If not in Ireland, they would be educated elsewhere in Europe, probably in another Catholic country. That would be worse. Priests were one of the main sources of political advice to the Irish people. It was important that they should be educated somewhere where the British Government could watch over the doctrines they were taught (2 June 1845, *Hansard* 182: 1160 ff, 1162 ff).

On Repeal, Wellington's strategy was the same. He said not a word in favour of free trade. The reasons he gave to persuade the House of Lords not to reject the Bill were all constitutional:

- It was recommended by a speech from the Throne.
- It was passed by a majority of the House of Commons.
- Were the House of Lords to reject it, it would be the only branch of the legislature to do so. He reminded his audience that without the

House of Commons and the Crown the House of Lords could do nothing.

- The House of Lords had vast influence on public opinion.
- If it did not pass Repeal then, it would merely be postponing it to the next Parliament, where it would come up again (*Hansard* 188: 1401 ff, 28 May 1846).

Repeal was passed in the Lords by 211 to 166 on the second reading on 28 May 1846. That was equally crucial with the much better known Commons vote.

1.6 Peel and Classical Economics.

A contemporary economic debate, recently revisited, concerned the welfare effects of unilateral tariff reductions, such as those of 1842 and 1846. If Britain was a relatively large country in the world economy, so that it was able to influence world prices, abandoning tariffs might cause it to lose more in revenue than it gained from increased allocative efficiency. (For the contemporary debate see Senior, 1843, Torrens, 1844; for its revival see Irwin, 1988, McCloskey, 1980). If hegemonic ideology explains politicians' language, we would expect Peel to side with Senior and assert that the gains would outweigh the losses, and the protectionists to side with Torrens and assert the reverse. However, arguments from classical political economy did not work this way on either parliament or the Cabinet. Peel did engage with classical economics, but in a different way.

Classical economists asserted that protection for corn was a disguised transfer from non-farmers to farmers. If protection were removed, the price of food would come down. In the transfer from academic to popular rhetoric, the argument then branched. One branch, used in talking to working-class audiences, asserted that therefore the working man and his family would gain. The other, used in talking to capitalist audiences, asserted that the gains would flow entirely to the capitalist because an iron law of wages would hold them down in that era of high un(der)employment. The latter branch had better academic credentials at the time than the former.

A related welfare question is on the effects of Repeal on labour. By the Stolper–Samuelson theorem, Repeal could be expected to be unambiguously in the interests of industrial capital, contrary to the interests of land – and ambiguous on the interests of labour (Stolper and Samuelson, 1941: 72). Labour was employed in both agriculture and industry. Would agricultural labour's losses be outweighed by industrial labour's gains? There was no clear answer to this question at the time, though Cobden presented himself as the friend of the farmworker by arguing that as the farmworker had the lowest wages of any labourer, so he spent proportionately the most on food and would therefore gain from Repeal (*Hansard*, 12 March 1844, volume 73, columns 862–895, especially at 879 and 890).

Peel frequently expressed the view that if labour would not gain from Repeal he was not justified in repealing the Corn Laws, for to do so would simply be to transfer resources from one special interest to another. He maintained that the evidence from the tariff reductions of 1842 showed that wages did not go down with the cost of living, and that therefore there were real gains for labour as well as for capital. [Between the 1842 tariff reductions and the end of 1845] *the opinions I had previously entertained on the subject of protection to agriculture had undergone a great change* because 'experience has shown that a high price of corn is not necessarily accompanied with a high rate of wages . . . speaking generally of the industrious classes of this country, I think it impossible to demonstrate that it is to their advantage that there be permanently a high price of corn' (speech in Parliament, 10.6.45, quoted by Irwin [1989] 1997: 298).

Peel distanced himself from political economists (see his remarks in Irwin [1989] 1997 *passim*). He convinced himself by experience that the net welfare effects of Repeal on the UK population were positive. It has taken economists 150 years to study the same question and even yet they are not as conclusive as Peel was. On the whole, they seem to agree with him. Bliss (1998), using data from Crafts (1985), finds that the net effect of Repeal was to increase wages. But as he admits, this depends on unreliable parameter estimates.

2.   INTERESTS AND IDEOLOGY IN THE HOUSE OF COMMONS

2.1   Data

This section studies in more detail what sorts of Tory MPs supported and opposed Peel. The data sources used are the merged datasets of Aydelotte (1970) and Schonhardt-Bailey (1991a, 1991b, 1994), with some extra variables.[6] Over 25 years (1950–75 approximately), the late W. O. Aydelotte collected roll-calls in the 1841–7 House of Commons. For each of the 815 men who sat in that House, Aydelotte recorded his vote on as many of the 186 principal roll-calls as he participated in. He also collected up to 200 pieces of contextual information on each MP from contemporary sources. Most of these record the member's networks (club membership, relationship to the aristocracy, school attended) and material interests (business interests, military service, wealth at death and so on). Schonhardt-Bailey collected further data, originally for her doctoral dissertation, intended to facilitate a direct test of endogenous tariff theory. Accordingly, her data record the economic interest of each constituency and the degree of portfolio diversification since 1815. Of her variables, the one reported below, now called CSBDPREF,[7] records the expected trade orientation of each constituency. The more it depended on industry vulnerable to imports (specifically agriculture), the more its MP could be expected to have a constituency interest in voting for protection. Conversely, the more it depended on exporting industry (such as textiles, machinery or cutlery), or on international transport (docks), the more its MP could be expected to have a constituency interest in voting for free trade.

Both the Aydelotte and the Schonhardt-Bailey variables concentrate on interests rather than ideology. Material interests are easier to measure, but we have been able to import a few measures of ideology to the database. From Hilton (1988) and his sources, we marked all those known to be religious evangelicals (and the few known vocal opponents of evangelicalism). From the records of the *History of Parliament*, which end in 1832, we coded for the attitudes of the longer-serving MPs in our set to the religious and constitutional crises of 1829–32 over the position of the Catholic and Anglican churches.[8] And from the 1851 census we add details of religious attendance in England, Scotland and Wales (1851 being the only time in British history that these data have been recorded). There was no census of religious attendance in Ireland, but the 1851 census yields data of excess mortality for the Irish census districts, 1841–51, which we have coded as a new variable DEATH for Irish members. (It is not significant in the analyses below, perhaps because the horror of the Famine had not yet struck in full force by June 1846.) For a fuller evaluation of the Aydelotte dataset see McLean and Foster (1992). For other uses of it by political economists see Schonhardt-Bailey, (1997a, volume 4: 53–84, 309–38).

Riker's concept of heresthetic depends on multidimensionality. As is well known, when opinion is unidimensional, the median voter's optimum is unbeatable under majority rule. Parliamentary procedures are majoritarian. Therefore, at least in the long run and assuming that legislators are moderately well informed, the opinion of the median legislator will prevail in each house, and political manipulation cannot shift voting from this robust equilibrium position. This is well documented in studies of the US Congress (see especially Poole and Rosenthal, 1997); and, of course, it underlies endogenous tariff theory, reviewed above. However, when opinion is multidimensional, the median voter theorem does not hold. When the median voter theorem fails, it can fail catastrophically, so that chaotic outcomes and majority rule cycling over the whole issue space become possible. Riker (1982, 1986) used this to underpin his notion of heresthetic. A heresthetician knows that no outcome in multidimensional space is stable under majority rule. So he structures the world so that he can win for his favourite option.

Riker's ideas have been fiercely criticized (most effectively by Green and Shapiro, 1994: 107–13). We agree with the critics that he probably exaggerated the frequency that cyclical outcomes arise in real politics. But that does not invalidate his stress on the extraordinary political events when they may do. The election of Abraham Lincoln in 1860 was one such case. Repeal of the Corn Laws was another. Peel structured the world so that almost the whole of the opposition in the Commons voted for Repeal. (Only ten non-Tory MPs voted against Repeal in the third reading vote, on 18 May, 1846, on which this analysis is based).

The Aydelotte dataset encompass votes not only on Repeal but also, *inter alia*, on railway, bank and factory regulation; political reform; educational reform; working-class distress; individual railway proposals; and the abolition of flogging in the army. It can therefore be used to test, not only the roles of interest and ideology in determining MPs' votes, but also whether the number of issue dimensions was high enough to promote chaos and heresthetic. In other work (McLean, 1995, 1998; McLean and Bustani, 1999; McLean and Foster, 1992), we have explored the dimensionally of roll-call voting in the 1841 House. That work confirms Aydelotte's original finding that politics in that parliament were multdimensional. Aydelotte (1970) originally found no fewer than 24 dimensions to the voting, using Guttman scaling. This is both too many and too few. It is too many in that most of the scales are inadequately labelled, uninterpreted and seriously overlapping. (Nevertheless, Aydelotte's work is extraordinarily adventurous for its time, given the techniques and hardware then available). It is too few in that it does not pick up the dimension of regulation. An MP's position on Aydelotte's Big Scale, which links the Corn Laws, Ireland and relief of working-class distress into a single ideological dimension, fails to predict his position on regulation. For instance, if he was 'right-wing' on the Big Scale, he was equally likely to be 'right-wing' or 'left-wing' on regulation. This is not too surprising, as it was (then as now) not clear whether being in favour of stringent government regulation is a right-wing or a left-wing position.

Attitudes to regulation formed a dimension orthogonal to that of the Big Scale. However, regulation is not a big enough exception to the generalization that opinion among MPs was one-dimensional. Although it is true that Peel threatened to resign if factory legislation he opposed were carried, and it is also true that the Ten Hours Act 1847 was carried by a 'left–right' coalition to punish the Repealers of the Corn Laws, Peel's threat was not really credible. Governments did not stand or fall on issues of regulation.

2.2.   Results of Bivariate Analysis

All the analyses reported below take the dependent variable as vote on the 3rd Reading of the bill to repeal the Corn Laws on 15 May 1846. (The vote on the 2nd reading, on 27 March 1846, was almost identical – the analysis is not affected by choosing one vote rather than the other.) The first step is to take likely predictors one at a time. Taking all cases, the results look quite promising. MPs who voted for Repeal sat for more urban seats than those who voted against. Viewing the data the other way round, the probability of voting for Repeal rose for each class of constituency except the last (there was no difference in vote between MPs representing moderately free trade and strongly free-trade constituency interests). Table 4.1 summarizes the main results.

Table 4.1 gives reasonable support to endogenous tariff theory (ETT). The probability of voting for Repeal varies in the expected direction for constituency characteristics, and also for whether the MP was an active businessman. It also shows that ideology mattered: for instance, either that MPs' attitudes to the constitutional questions of 15 years earlier coloured their attitudes to Repeal, or that both were coloured by some common background factor. The influence of evangelicalism fits the inverted U-shaped pattern predicted by Hilton (1988), although this effect is less strong and there is some risk of circularity in the data. Hilton's hypothesis is that 'moderate' evangelicals welcomed Repeal whereas 'extreme' ones merely saw in the Famine evidence for God's punishment for Britain's wickedness (rather blasphemously implying that God has a poor aim – punishing the English by killing the Irish). But in such data there is a risk of defining evangelicalism from public statements made during the Corn Law crisis, thus reversing the direction of causation.

However, these conclusions need to be shaded and qualified. First and most important, although the trends are as predicted by ETT, the outcome is not. If the data were regression data, we would say that the slope was correct but the intercept was wrong for ETT. True, the more rural the constituency, the likelier was its MP to vote against Repeal. But in all categories except the most rural, a majority of Members voted for Repeal. Disregarding coding errors and missing data, the median constituency is in category 2 (next-to-most protectionist). But Table 4.1 shows that a majority of Members who sat for category 2 constituencies voted for Repeal. Second, the analysis so far assumes that party is irrelevant. This is in the tradition of ETT and of US roll-call analysis. In these traditions, party is treated as an intervening variable, which confuses more than it clarifies. Even in the weak party system of the 1840s, that approach is wrong for UK data. True, there is a reasonable association[9] between rurality and Toryism,

Table 4.1 Repeal of the Corn Laws. Bivariate analysis: all votes

	Value	Prob. of voting for Repeal	No. of cases	d.f.	F	Sig. F
Predicted trade orientation	1 (Most protectionist)	0.19	99	4	26.844	0.000
	2	0.56	176			
	3	0.72	79			
	4	0.89	36			
	5 (Most free trade)	0.86	22			
Evangelicalism	Anti	1.00	3	3	2.625	0.050
	No info	0.58	573			
	Evangelical	0.79	14			
	Extreme evangelical	0.30	10			
Business	Not active businessman	0.55	498	1	9.180	0.003
	Active businessman	0.72	102			
Catholic emancipation	Was against	0.24	33	2	9.704	0.000
	No info	0.59	525			
	Was pro	0.71	42			
Church and state	1 (Strongly anti-reform)	0.42	24	4	9.843	0.000
	2	0.33	3			
	3 (No info)	0.54	498			
	4	0.80	20			
	5 (Strongly pro-reform)	0.93	55			

Table 4.2 Repeal of the Corn Laws. Bivariate analysis: Tory votes only

Variable	Value	Prob. of voting for Repeal	No. of Cases	d.f.	F	Sig. F
Predicted trade orientation						
	1 (Most protectionist)	0.10	86			
	2	0.38	116	4	8.189	0.000
	3	0.46	41			
	4	0.64	11			
	5 (Most free trade)	0.40	5			
Evangelicalism						
	No info	0.31	337			
	Evangelical	0.67	9	2	2.719	0.067
	Extreme evangelical	0.22	9			

Notes: For Tories, attitudes to Catholicism or church and state, and whether the MP was an active businessman, were not significant predictors of vote on Repeal.
Only ten non-Tories voted against Repeal. They were all from deeply agricultural seats (mean value of the trade orientation variable = 1.67; mean trade orientation for non-Tory pro-Repeal voters = 2.89). Taking the vote as the dependent variable, trade orientation was the only significant predictor for the non-Tories ($F = 8.189$ for 4 d.f; sig. of $F = 000$).

but it is far from perfect. The strong Tory Government was a strong constraint on those whose party label was Tory, even though it could only induce a third of them to vote with the Government.

Therefore, we repeat the analysis of Table 4.1 for Tories only. Peel's heresthetic, and Russell's characteristic combination of firmness (the Edinburgh letter) and dithering (the failure to form a government) had delivered all the Whig, Liberal, Reform and Repealer votes, bar ten, to the Government. The swing voters would be those Tories who, torn between their Government on one hand and their traditions and interests on the other, chose the former. Table 4.2 shows the results of repeating the analysis of Table 4.1 on just the Tory MPs.

In Table 4.2, three of the five predictors drop away. These variables are themselves strongly associated with party, so their significance in the all-MPs analysis tells us nothing about the comparison between the swing voters (the Peelites) and the protectionist Tories. We are left with trade orientation and evangelicalism, both of them still subject to the qualifications just mentioned. Note in particular that the median MP in this category still sits for a seat with the next-to-most protectionist trade orientation. As expected, a majority of them, like a majority of all Tory MPs, voted against Repeal, but 38 per cent of them voted in favour – roughly the same proportion as among Tory MPs at large, and enough to secure Peel his Commons majority.

2.3 Logistic regression analysis

If bivariate analysis tells us little about the Peelites, can multivariate analysis do any better? In earlier work (McLean, 1998), we reported that an ideological model performed better than an interest-based one, but that both were poor predictors. The recent improvements to the trade preference variable CSBDPREF change that conclusion, but not by very much.

All the variables that were tried for the bivariate associations reported above were tried again, including those found not to be significant in the bivariate model (since bivariate analysis can conceal true associations as well as reveal misleading ones). As the dependent variable (vote on the 3rd Reading of the Corn Law Bill) is binary, we use logistic regression. Beginning with a saturated model, we progressively eliminated non-significant predictors. The best fitting model has the properties reported in Table 4.3.

Logistic regression is notoriously hard to interpret, and none of the standard packages make it easy for the reader. The first block of Table 4.3 shows the prediction without the model (initial log likelihood) and with the model. One measure of the information improvement is the model chi-square as a proportion of the initial log likelihood. The classification table shows how many cases the model predicts successfully. Note that it is good at predicting negative votes (that is, votes against Repeal), but bad at predicting positive votes, in favour of Repeal. It successfully predicts only 40 per cent of these.

Of the four predictors that work in this model, one is ideological, one relates to personal interests and the other two are environmental. Most of the work is done by the constituency variable TYPECON2, which distinguishes county members from the rest. Note that in this model, small borough members do not behave distinctively from anybody else. Being in a constituency with a high proportion of Anglican churchgoers on census Sunday 1851 predisposes the member against Repeal. The personal interest variable that works is GENTRY. Earlier work had shown that the relationship between Repeal vote and membership of the landed interest was non-linear. The very largest landowners in the Commons actually voted in a majority in favour of Repeal. They were likelier to have diversified asset holdings than the next class down, classified as GENTRY, the only set of landowners to vote by a majority against Repeal. This finding is consistent with earlier economic history (Moore, 1965; Schonhardt-Bailey, 1997a). Support for Catholic emancipation in 1828–30 predisposes a Member in favour of Repeal. The variables relating to district trade orientation and evangelicalism have dropped out.

Another measure of the success of the model in classifying cases is τ_p. This is a proportional reduction of error statistic of the form (errors without model – errors with model)/(errors without model). At 0.54, it is reasonably high. But note that this is because there are very few incorrectly predicted votes against Repeal. There are a lot of incorrectly predicted votes for Repeal. The best available multivariate model cannot account for 55 out of the 93 Peelites for whom data are available. Thus we are led to a conclusion with which only Namierites, Marxists, new trade theorists and public choice theorists could disagree: ideology and interests both matter.

Schonhardt-Bailey (2000: 17, see especially table 7, model 3) has now strengthened these conclusions using the bespoke Poole and Rosenthal program *NOMINATE* (Poole and Rosenthal, 1997), which reduces the number of wrongly predicted members to just 23, of whom only 14 supported Repeal when the model predicted that they would oppose it. She finds that a

> single underlying ideological dimension that divided ardent protectionists from free trade crusaders captures the overall voting patterns of the 1841–47 Parliament extremely well. . . . MPs' ideology . . . reflected both their own personal beliefs and those of their constituents.

This chapter, however, disagrees with her conclusion (Schonhardt-Bailey, 2000: 16) that the switch of 1846 results from the swing Peelite MPs

Table 4.3 Logistic Regression (Tory votes only)

Dependent Variable: Vote on Corn Laws 15 May1846
Number of cases included in the analysis: 296

		Predicted					
		Negative Vote		Positive Vote		Percent Correct	
		N	I	I	P		
Observed							
Negative Vote	N I	176	I	I	27	I	86.70%
Positive Vote	P I	55	I	I	38	I	40.86%
						Overall 72.30%	

Variables in the Equation

Variable	B	S.E.	Wald	df	Sig	R	Exp(B)
COFE	-0.0590	0.0224	6.9151	1	0.0085	-0.1155	0.9427
CATHOLIC	0.6675	0.3817	3.0584	1	0.0803	0.0536	1.9494
TYPECON2			28.9675	2	0.0000	0.2603	
TYPECON2(1)	-1.3957	0.3808	13.4348	1	0.0002	-0.1762	0.2477
TYPECON2(2)	0.3863	0.3426	1.2710	1	0.2596	0.0000	1.4715
GENTRY	-0.7218	0.3221	5.0231	1	0.0250	-0.0906	0.4859
Constant	0.9613	0.5122	3.5221	1	0.0606		

Variables entered
COFE (C of E attenders/population, 1851) * 100
CATHOLIC attitude to Roman Catholics
TYPECON2 newly coded constituency type
GENTRY member of gentry

Notes:
1. Tau-p for this model = 0.54 (cf Menard 1995, pp. 24–9).
2. Cox and Snell – r^2 for this model = 0.163. This is a version of proportion of sum of squares explained in terms of likelihoods rather than sums of squares (personal communication, Sir David Cox).
3. Initial -2 Log Likelihood: 368.46766. Model -2 Log Likelihood: 315.678
4. In TYPECON2, a value of 1 denotes a county constituency; a value of 2 denotes a large borough constituency. The model shows how these differ, in opposite directions, from the reference category 3 (small borough constituency).

paying relatively more attention to their constituents' ideology than to their own. Rather, this chapter argues that it was Peel's highlighting the Ireland public order dimension of ideology that tended to swing them.

3. THE HERESTHETIC OF PEEL AND WELLINGTON

Riker coined the word *heresthetic* because he was convinced of the importance of changing the number of political dimensions. In his canonical example (Riker, 1982, 1986), the persistent losers in US national politics from 1800 to 1860 reorganized politics around the issues of slavery and secession, split the hegemonic Democrats and got Abraham Lincoln elected. The trick was to turn one political dimension into two, and induce instability. Heresthetical politicians are those who can exploit this chaos and construct a winning platform as, according to Riker, Lincoln and the Republicans did between 1852 and 1860.

There is one vital difference between the Republican and Peelite coalitions. Peel, Wellington and Graham controlled a winning coalition before the Repeal vote. They deliberately destroyed it and substituted another, temporary, one. The latter did not outlive the Repeal vote. After 1846 there was a Commons (though not a Lords) majority for a free-trading capitalist coalition but Peel did not actively try to lead it. No doubt if he had not fallen from his horse in 1850 he, rather than his follower Aberdeen, would have become Prime Minister in 1852, and a Peel administration would surely have handled the Crimean war more competently than did Aberdeen, whose ministry it killed. After the fall of the Aberdeen ministry, the Peelites lost what coherence they had had as a group. Most who remained active went into the Liberal Party, and became one of the sources of its liberal capitalist orientation.

Conventional Downsian political science both misspecifies Peel's utility function and fails to understand how a politician's utility function may change over time. Having achieved Repeal, he was delighted to cease being Prime Minister and no longer have to 'listen to such trash in the House of Commons'. In August 1846 he wrote to Aberdeen:

> I do not know how other men are constituted, but I can say with truth that I find the day too short for my present occupations, which chiefly consist in lounging in my library, directing improvements, riding with the boys and my daughter, and pitying Lord John and his colleagues (quoted in Gash, 1972: 616).

There is no inconsistency here with his statements in December 1845 of his delight at re-election:

Sir R. Peel to Princess Lieven, at Paris.

Whitehall, December 26, 1845.

My dear Madame de Lieven,

Many thanks for those few lines in which you say all that could be said in volumes.

However unexpected is the turn which affairs have taken, it is for the best.

I resume power with greater means of rendering public service than I should have had if I had not relinquished it.

But it is a strange dream.

I feel like a man restored to life after his funeral service had been preached, highly gratified by such condolences on his death as I received from the King and our valued friend Mr. Guizot.

Believe me, &c.,

R. Peel.

In December 1845 Peel had a job to do, which in his perception only he could do. By June 1846 he had done it. He could still influence political outcomes – the Russell administration barely made a move from 1846 to 1850 without anxiously consulting Peel. He had lost all interest in his party (not that he had ever had much), as his gratuitous references to Cobden in his resignation speech show.

What was Russell's motive in refusing office – the event that put Peel so firmly in the saddle? We have not studied Russell from primary sources (but see Prest, 1972: 200–10). It has been suggested that Russell used the squabble between Grey and Palmerston as an excuse to duck the responsibility for Repeal, in the knowledge that it was likely to come in any case and it might as well come through Peel as through himself. He may have realized that he could not carry the Lords whereas Peel could. Wellington's services would not have been available to a Russell administration. If true, this shows that office was not necessarily Russell's overriding maximand, either. Note, once again, the extreme alacrity of Peel's resumption of office. Peel's maximand in December 1845 was very different to his maximand in July 1846. He probably did not guess that Russell would fail in the precise way he did, but he created the conditions for it by refusing to write Russell a blank cheque of support, and getting promises from Wellington and Stanley that they would neither form a protectionist government nor support anyone else who tried. Russell could not carry the Lords unless Peel and Wellington let him. Peel would give him no such promise, thus manoeuvring himself into the position that only he could form an administration. The protectionist Tories in both houses then faced a dilemma: to accept Repeal from Peel, or to defeat him and accept the risk of a radical victory in the ensuing election, and then have Repeal and many other disagreeable things forced on them anyhow.

Was Ireland really no more relevant to Repeal than Kamchatka? Croker, who made the allegation, was editor of the protectionist *Quarterly Review* and almost the only person who could write to Wellington in colloquial, bantering, tones. Wellington agreed with him. His analysis of the famine was a precognition of Sen's (1981) theme that famine is usually a failure of entitlement, not a failure of food. The starving peasants of the west of Ireland were locked into a sharecropping contract (known there as 'conacre') and had no cash with which to buy alternative food. That Wellington (and Sen) saw further into the causes of the famine than did Graham (and Woodham-Smith) is attested by at least three things. First, the crop failure was worst in eastern Ireland (Gray, 1999: 101), but the excess mortality was by far the worst in the west. Eastern Irish farmers were in a cash economy and could buy substitutes for potatoes. Western Irish farmers were not and could not. Second, the entitlement theory explains why the starving westerners could not eat the fish that teemed off their shores. The only extant fishing boats were curraghs which, if caught in an easterly wind, had no port of refuge until Halifax, Nova Scotia. Fish were caught, and piled up, rotting, on Galway quays, because nobody had money to buy them and there was no railway to move them to places where people had money. The entitlement to fish from Galway, the best port on the west coast, was restricted to the hereditary community of Claddagh fishermen, who would not surrender it during the Famine (Woodham-Smith, 1991: 289–93). Third, there is therefore no surprise (although there has always been great anger) that a great deal of grain continued to be exported from Ireland throughout the Famine. Policy-makers needed to transfer not food, but entitlements to food.

Unfortunately, Wellington's analysis was not matched by prescription. He was not, in any case, an executive minister. Neither he nor anybody else in British public life, in either the Peel or the Russell administration, found a solution that matched the scale of the problem. Peel's and Graham's insight, in simultaneously seeing in October 1845 that the crisis was desperate, was deeper. It was deeper not only than their contemporaries', but than that of historians who have almost wilfully failed to see that there was a real connection between famine and repeal (see, most recently, Lusztig, 1996: 39). In this, Graham was certainly moved by his gloomy evangelicalism. Note his frequent references to *Heaven* and *Providence*. Evangelicals, according to Hilton (1988), believed that God had set the affairs of earth in order. Humans were always tempted to meddle with God's creation, usually with disastrous results. Protection was an instance of such meddling. Therefore free trade was in accordance with God's law (or, for the blasphemously literal, the famine was an expression of God's wrath). Evangelicals who wrote to Peel or Graham about the famine did see a clear connection between famine and Corn Laws (Gray, 1999, chapter 3 *passim*, especially p. 103). Graham did not believe in such simplicities, but there seems no doubt that his support for Peel derived from evangelicalism.

Peel was not an evangelical in any serious sense. His adoption of Ireland as the peg on which to hang the conversion to free trade he had already intellectually made was heresthetical. However, this is not to imply that he was not sincere in his wish to minimize the famine. The following outburst is decisive evidence:

> Are you to look to and depend upon chance in such an extremity? Or, Good God, are you to sit in cabinet, and consider and calculate how much diarrhoea, and bloody flux, and dysentery, a people can bear before it becomes necessary for you to provide them with food? (Speech in the House of Commons, 27 March 1846, *Hansard* 3rd ser. 85: 217).

As shown in section 2, Peel and Graham considered that the prospect of famine made the Corn Laws unsustainable. Their reasoning was more profound than their Protectionist, and Irish, critics seem(ed) to understand.

Wellington did not share their reasoning. But once he let himself be convinced that the Queen's government required him to stay at his post, he proved as doughty a heresthetician as Peel. Wellington's secret weapon was not so much his lofty dismissal of the angry protectionists as his remarkable agreement with Stanley (later to become the 14th Earl of Derby; Conservative leader from 1846 until 1868). Wellington and Stanley had an identical diagnosis of the situation, differing only in their prescriptions. As in 1829, a split in the Tory Party could not be avoided. It must then be patched up as soon as possible. This required its current and future leaders in the Lords to do everything to minimize the damage. Wellington would stay in office until the controversial bill was through, then hand over the leadership of the Tories to Stanley. Stanley wrote:

> We cannot disguise from ourselves that the unfortunate measure now under consideration has, for the time at hand, completely dislocated and shattered the great Conservative party in both Houses. . . . But when, with that disregard of yourself which you have shown throughout your life, you advise that I should now endeavour to rally the Conservative party, I am forced to remind you that in the present state of affairs and feeling, they could only be so rallied in opposition to the measures of your own Government. I may be compelled, by my strong sense of the impolicy of the present measures, to give my vote against them; but I have resisted, and I shall continue to resist, entreaties that I would take an active part, and put myself at the head of a movement to throw them out.

Wellington replied:

That which I look for therefore is, the holding together in other hands the great, and at this moment powerful, Conservative party; and this for the sake of the Queen, of the religious and other ancient institutions of the country, of its resources, influence, and power. . . . It is quite obvious that I am not the person who can pretend to undertake, with any chance of success, to perform this task . . . You will see, therefore, that the stage is entirely clear and open for you, and notwithstanding that I am, thank God, in as good health as I was twenty years ago, I am as much out of your way, as you contemplated the possibility that I might be when you desired to be removed to the House of Lords.

In a 'memorandum upon the leadership of the Conservative Party in the House', apparently addressed to Stanley, he added, 'I am *most anxious* for Lord Stanley's success. He will always find me ready to promote his views for [the] consolidation of the Conservative party'. Wellington conceded that 'my position is certainly anomalous', but added that he had taken the same line while leader of the Tories in the Lords during the Grey and Melbourne administrations.[10]

Stanley had written to Bentinck, whose violence in the Corn Law debates horrified him:

I own that I would rather accept from the present Administration a measure of which I did not wholly approve . . . than the risk of all the evils which must result from a long interregnum in the formation of an Administration or from a long continued struggle on such a subject as Corn Laws, to be finally decided by an appeal to the excited passions of a general Election.[11]

Thus Stanley, whom Disraeli had nicknamed the Rupert of Debate, turned into a Macavity of Crime. He said nothing throughout the Corn Law debate, attended the house as little as he could, and held totally aloof from the activities of Disraeli and Bentinck (Stanley to Duke of Rutland, 7.3.46, quoted by Stewart, 1971: 67). When he did succeed Wellington as leader of the Conservative peers, he maintained his detachment, to the detriment of the Tories' effectiveness.

What are we to make, finally, of Wellington's strategy? It was vulnerable to the objection, pressed rudely by Redesdale, pugnaciously by Croker, and politely by Stanley, that there was no policy, however un-Conservative, that it could not be used to justify. Wellington's tactic of warning the protectionists that if they did not accept Peel they might get Cobden was cruelly undermined by Peel's 'panegyric' of Cobden. On the other hand, it is not obvious that an Ultra leadership would have served the Ultra interest any better. The example of 1909–14 (McLean, 2001, chapter 6) suggests that Ultra leadership of the House of Lords does not always get ultras what they want. At all events, Wellington's loyalty was as important as Peel's heresthetic in securing Repeal of the Corn Laws.

5. CONCLUSION: REPEAL, ENDOGENEITY, IDEOLOGY, INTEREST AND HERESTHETIC

Thus two extreme views are equally false: that Repeal inevitably flowed from the spread of a hegemonic ideology, and that it inevitably expressed the increasing dominance of urban over rural interests. The former hypothesis quite fails to show how ideology is translated into action, and the latter one quite fails to show why some prominent people acted against their obvious material interests.[12]

Consider again Schonhardt-Bailey's (1997a, volume 1: 1–2) summary of the modern literature on Repeal:

> Britain's unilateral move to free trade is said to have signified the triumph of Manchester School Liberal thinking; marked the birth of its international economic hegemony; launched a new form of British imperialism; paved the way for the disintegration of the Conservative party for a generation; been the catalyst for class conflict between the rising industrial middle class and the politically dominant landed aristocracy; given testimony to the organization, political astuteness and tenacity of the pro-repeal lobby, the Anti-Corn Law League; been an inevitable result of changes in the financial system and industrial structure; and illustrated the dramatic and abrupt change of mind of one absolutely pivotal individual – Prime Minister Sir Robert Peel

to which we added the Hilton hypothesis that evangelicalism drove Repeal. How do these theories fare in the light of our evidence?

A triumph of the Manchester School?   Not according to Peel (section 2.6). To maintain that he was nevertheless subconsciously a captive of the Manchester School is to enter the dangerous ground of false consciousness, where we do not wish to tread.

The birth of British international economic hegemony; a new form of British imperialism?   Repeal may indeed have launched either or both of these – we take no position on that. But we have found no evidence that either was in the minds of the people who launched it.

A harbinger of Conservative disintegration?   It certainly was. The Conservatives did not again form a majority government until 1874. Patently, by June 1846 Peel had lost interest in either his own or his (former) party's electoral survival, while Wellington's heresthetic had required him to state again and again that he stood above party. Our case falsifies the conventional Downsian axiom that politicians maximize the subjective probability of re-election.

A catalyst for class conflict?   This is how Marx and Engels saw Repeal (see the citations in McLean, 1992). Peel and Wellington saw it as exactly the opposite. They argued that the landed interest must give way in order to *reduce* class conflict. Peel's public ideology entailed the governing class considering the interests of other classes in governing. To ascribe to him a contradictory 'real' ideology is again to enter the dangerous ground of false consciousness.

The organization of the Anti-Corn Law League?   We have not specifically considered this, but others have pointed out a problem of chronology. The League was at its peak in 1842–3, but played no direct role in bringing about Repeal in 1845–6. Schonhardt-Bailey (especially 1991b) has argued that fear of electoral pressure from the League, and/or constituency interests, drove those Conservatives representing more urban or more diversified seats towards the Peelites. However, the results in Section 3 above show that district interest and portfolio diversification perform only modestly in predicting the decision of Tory MPs to go with Peel or not.

Changes of the financial and industrial structure?   The finance capital hypothesis due to Cain and Hopkins (1980) fails. Bankers split no differently from the general population of MPs on Repeal. Industrial structure is more plausible, especially if 'industry' includes the farming industry – see our comments on the performance of GENTRY in section 3. But structural variables work rather poorly at predicting both legislators and policymakers (see comments on Peel and Cobden *passim*). *Evangelical religion* only weakly explains legislators (section 3); but works quite well to explain why Peel's closest confidant, Graham, shared Peel's view of the famine and Repeal.

The dramatic and abrupt change of mind of one absolutely pivotal individual Yes, Peel was absolutely pivotal. But so was Wellington, whose role has not been previously noted by political economists. Peel's change of mind was dramatic but not abrupt – he lost faith in the Corn Laws over a long period starting before 1841. What was abrupt was his decision that the famine killed the Corn Laws. This was heresthetic, but not purely heresthetic as Peel did care about the famine as a substantive issue. The fall of Peel marks a great break. Peel knew that the British disliked the Irish too much for private charity to work; he set the best scientists of the day on the case; above all, he was a hyperenergetic administrator. Lord John Russell had none of these attributes. Russell, not by Peel, made the truly catastrophic decisions: especially the decision in 1847 to make Irish relief entirely an Irish affair (Mokyr, 1983: 291; Woodham-Smith [1962] 1991: 407–13).

If we are to reject endogenous trade theory without endorsing simplicities about hegemonic ideology, we need to come to a nuanced conclusion. Interests and ideology both played a great part. But, for élites as well as for legislators, ideology was probably the greater.

The ideological dimensions
Rikerian heresthetic requires more than one issue dimension. In ordinary politics, with most issues capable of being fitted onto a single issue dimension, the median optimum is a stable equilibrium. Empirically, Aydelotte demonstrated the existence of a dominant issue dimension in the issues where votes fitted his Big Scale. But, as reported above, there were other issue dimensions. Regulation provided a dimension orthogonal to the main one. However, the issues involved in regulation were not salient enough to cause disequilibrium. The dimension which did that was public order. In the 1840s, governments were very worried about threats to public order from the underclass (see, for example, Stevenson and Quinault, 1974, chapters 3–5). The minister who cared most about public order was Wellington, the victor of Waterloo. Most of his haranguing of the Cabinet was about the French threat, but he was easily alarmed by domestic threats to public order as well. In Britain, Chartism was at its height; in Ireland, it was well known that British government lacked legitimacy.

Every commentary on the period stresses the importance of English stereotypes of Ireland and the Irish, in which Irish people were regarded as lazy, disloyal and incompetent. This incomprehension reached tragic depths during the famine. Peel and Wellington shared it, as their writings show. But they both rose above it. Wellington's speech on Maynooth reminded the Lords of some strategic truths. Ireland was a weak link in the defence of the UK. The more disaffected the Irish, the more likely they were to welcome invaders, as had already happened in 1689 and 1798 (and was to happen again in 1916). Parliament could not prevent the Irish from being Roman Catholics, as Wellington pithily said. Therefore, the British Government had to approve things that they would not otherwise have approved, such as the Maynooth grant. Wellington used the same argument about Repeal of the Corn Laws. If Peel thought it necessary for the good government of the UK, that overrode Wellington's opinion on the substantive issue of protection.

It may be objected that public order does not provide an issue dimension in the ordinary sense. Nobody was against it, except some Irish revolutionaries. It was a valence issue, in Butler and Stokes' (1969) terminology. But it did have the necessary property for an application of Rikerian heresthetic. It could generate cyclical majorities. And it generated the manufactured Commons majority that defeated Peel's Irish Coercion Bill and led to his fall, in June 1846.

The farming institutions

It is a prevalent idea in modern political economy that institutions determine outcomes. 'Institutions are the rules of the game in a society or, more formally, are the humanly devised constraints that shape human interaction' (North, 1990: 1). And yet, as we have seen, the conventional mapping from inputs to outcomes via a set of institutions is embodied in the theory of endogenous protection, which fails to explain the Repeal of the Corn Laws. The inputs to trade politics in Britain in the 1840s were little different to those in other places and times. In particular, those industrial sectors which benefited from protection lobbied for its continuance ('Copper, Tin, Zinc, Salmon, Timber, Oil, Saltmeat, all are to be ruined, and all in arms', Gladstone's Diary for 15.3.1842). What are the institutions that led to such an unusual outcome? Plausible candidates include:

The Anti-Corn-Law League: embedding free trade and nationalizing an interest   It is well established (McCord, 1958; Schonhardt-Bailey, 1997a) that the Anti-Corn Law League was one of the first and most effective lobby groups in British political history. While it represented the sectional interest of capital (and to a small extent labour) in those sectors of the economy that stood to gain from free trade, it spread its lobbying efforts widely. In particular, it contested or threatened to contest by-elections in a wide range of seats. This tactic cannot have worked unless the median voter in these constituencies was (believed to be) a free trader. But, as there were more farm than industrial producers, naïve theory would predict that the Anti-League (Agricultural Protection Society) was stronger than the League. That it was not may be due to an Olsonian failure to carry its own free-riders, whereas the League succeeded. But there has been no analysis of League and Anti-League in Olson's (1965, 1982) framework.

Perhaps the best example of an institution that embedded free-trade values was the Board of Trade. As Brown (1958) has shown, the Board was captured as early as 1830 by free trade ideologues. The 1840 Select Committee Report on Import Duties (see especially the evidence of McGregor and Deacon Hume) gave a solid platform for Peel's and Gladstone's tariff reductions of 1842. Gladstone came to the Board of Trade in 1841 disappointed that he had not been sent to govern Ireland ('the science of politics deals with the government of men, but I am set to govern packages'). He wrote much later that:

> I was totally ignorant both of political economy and of the commerce of the country. I might have said . . . that my mind was in regard to all these matters 'a sheet of white paper', except that it was doubtless coloured by a traditional prejudice of protection, which had then quite recently become a distinctive mark of conservatism (quoted by Morley, 1908, volume I: 181).

The ideologues of the Board of Trade helped to convert him from protection to free trade within the ensuing 12 months.

The 'Great' Reform Act of 1832   The Reform Act shifted the balance of interests represented in Parliament somewhat from the countryside towards the towns. Not by very much, nor quantifiably. Before 1832, 'virtual representation' ensured that territorial interests which could not be represented in Manchester or Leeds (which had no seats) could turn up as the representatives, say, of Grampound or Old Sarum; therefore the shift from land to capital in 1832 cannot be measured.

Perhaps a more important consequence of 1832 was a decline of 'independence' – 'real Independance' as Wellington put it to Redesdale. In Burkean terms, an MP was independent if he was free to exercise his judgement unhindered by constituency pressures. That was easy if you sat for a rotten borough. The MP for Old Sarum, which had no electors at all, had total Burkean independence. Wellington's point to Redesdale was, in ETT terms, that it was harder after 1832 than before for legislators to 'shirk' on their constituents' interests. Indeed, the entire House was more likely to be called to account if the League could persuade the median voter in the median district to support a free trader.

Yet, if 1832 led to a reduction in independence, which in turn led to the interest of capital being promoted at the expense of land, the process was indirect and incomplete. It could not account for Wellington and the majority of peers. Whatever constrained them to vote against their material interest, it was not a lack of Burkean independence.

Constitutional conventions about government formations and resignations   By the 1840s, the convention that an administration that could not command a parliamentary majority must resign was firmly established. But neither Melbourne's resignation in 1839, nor Peel's in 1845, was caused by the loss of a parliamentary vote. And what should follow an unforced resignation was correspondingly fluid. In 1839 the resigning Melbourne advised the Queen that she should send for the Tory leaders. She did, but told Peel that he could not remove any of her Whig Ladies of the Bedchamber. Melbourne resumed office. However, the Bedchamber crisis weakened the power of the queen – in Halévy's ([1923] 1961, volume 3: 245) magisterial judgement:

> It was evident that the queen had been very stupid and very obstinate, Melbourne very dishonourable or very weak, his colleagues too eager to resume office at any cost.

Thus by 1845 the institution of the monarchy had already changed from 1839. Queen Victoria continued to grumble about prime ministers she disliked. But she had changed her mind about Peel; and the Bedchamber incident had warned her that, after an administration resigned, she should not interfere with the attempts of those she approached to form an administration with majority support or acquiescence. In 1845 she preferred Peel to Russell; but she did not actively try to influence the Cabinet-making of either. Therefore Peel was able to weave the web he did in December 1845 without royal interference.

Another fluid institution concerned prime ministerial control over the Cabinet. In early November 1845, Peel did not resign although he was in a minority of three in his own Cabinet. A month later, he did resign although he had carried all but two. This may seem quixotic; but it illustrates that no humanly devised constraint bound these two decisions. More recent Prime Ministers including Gladstone, Asquith, Thatcher and (allegedly) Blair have similarly refused to be constrained by a hostile Cabinet majority.

Finally, the options of resignation with, and without, an accompanying dissolution, were both open, and it was common knowledge that they were both open, in 1846. Peel rejected the requests of both Wellington and Cobden, from their opposite directions, for a dissolution. Both calculated that Disraeli's heresthetic move to defeat Peel on the Irish Coercion Bill would be repudiated by the electorate, so that a Peelite administration would be returned with the support of the median voter. But Peel judged that it would be too dangerous to hold an election in Ireland in these circumstances – turning Wellington's favourite public order argument against him. And, as amply demonstrated in his own writings and behaviour, he no longer cared about being Prime Minister.

We must return, then, to the question we started with. Why does the dominant school of political economy do so poorly at explaining the Repeal of the Corn Laws? Our answer is remarkably old-fashioned. Not only does the conventional school misspecify some politicians' utility functions, but it fails to allow for the occasional politician who can take advantage of heresthetic and fluid, non-binding institutions, to wrench politics in totally unexpected directions. In 1846 there were two such – Peel and Wellington.

Bicameralism   The House of Lords was a veto player. Only Wellington, in alliance with Peel, could deliver a Lords majority for Repeal. Peel's genius lay, first in converting Wellington, and then in ensuring that neither Stanley nor Russell had a bicameral majority to form an administration. Stanley could have carried the Lords but not the Commons; Russell, the Commons but not the Lords. This is the most ingeniously constructive use of the Lords' blocking power between 1832 and its restriction in 1911.

APPENDIX   VARIABLES USED IN THE ANALYSIS

Table 4.A1   Measures of MPs' ideology

VARNAME	Description		Values	Source
BIGBIGSC	Scale position on Big Scale	1.00 5.00	Most 'left-wing' Most 'right-wing'	Aydelotte, recoded
BIGENCAN	Scale position on enlarged Canada Wheat scale	1.00 5.00	Most 'left-wing' Most 'right-wing'	Aydelotte, recoded
CATHOLIC	MP's attitude to Roman Catholics	−1.00 0.00 1.00	Against emancipation or change No information Pro-emancipation or change	*DNB*, Dod, Thorne, Histparl
CHUSTATE	MPs' attitude to church–state relations	−1.00 −0.50 0.00 0.50 1.00	Strongly anti-change Weakly anti-change No information Weakly pro-change Strongly pro-change	*DNB*, Dod, Thorne, Histparl
DENOM	MPs' denomination if not C. of E.	0.00 1.00 2.00 3.00 4.00 5.00 9.00	No information RC Church of Scotland Free Ch. of Scotland Quaker Unitarian Other nonconformist	*DNB*, Dod, Histparl

Table 4.A1 (cont.)

VARNAME	Description		Values	Source
EVANGEL	MPs' attitude to evangelicalism	−1.00 0.00 1.00 2.00	Anti-evangelical No information Evangelical Extreme evangelical	*DNB*, Dod, Hilton, Histparl, Thorne, Brent, Bradley
MILITARY	Any military service	0.00 1.00	No Yes	Regrouping of Aydelotte vars Army1, Navy1
PEELITE	Tory who voted with Peel in May 1846 in favour of Repealing the Corn Laws	0.00 1.00	No Yes	Aydelotte (recoded)
PLEDGE	Whether MP gave pledges	−1.00 0.00 1.00	Gave no pledges No information Gave a pledge (to anything)	Dod

Table 4.A2 Measures of constituency ideology

VARNAME	Description	Values	Source
COFE	(C. of E. attenders/population, 1851)*100		1851 census
PROTDISS	(Protestant dissenters/population, 1851)*100		1851 census
RC	(Roman Catholics/population, 1851)*100		1851 census
RELIGIOS	(Total attenders/population, 1851)*100		1851 census

Table 4.A3 Measures of MPs' interests

VARNAME	Description	Values		Source
AGE1841	MP's age in 1841			Aydelotte
BANK1	MP had interests in banking	0.00	No	Aydelotte (recoded)
		1.00	Yes	
BUSINT	MP had any business interests	0.00	No	Aydelotte (recoded)
		1.00	Yes	
CONTEST	Election to 1841 parliament contested	0.00	No	Aydelotte (recoded)
		1.00	Yes	
GENTRY	Member of gentry	0.00	No	Derived from SOCCLSUM
		1.00	Yes	
PATRON	N. of livings of which patron			Dod
SOCCLSUM	Social class – summary	1.00	Peerage	Aydelotte
		2.00	Gentry	
		3.00	Baronetage	
		4.00	Otherwise related	
		5.00	Related by marriage	
		6.00	Unrelated to landed	
WEALTH	Wealth at death			Aydelotte

Table 4.A4 Measures of constituency interests

VARNAME	Description	Values	Source
CSBDPREF	District trade preference	1.00 Most pro-protection 5.00 Most pro-free trade	Schonhardt-Bailey
DCDIST	Nature of district	0.00 Agricultural 1.00 Mixed 2.00 Industrial	Deane and Cole
DIVS15CO	Diversification score 1850		Schonhardt-Bailey
EOVRSSUM	Electors per seat in the constituency		Aydelotte
NENGLAND	Constituency in England/Wales north of line from Wash to Avon	0.00 No 1.00 Yes	Aydelotte
POVRESUM	Population/electorate in the constituency		Aydelotte
SCOTLAND	Constituency in Scotland	0.00 No 1.00 Yes	Aydelotte
SIRELAND	Constituency in Ireland excluding Ulster	0.00 No 1.00 Yes	Aydelotte
TYPECON2	Type of constituency	1.00 County 2.00 Small borough 3.00 Large borough 4.00 University	Aydelotte
ULSTER	Constituency in Ulster	0.00 No 1.00 Yes	Aydelotte

NOTES

1. Most of the documents quoted in this and the next two subsections were first published in Peel's posthumous *Memoirs* (Peel, 1856–7). Documents from other sources are identified individually. In the extracts from Peel's *Memoirs*, the original documents are in inset standard type; Peel's commentary in italic.
2. 'The Duke' when not labelled as the duke of anywhere, always means the Duke of Wellington in this period.
3. Wellington to Redesdale, 25.12.45. He failed to persuade Redesdale, who replied, 'I decline all connexion with the Government at present', 28.12.45. In the new year Wellington therefore had to act as his own chief whip in the Lords, WP 2/135/35; 2/135/49.
4. Wellington to Croker, 6.4.46, in Jennings, *Croker*, iii, p. 65. See also the peroration of Peel's Commons speech of 16.2.46: *Hansard* 3rd ser., 83: 1043, and from his speech of 27.3.46, *Hansard* 3rd ser., 85: 217.
5. The 'panegyric' was probably influenced by a remarkable exchange of letters. Peel and Cobden, who had never met face to face, had bitterly attacked one another. On 23 June Cobden wrote warmly to Peel, urging him to dissolve Parliament on his expected defeat and run for election as the head of a new free-trade party. Peel replied, while listening to the debate, with equal friendliness but firmly refusing to do what Cobden (and, ironically, also Wellington) advised. The letters are in Morley (1903: 391–400). Nevertheless, the panegyric remains unexplained. Why gratuitously offend Wellington and the entire parliamentary Tory Party? One hypothesis is that, having achieved Repeal, Peel had immediately lost interest in office. See his comments to Gladstone quoted above. His wife, to whom he was devoted, was severely depressed. The 'Cobden' speech burnt many bridges, and Peel rode straight home to Drayton to be with his wife having (perhaps) signalled that he had made his position as party leader forever untenable. For this hypothesis see Heesom (1973: 91).
6. The merged dataset is available to interested users in SPSS format from the following website: http://www.nuff.ox.ac.uk/users/mclean/.
7. This is a revision of her earlier variable DISTPREF, the results from which have been reported in both her and my earlier work. Some dubious cases have been reclassified with new data, and the new variable gives better results.
8. By kind permission of Valerie Cromwell, Director of the History of Parliament, and of D. R. Fisher, editor of the projected volumes for 1820–32. The Aydelotte database was originally supplied (on punched cards) without the MPs' names. None of the operations described in these paragraphs would have been possible but for the detective work of Mrs. Aydelotte, which we acknowledge with enormous gratitude. In her late husband's papers, she found the name key to his database. This alone has made the merging and additions possible.
9. Cross-tabulating CSBDPREF (district trade orientation) against PARTYBK5 (5-way party breakdown) gives a Kendall's tau-β value of 0.345.
10. Stanley to Wellington, 18.2.46, WP 2/138/15–16; [Wellington], Memorandum upon the leadership of the Conservative Party in the House, copy not in W's nor his secretary's hand, marked 'From Lord Derby 1870', WP2/138/33; Wellington to Stanley 19.2.46, WP 2/138/39–44. Wellington's handwriting in the last, which is badly faded, is so bad that I have relied on the transcription in G. R. Gleig (1864: 416–17), *Life of Wellington* (People's Edition, London). However, a comparison between the original and the transcription shows that even Gleig was defeated by the Duke's hand in places.
11. Stanley to Bentinck 14.1.46, Derby Papers Box 132/13, quoted by Blake (1970: 63). Also quoted, with a different reference, by Stewart (1971: 55).
12. Cobden claimed that he was motivated by the economic interests of the class to which he belonged:

   I am afraid, if we must confess the truth, that most of us entered upon this struggle with the belief that we had some distinct class interest in the question, and that we should carry it by a manifestation in [?of] our will in this district against the will and consent of other portions of the community (Cobden, 1870: i. 97, quoted by Irwin, 1989: 42)

But a familiar fallacy prevents this from being taken at its face value. Cobden may well have been consciously acting in his class interest. But the Anti-Corn Law League bankrupted and exhausted him. This explanation, even from Cobden's own mouth, fails to explain why the individual Richard Cobden should have sacrificed his interests to those of a wider group.

5. The strategic use of ideas: nationalizing the interest in the nineteenth century

Cheryl Schonhardt-Bailey

1. INTRODUCTION

Politics is about choices and choices are about preferences. But, oddly enough, political scientists rarely question the genesis of preferences. Having borrowed heavily from economic theory, rational choice-oriented political science considers preferences to be intuitively self-evident. But are they? Few would disagree that economic interests are central to explaining preferences, yet several authors have started to identify the limitations of theories of political behaviour that rely solely on economic interests. Ideas and ideology are beginning to capture the attention of authors who are dissatisfied with the sometimes sterile and mechanistic framework of rational choice political science.[1] But if rational choice can be accused of being sterile and mechanistic, so too can the ideas literature be criticized as woolly and unscientific. For those who accept the broader and less controversial proposition that interests *and* ideas (in some combination) determine preferences, the challenge of dissecting their respective influences is formidable. This study takes a small step in that direction by focusing on how interest groups use ideas to pursue policy objectives. I argue that some interest groups are able to *nationalize their interest* – that is, they use ideas or ideologies to gain support for their policy objective (support that is not available from interests alone).[2]

Interests-based approaches such as pluralism, public choice and élite theory all purport to explain why some groups are more successful than others in shaping public policy. For pluralists, larger groups are likely to enjoy greater success than smaller groups. For public choice theorists, groups that are able to overcome the free-rider problem are the ones that shape public policy. For élite theorists, socio-economic class elevates interest groups of one class over those of another class. In short, success is contingent upon internal characteristics of the group – its size, its organizational ability or the socio-economic make-up of its members. Of course, some refinements to these approaches factor into the equation structural/institutional features (for example, concentration of interests, the nature of the electoral system and so on) that also condition the success of one group over another. What is rarely discussed, however, is how groups communicate with non-group members – that is, how they appeal to the general public for support. I contend that such appeals are very often based on unifying themes or ideas, particularly ones that are linked with the broader societal welfare. It is the use of ideas, *ceteris paribus*, that enables some groups to succeed where others fail.

This chapter examines how and under what conditions economic interests persuade non-group members to support the group's policy objective. Central to my focus is the role of institutions, and in particular political parties, in facilitating the strategy of nationalizing the interest. I apply a couple of hypotheses to three cases of trade policy in the nineteenth and early twentieth century – Repeal of the protectionist Corn Laws in Britain (1846); the tariff reform challenge to Britain's free trade policy (1903–6); and Germany's protectionist backlash of the early 1890s freer trade policies. In two of these cases – Repeal of the Corn Laws and post-Caprivi Germany – we see an interest group that successfully nationalized the trade-related interest of its members. For the Anti-Corn Law League in Britain, this interest was in free trade, while for the *Bund der Landwirte* in Germany, the interest was in protection. In the third case of tariff reform in Britain, an example is found of an interest group that tried but failed to nationalize its interest.

Sections 2–4 develop an operational definition for ideology, identifying the strategy of nationalizing the interest as one important function. Sections 3 and 4 provide flesh to the various dimensions of nationalizing the interest, and discuss the institutional context within which success is more or less likely. Finally, section 5 applies two hypotheses to the three cases, illustrating how the various groups fared in their attempts to acquire a national following.

2.   DEFINING IDEOLOGY

One fairly common misunderstanding of ideology is that it suggests some form of non-rationality, that is, some 'residual or random component of conscious human decision making' (Hinich and Munger, 1994: 236). Hinich and Munger, who rightly object to this characterization of ideology, note that Marx's definition of ideology as false consciousness is chiefly responsible for giving ideology a bad name:

> With hindsight, we can paraphrase Marx's theory of ideology as the barrier that
> prevents the masses from taking their rightful place in society as follows: (a) cit-
> izens *should* act collectively to pursue their interests; (b) ideologies are (menda-
> cious) means of preventing this; (c) societies that are not ideological, but
> encourage true consciousness, are morally superior to societies stupefied by
> ideological galimatias: (d) most important, societies that are not ideological will
> win the evolutionary efficiency contest, and will overwhelm those that do not rid
> themselves of ideology. . . . The definition of ideology as false consciousness was,
> no doubt, rhetorically useful to Marx, but it provides a tenuous basis for social
> science. The false consciousness, or nonrational, view of ideology has largely
> been accepted into social science, without reflection or good reason.

Indeed, so distasteful is the word 'ideology' that the international relations
literature avoids it altogether, and instead speaks of 'ideas':

> For analytical purposes, the term *ideology* has become . . . 'too ideologized'.
> Modern uses of 'ideology' invariably imply partisanship, bias, propaganda,
> oversimplification, and so forth. . . . In view of all the problems associated with
> the term *ideology*, it is perhaps not surprising that the term *ideas* has come to be
> preferred in international relations. The term *idea* is ostensibly simpler and less
> loaded with the connotations that come with the term *ideology* (Woods, 1995:
> 163; my italic).

And yet, ideas are not ideologies, since the latter usually implies some fairly
coherent collection of the former. The intent here is not to ring fence ideas
from ideologies, but rather to analyse the uses to which ideas *and* ideologies
are put – particularly by economic interests. Hence, I develop an operational definition for ideology, and leave the more sociological and abstract
discussions of ideology to others.[3]

Recent work in the 'ideational' literature offers a good foundation for an
operational definition of ideology. This literature notes that ideology performs three functions: (a) it may become encased in institutions, and then
affect the evolution of public policy; (b) it offers a 'roadmap' for both voters
and policy makers; and (c) ideologies provide 'images' (or 'brand names')
on which voters, politicians and parties rely to distinguish one political
party from another.[4] I introduce a fourth function of ideology, which I call
'nationalizing the interest'.

a.   Ideas in Institutions

If institutions can be thought of as 'formal rules, compliance procedures,
and customary practices that structure the relationships between individuals in the polity and economy',[5] their potential impact on policy making
is substantial. Institutions may influence *which* ideas or ideologies gain
political access, as well as the *access* of political leaders to these ideas or

ideologies. Moreover, when ideologies are recognized as legitimate by authoritative institutions, they acquire an added permanency by virtue of becoming established or conventional wisdom.

b. Roadmaps

Political parties must compete for the votes of individuals who are not only concerned with their own (and their community's) economic well-being, but who must also gauge the reliability of candidates to deliver on their promises. One important way to gauge this reliability is by considering the ideological reputation of the candidate, and the simplest way to measure reputation is his party label. Thus, for Hinich and Munger (1994: 101–2), voters use the ideological positions of candidates 'as a cue, a predictor of the positions of the candidate once he takes office, based on *the particular correspondence or mapping* between ideology and policy'. Goldstein, too, sees ideology as serving the 'roadmap' function, but for her ideology constitutes the causal ideas that help politicians to select from a number of possible policy options. In providing a roadmap between the causes of the problem and its likely solution, ideology provides voters and policy-makers a way to deal with the uncertainty of candidates' promises and policy outcomes.

c. Brand Names

Hinich and Munger (1994: 99–100) are not the first authors to find that parties provide 'images' or shorthand understandings for candidates' ideologies, but their work makes explicit that such images provide cues to voters about the policies that candidates are likely to adopt once in office:

> [The] investment in ideology as an asset, or brand name, suggests that ideological reputations can be thought of as cues. The cues serve as signals to voters about how certain types of outcomes are related to the choices that they and others make. . . . (I)deology provides voters with some means of comparing candidates and parties.

The authors maintain that political parties – particularly new parties – cannot be successful without a 'coherent and understandable ideology' (ibid., p. 61). Indeed, parties do not organize themselves around policy positions, but rather around ideologies: '(p)latforms are more than a point in an n-dimensional space; they become abstract, even ethical statements of what is good, and why' (ibid., p. 3). Policy positions of parties (and politicians) are constrained by their ideological reputations; too much movement diminishes the credibility of the party image. Hinich and Munger are correct to emphasize ideological reputation, but one must not underestimate the ability of parties to change their images or brand names over time. That is, parties almost invariably modify their ideologies as they adapt to economic, social and other changes that affect the median voter. Party images, or brand names, are malleable in the long run – even, for instance, complete reversals on policy positions such as occurred with the Republicans and Democrats on trade policy from the nineteenth to the twentieth centuries, or any number of recent British Labour Party policies. In the short run, however, voter-maximizing parties in stable polities may modify their images at the margin, but do so cautiously as such changes lessen the credibility of the party label. Clearly there is a balance which must be struck between maintaining a clear ideological reputation and adapting to shifts in the median voter.

While the roadmap and brand name functions of ideology are distinct, they are interrelated. The roadmap function might be conceptualized as the voter or politician using an existing map to guide the choice of candidate or policy. Because the voter and politician cannot draw the map themselves (since the uncertainty that requires use of a map in the first place makes such a task impossible), they must obtain the map from some other source. In most cases, this other source is the brand name. Political parties are, using the same analogy, the cartographers of the maps.

From this analogy we can see that in its roadmap function, ideology is exogenous (that is, it is not constructed or reconstructed by individual voters or politicians). But in its brand name function, ideology is endogenous to political parties. That is, parties construct and modify ideologies as a way of presenting a distinct brand name to the electorate. Yet this analogy also reveals the limited value of these two functions. First, if we think of ideology as having an exogenous effect on individuals, that effect is not limited to simply providing a prescriptive roadmap. Ideology may also motivate political action, provide group cohesiveness and even shape the way that individuals perceive their interests. It does so not by prescription but by persuasion. As John Plamenatz notes, the prescriptive (or roadmap) element of ideology is secondary to its persuasive role. He likens an ideology to a fable by Aesop, in that it tells 'a tale that points to a moral'. The tale is always put into words, though not always with the moral. 'What makes the tale ideological is that [the] audience, consciously or unconsciously, draws a moral from it' (Plamenatz, 1970: 75–6).

Second, the brand name function helps us to identify one source of ideological thinking – political parties. But we know that many ideologies form distinct identities outside political parties (for example, feminism, environmentalism and Marxism), and we know that political parties are often not ideologically cohesive. While this is not the time to embark upon a discussion of the origins of ideology, suffice it to say that parties do not hold a monopoly on ideological thinking. What ideological thinking they do, moreover, is rarely done as a group but rather as individuals pursuing individual political careers. Political parties are, after all, collective entities not unitary actors. Hence, to the extent that brand names serve a function, they must be flexible and adaptable to accommodate intra-party ideological disputes, without being so loose as to forfeit the party's distinct identity. The limitations of the roadmap and brand name functions may be summarized as: (1) ideology has less to do with prescription and more with persuasion; (2) political parties are not the only source of ideological thinking; and (3) cleavages within political parties will invariably shake the foundations of their brand names or political images.

d. Nationalizing the Interest

Nationalizing the interest means that parochial interests create the illusion (which may or may not be based in fact) that their political objective is (or should be) shared by the larger citizenry (or by a particular social or economic class) – more succinctly, the particular is represented as the general. The goal, of course, in representing the particular as the general is to create a large (even national) following. However well groups pursue the interests of their members, they will not gain the support of the general public without some recourse to ideology, or at a minimum, ideas. Ideology persuades the general public to support or to become indifferent to the groups' policy preferences; that is, it makes the policy goal palatable to non-members of the group. Groups that nationalize the interest may even use ideological persuasion to *shape the economic interests* of individuals, particularly insofar as changes in policy (for example, economic policy reform) make it difficult for individuals to calculate what their interests actually are. Bates and Krueger (1993: 456) emphasize the importance of ideology in shaping individuals' interests:

> A result of this uncertainty [in economic policy reforms] is that people can be persuaded as to where their economic interests lie; wide scope is thus left for rhetoric and persuasion. In such situations, advocates of particular economic theories or of ideological conceptions of how economies work can acquire influence. . . . Under conditions of uncertainty, people's beliefs of where their economic interests lie can be created and organized by political activists; rather than shaping events, notions of self-interest are instead themselves shaped and formed. In pursuing their economic interests, people act in response to ideology.

It is no doubt feasible for a fractional, interests-based party to attempt to nationalize its party's interest, and for politicians to nationalize a policy objective, but for simplicity I focus on the motivation and ability of interest groups to nationalize the economic interests of their members.

Stated succinctly, *economic interests will be more successful in obtaining their political objective(s) when, as a collectivity, they are able to 'nationalize the interest'* (Hypothesis 1). Groups that do not engage in a nationalizing the interest strategy would be expected to fare less well in the policy arena. But what happens if two opposing groups both attempt to nationalize the interest on a single issue? Who wins? In order not to confuse internal attributes (group size, ability to overcome free rider problem and socio-economic make-up of members) with external relations, it must first be assumed that both groups are equivalent in *potential* political strength. That is, their capabilities need not be identical, but neither should suffer a serious handicap nor overwhelming advantage that would predetermine the outcome. The question is then, what are the conditions that favour one nationalizing the interest strategy over another? Before we can address this question, however, we must be clear about a basic distinction in types of interest group – the interests-based group and the ideology-based group.

3. NATIONALIZING THE INTEREST

a. Interest-based versus Ideology-based Groups

E. E. Schattschneider argued that these two types of group are distinguished by whether members can expect to benefit personally from the goal of the group. For example, the members of the National Association of Manufacturers expect to benefit personally from policies promoted by the association, while the members of the American League to Abolish Capital Punishment do not expect to escape execution as a result of membership, since obviously membership includes *anyone* opposed to capital punishment, not just those persons on death row (Schattschneider, 1960: 26). So, according to Schattschneider, interest-based groups provide exclusive benefits to members, while ideology-based groups provide non-exclusive benefits. Yet this distinction becomes blurred if one considers the 'logic' of collective action (Olson, 1965), since ideology-based and interest-based groups both provide public and possibly also private goods (selective incentives). The abolition of capital punishment, a clean environment and a nuclear-free world (that is, goals pursued by ideology-based groups) are enjoyed by contributors and non-contributors alike,[6] and the enjoyment by one individual does not detract from that of another.[7] They may also provide private goods to contributing members, such as newsletters, invitations to special events, a sense of personal gratification and so on. An interest-based group also provides both a public and a private good – for example, favourable corporate tax policy may benefit all businesses regardless of whether or not they contribute to the corporate lobby organization, while selective incentives (group pension schemes, newsletters) are enjoyed only by contributing members. I argue that the distinction between ideology-based and interest-based groups has less to do with the exclusivity of benefits and more to do with the tendency of the latter to 'rationalize their special interests as public interests'(Schattschneider, 1960: 25) and thus obfuscate the value of the public good to individuals who do not share their special interests. It is at this point that interest-based groups may invoke ideology as a tool of obfuscation – that is, they may engage in a strategy of nationalizing the group interest. Ideology-based groups, on the other hand, begin and end their appeal with the tool of ideology, while interest-based groups begin with shared interests and then invoke the tool of ideology only when and as necessary. Interest groups that use ideology to obfuscate the public good benefits accruing to their members are indeed exploiting the ideology in pursuit of (an) ulterior motive(s).[8]

b. Conditions for Nationalizing the Interest

Why are some interest groups more successful at nationalizing the interest than others? At least three conditions favour some groups over others: (1) the existence of positive externalities to the public good that is sought by the group, externalities that may be linked to an idea or ideology; (2) good organization and strong leadership; and (3) a conducive institutional environment. Condition (1) is unique to the theory of nationalizing the interest, while conditions (2) and (3) are widely accepted as keys to successful lobbying. Organization, leadership and conducive institutions can surely be helpful, but not all three are absolutely essential. What *is* essential, however, is condition (1) – the existence of positive externalities.

1. Positive externality
A positive externality to a public good is some benefit that accrues to non-interested, non-members of the group. While the tangible benefit may be difficult, if not impossible, to measure, the *idea* or image behind it is appealing to most people. This idea or image is generally couched in terms of the broader societal welfare – for example, a prosperous economy, national pride, family values and a clean environment are all potential positive externalities. Consider contemporary farmers groups that seek to obtain or retain trade protection. Appeals to the public are phrased in terms of the broader societal welfare: 'self-sufficiency in agriculture is necessary for the nation's security' (Ruppel and Kellogg, 1991; Winters, 1990); 'agriculture

must be protected as an environmentally friendly "green" industry'
(Anderson, 1992b); and 'the family farm must be protected in order to preserve traditional rural values,' and/or 'the countryside'. A recent statement
by the European Union (EU) Farm Commissioner invokes positive externalities to defend Common Agricultural Policy (CAP) subsidies: 'If
European society is interested in the European model of agriculture,
meaning that agricultural output is not measured only in cereals or beef but
also in the landscape and the environment, it needs to pay the additional
cost' (Anon., 1998a). The French are particularly adept at invoking positive externalities to defend their status as the main beneficiaries of CAP
subsidies, arguing that these subsidies are part of the 'spirit and heritage'
of the EU (Anon., 1999). Because the French see themselves as a farming
nation (though only 4 per cent of the workforce is devoted to farming) they
are sympathetic to their farmers as 'they burn down buildings, block
motorways, dump tonnes of imported fruit and vegetables on the streets
and stage other violent demonstrations in defence of what they consider
their right to cash from the public purse' (Anon., 1998b).

William Browne's depiction of the myths behind US agricultural policy
offers an apt illustration of how US farmers invoke positive externalities to
garner support for agricultural subsidies (Browne et al., 1992: 11–15). He
maintains that US farmers perpetuate the idea that family farms are central
to the nation's cultural heritage, purporting that (a) farms are necessary for
preserving individual liberties in capitalist societies, and (b) family farms
are 'repositories for family values and hence for traditional ways of defining personal loyalties within a framework of community' (ibid., 11). As a
consequence, '(a)grarian populist arguments have . . . been applied to
public policy as reasons to preserve family farms or, more frequently, to
preserve farming as a way of life in general' (ibid., 13). It is precisely the
ambiguity of the ideas and images behind the 'agrarian ideal' that makes
them so politically attractive, for as Browne notes:

> (T)hey are contested symbols, vague images of how agriculture ought to be, or
> once was. Their lack of specificity means that competing political interests can
> easily appropriate them. . . . There is irony in the fact that an agrarian philoso-
> phy that stresses the importance of community and the public good should be
> used to promote the interests of a few (ibid., 13–15).

It is because US farming lobbies use family values and community spirit as
images or ideas that they have been so successful in persuading urban consumers to pay higher prices for subsidized food.

But how do these images or ideas actually work to persuade non-group
members to accept the policy objective of the interest group? Kenneth
Shepsle depicts the role of ideas quite simply as 'the hooks on which

politicians hang their objectives and by which they further their interests' (Shepsle, 1985: 233). But how, exactly, do these hooks work? In the agricultural examples given above, ideas 'hook' non-group members by getting them to think of the price paid from a commodity as including a package of goods and not just the one item. That is, the commodity becomes multidimensional.[9] The package price includes not just the food product, but other items as well, such as supporting the family farm, preserving the countryside and alleviating rural poverty. The positive externalities to the public good thus provide the ideas that transform a commodity valued by a single dimension (private consumption) to one with value in other dimensions. In the historic case of the Repeal of the Corn Laws, the free-trade interest group persuaded workers not to see free trade in terms of its possible negative consequence for wages, but rather in terms of fighting against a landowning aristocracy (that is, monopolists). The job of interest groups engaged in nationalizing the interest is to (a) convince non-group members that the commodity is multidimensional, and (b) persuade them of the value of the other bits of the package. Non-group members then become willing to pay more for the same product because they give higher salience to the other bits of the package.

As noted earlier, interest groups are not alone in appealing to positive externalities for support. Political parties may use it to enlarge their membership, or as one author aptly puts it: 'National societal goals transcending group interests offer the best sales prospect for the party intent on establishing or enlarging an appeal previously limited to specific sections of the population' (Kirchheimer, 1966: 54). Political leaders may also appeal to positive externalities to garner support for their policies. Positive externalities may be linked to a specific idea or to a wider ideology, but in either case they are seen to enhance the broader societal welfare.

2. Leadership and organization

Interest groups that enjoy strong leadership and good organization are better situated to nationalize the interest. The importance of leadership is fairly self-evident, for '(t)he best ideology, in terms of internal logical consistency and emotional appeal, is as nothing without committed apostles to spread it' (Hinich and Munger, 1994: 21). Group *leaders*, therefore, almost certainly will be true believers of the ideology they invoke to nationalize the interest. Almost as self-evident is the need for organization, since only when ideologies are backed by organizations will they take hold. Sartori (1990: 169–170) boldly states that 'no idea has ever made much headway without an organization behind it . . . Wherever ideologies seem to be important in politics they have a firm organizational basis.' . . . (I)deological persuasion requires a powerfully organized network of communications'.

Undoubtedly leadership and organization are vital, but it is difficult to quantify how much of each is actually required for a successful nationalizing the interest strategy. In the British case, the Anti-Corn Law League enjoyed superb leadership and an unprecedented organizational apparatus – and it succeeded in its policy objective of repeal. But the Free Trade Union exhibited rather average leadership and never attained the national organization of the League – and yet it, too, succeeded in persuading the electorate of its free-trade goal. Hence, while some leadership and organization are necessary, extraordinary quantities of either do not appear essential.

3.   Institutions

Institutions as 'formal rules, compliance procedures and customary practices' (Yee, 1996: 92) might refer to any number of entities; however, I specify three that are of particular relevance for nationalizing the interest. Changes in the franchise, party system and governmental agencies or departments can each (or in concert) facilitate or block the efforts of interest groups that attempt to nationalize the interest. For instance, laws that enfranchise new groups of individuals (middle class, working class and women) will undoubtedly provide a window of opportunity for those individuals to nationalize their interests. This may arise as a consequence of a newly enfranchised group sharing some common ideas of what contributes to the broader societal welfare: middle-class voters might share an antipathy towards aristocratic traditions; working-class voters might share a commitment to fair practices in the workplace; and women voters might share a commitment to non-discrimination in employment. 'Anti-aristocracy', 'workers' rights' and 'women's rights' then become ideological fodder for much narrower goals of economic interest groups.

A polity in which parties are highly ideological can limit the opportunity for interest groups to nationalize the interest, since party cleavages may dominate the ideological debate. Conversely, a polity of ideologically weak parties may allow interest groups more freedom to exploit ideology as they seek to nationalize their interest.

Finally, recalling that one of the politically relevant functions of ideologies is that they may become encased in institutions and thereby 'take on a life of their own', we should expect that this would have repercussions for interest groups that seek to exploit ideologies. When ideologies become encased in governmental agencies or departments, they acquire added legitimacy which in turn can benefit interest groups that seek to exploit these same ideologies and hinder groups whose goals conflict with these ideologies.

However important nationalizing the interest may be to a group's policy success, its applicability is inevitably limited by the nature of the policy in question. Three types of policies provide less fertile ground for nationalizing the interest: (1) very narrow or localized policies (for example, preservation of a neighbourhood woodland); (2) highly specialized or technical policies (for example, reserve requirements for commercial banks); and (3) secretive policies (for example, military planning and expenditures). Very local policies affect too few people, specialized policies are too difficult to understand and secretive policies (by definition) lack an open forum for discussion. On the other hand, distributive and redistributive policies such as international trade, social welfare and fiscal policy allow greater scope for nationalizing the interest since the numbers affected are substantial, the issues are fairly intuitive and they are subject to public debate.

Just as some policies have greater scope for nationalizing the interest than others, some types of group will be more likely to use the strategy than others. Groups comprised of 'insiders' – that is, individuals who are either part of or have easy access to the policy-making élite – tend not to engage in nationalizing the interest, since to do so would only dilute their privileged access to the policy-makers. 'Outsider' groups – that is, those that have little or no direct access to policy-makers – are more likely to seek to nationalize their interest as a way of placing greater political pressure on policy-makers. (Protectionist MPs and the Anti-Corn Law League provide a perfect example of the propensity of outsiders to nationalize their interest while insiders relied on their presumed strength in Parliament.)

This distinction between insider and outsider groups parallels Schattschneider's (1960: 38–39) observation that it is the weak, rather than the strong, who seek the involvement of more and more people in a conflict:

> [T]he notion of 'pressure' distorts the image of the power relations involved [in political conflicts]. *Private conflicts are taken into the public arena precisely because someone wants to make certain that the power ratio among the private interests most immediately involved shall not prevail.* . . . Since the contestants in private conflicts are apt to be unequal in strength, it follows that *the most powerful special interest want private settlements* because they are able to dictate the outcome as long as the conflict remains private. . . . Therefore, it is the weak, not the strong, who appeal to public authority for relief.

While the designation of weak/strong groups can lead to circularity in predicting policy outcomes (the strong win because they are strong), the private versus public debate helps us to see the link between policy type and group type. That is, policies that are narrow, highly technical or secretive have little scope for public debate, and are ones in which insider groups are more likely to hold sway. Hence, we would not expect to find a nationalizing the interest strategy at work. On the other hand, policies where the debate is open to the public are also ones with more outsider groups, and therefore are where we would expect to find the group(s) engaging in nationalizing the interest. Very often policies and groups do not separate into these two general types, and so we find insider and outsider groups competing against one another. In this case, nationalizing the interest may be a way for an outsider group to counter the insider access advantage.

c.   The Endogeneity and Exogeneity of Individuals' Preferences

Separating ideology from interests poses a methodological conundrum since not only are the two highly correlated (for example, the well-to-do tend to be conservative) but the direction of causality runs both ways. Hence, it seems sensible to accept this correlation and dual causality from the outset, and then to explore how actors – particularly interest groups – might exploit ideas in order to further their interests. But we must first have a clear notion of how individuals construct their policy preferences.

1.   Individuals' preferences
Think of interests and ideology as two dimensions of individual prefer-ences. That is, an individual may be motivated primarily (or even entirely) by economic interests, so that he advocates only those policies for which he perceives a clear and immediate economic benefit. At the other end of the spectrum is an individual who is entirely altruistic, so that he advocates policies that he discerns as benefiting society as a whole, or some disadvan-taged section of society. (For purposes of simplification, I collapse all dimensions of ideas and ideology onto a single dimension.) Figure 5.1 cap-tures these two extremes in motivation. In Figure 5.1(a), the individual is motivated by economic interests alone. His ideal line (in bold) designates his interests-motivated preference on a particular policy. His preference function, or utility function, is greatest on this line. His utility declines with distance from his ideal line, so that a policy that falls on, say, u_0 is preferred less than all others nearer to his ideal line. Note that the indifference curves, or lines above the ideal line, are flat, meaning that the ideas or ideology dimension has no bearing on his preference. The story is just reversed in Figure 5.1(b), where the individual is motivated solely by ideas or ideology. (Ideally, the lines would be drawn in a three-dimensional space, with utility representing the third dimension. For instance, an individual might imagine a three-dimensional hollow trapezoid, with the utility reaching its maximum at the apex.)

Most individuals fall somewhere in between these two extremes, with economic interests and ideological beliefs together shaping policy prefer-ences. In Figure 5.2, we see three types of policy preference where interests *and* ideas or ideology both have salience. In Figure 5.2(a) interests and ideas/ideology are weighted equally in deciding the policy preference. In

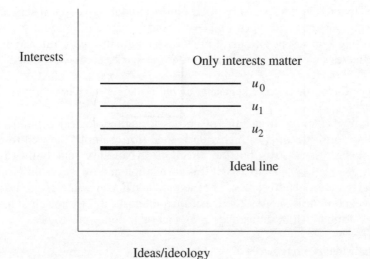

a. Preferences from interests only

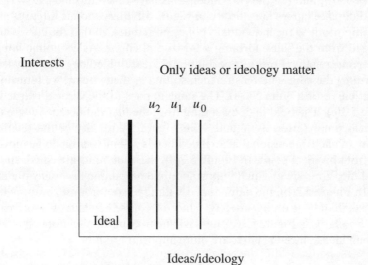

b. Preferences from ideas/ideology only

Figure 5.1   Two extremes for policy preferences

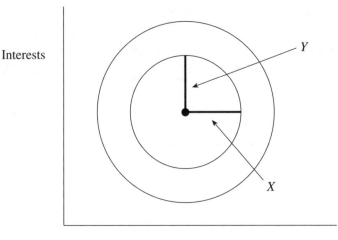

Ideas/ideology

a. Interests and ideas are equally salient

Figure 5.2   Variations in salience of interests and ideas/ideology

Figures 5.2(b) and (c), the two dimensions have different salience, so that the indifference curves are ellipses. In Figure 5.2(b), economic interests are more important to the individual's policy preference, so that the curves are squeezed from the sides, forming a horizontal ellipse. As economic interests become relatively more important (and ideas or ideology relatively less important) the ellipse flattens further, so that at the extreme, we return to the flat curves in Figure 5.1(a). The same applies to the vertical ellipse in Figure 5.2(c). The bold lines extending from the first indifference curve to the ideal point (given as *X* and *Y* in Figure 5.2(a)) depict the relative amount of each dimension that an individual is willing to forgo as he moves away from his ideal point. In Figure 5.2(a), these amounts are equal, since both dimensions are of equal importance in determining his policy preference. In Figure 5.2(b), the individual is willing to compromise far more on his ideas than he is on his interests, since of course he values his interests more. Similarly, in Figure 5.2(c), he is willing to compromise more on interests than ideas, since the latter are more important to him.

2.   Changing preferences through nationalizing the interest

A core tenet of rational choice theory is the proposition that once economic interests are correctly specified, the preferences of individuals or groups become self-evident. There is then no need to go further in explaining the

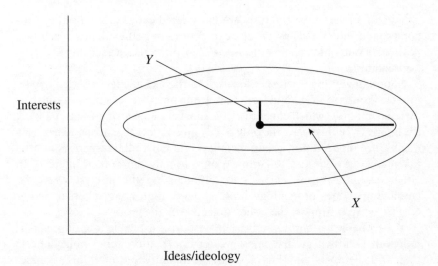

Ideas/ideology

b. Interests are more salient

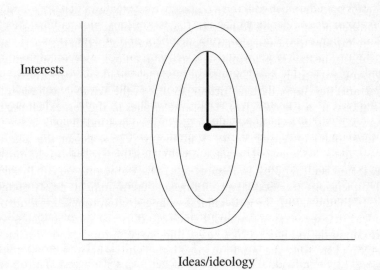

Ideas/ideology

c. Ideas are more salient

Figure 5.2 (cont.)

genesis of preferences. Interests are considered exogenous to policy outcomes, and individuals or groups can determine self-evidently whether a
particular outcome benefits or harms their interests. In fact, the reality is
not so simple.

Nationalizing the interest is focused on the use of ideas or ideology by
interest groups to shape and form non-group members' perceptions of their
own self-interest (which constitutes the most extreme form of nationalizing
the interest). In this sense, the only policy preferences that are endogenously
formed are those of non-group members. Yet individuals' interests may be
taken as exogenous and still allow groups to nationalize their interests. In
either case, the group engages in nationalizing the interest when, by
employing an idea or ideology, it *persuades* non-group members to acquiesce to, or even support the policy objective of the group.

A reasonable assumption (given the resources available to groups versus
individuals) is that groups enjoy greater information about policy effects
than do individuals, and thus enjoy an opportunity to exploit this asymmetry of information. The use or misuse of information does not, however, constitute nationalizing the interest since at the heart of this strategy is the use
of *ideas*. Groups have essentially two mechanisms to appeal to non-group
members – (mis)information and ideas. (The subjective element of
(mis)information may be linked with ideas, but clarity of analysis requires us
to draw a boundary between this and positive externalities that are founded
upon a clear idea or ideology.) The effectiveness of (mis)information depends
on how well informed are non-group members, and of course this will vary
from individual to individual, and may well vary over time (especially as individuals are exposed to other sources of information). As discussed later, the
further choice between information and misinformation depends on whether
the interests of the group and individual coincide or conflict. When group
and individual's interests coincide (Figure 5.3), the group merely needs to
inform individuals of this shared interest, thereby expanding the 'group'
from a collectivity of actual fee-paying members to one consisting of all individuals who share the interest. In this case, any recourse to ideas as persuasion is wasted effort. (For sake of simplicity, I assume some homogeneity of
interests among group members, so that aggregation of interests is unprob-
lematic.) When group and individuals' interests conflict, misinformation
competes with ideas as the mechanism of persuasion.

Table 5.1 presents the interplay between (1) individual and group interests, and (2) an individual's knowledge of her own self-interest. The objective relation between the interests of the individual and the group is
simplified as a dichotomy – either they coincide or they conflict. The three
rows in Table 5.1 depict the knowledge of the individual about her own economic interests. She may be clear about what her interests are and these may

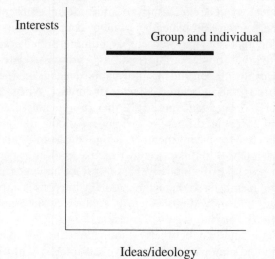

a. Uninformed individuals

b. Informed individuals

Figure 5.3   Group and individual's interests coincide

Table 5.1   The interplay between the mutuality of individuals' and groups' interests, and individuals' knowledge of self-interest

	Individual's and group's interests coincide	Individual's and group's interest conflict
Individual *knows* her interests	A. *Group provides confirming information* ('You really are one of us')	B. *Group persuades* ('Okay, we know you are not one of us, but X [the positive externality that our goal creates/enhances] benefits the broader societal welfare'.)
Individual *does not know* her interests	C. *Group provides information* ('You actually are one of us – you just didn't realize it')	D. *Group persuades* (using argument in cell B) *or provides misinformation* ('You actually are one of us – and here are the [altered] facts'.)
Individual *is mistaken* about her interests	E. *Group provides information* ('You were misinformed – the facts show that you are one of us'.)	F. *Group ignores or provides misinformation* (using argument in cell D)

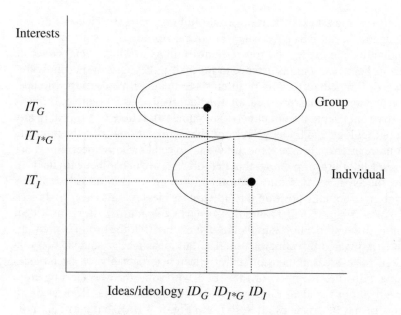

Interests

Figure 5.4   Group and individual's interests conflict (and group invokes ideas)

either coincide or conflict with those of the group. If her (immediate) interests coincide with the group's interest (cell A), the group merely confirms this mutuality of interests: it does not invoke anything other than common interests to garner her support. If, on the other hand, her interests conflict with the group's interest, the group may use positive externalities to persuade her both of the multidimensionality of the relevant commodity, and of the value of its added dimensions (cell B). Graphed in Figure 5.4, this scenario constitutes a powerful use of nationalizing the interest, since it entails a change in the individual's preference from one motivated predominantly by self-interest to one also motivated by an idea or ideology. The group therefore heads off potential opposition by persuading these individuals of at least a tangency of mutual interest (that is, the two indifference curves touch at IT_{I*G}, ID_{I*G}). At this point, both the group and the individual move outward from their ideal positions on both dimensions and towards the ideal positions of the other actor. Note, however, that the ideal point of each actor remains fixed. These individuals are persuaded to value the commodity not just in terms of its private consumption purposes, but also for its other dimensions. Of course, the group may attempt to use misinformation – rather than ideas or an ideology – to persuade the individual in cell B to support the group's policy objective, but since she already knows her interest such misinformation would fall on deaf ears. Hence, I do not include this in cell B as a realistic form of persuasion by the group.

Individuals in the second row are uncertain as to where their economic interests lie, a frequent occurrence in times of policy reform. For individuals whose (immediate) economic interests coincide with the group's interest, the group simply informs them of this fact (cell C). In Figure 5.3, this is shown as a movement from panel (a) to panel (b). It does not appeal to any idea or ideology and thereby does not engage in nationalizing the interest.

A more interesting case is the individual in cell D who is uncertain of her interests, but the group knows that her interests are in conflict with its own. Here, the asymmetry of information between group and individual allows the group to actually position the individual's ideal point as near to its own as possible. Figure 5.5 illustrates this scenario. In panel (a), the group's ideal point is situated in a horizontal ellipse, meaning that the group is predominantly motivated by economic interest, but ideas receive some expression as well. The ideas dimension may reflect heterogeneity of preferences among individual members of the group, with some members feeling more strongly about the ideas dimension than others. Or, the preferences of all members may be driven by interests (as in Figure 5.1(a)), but the image portrayed to the outside world is softened and massaged with ideas (that is, Shepsle's 'hook'). The dotted circle for the individual represents the feasible set of ideal points. (This is given as a circle, since no a priori reason exists to assume a particular elliptical shape.) She is uncertain where to locate her ideal point within this set, and so cannot identify a policy preference. By nationalizing the interest, the group is able to position the individual's ideal point on the perimeter of her uncertainty, nearest to the group's own ideal point. If the group were to expand its nationalizing the interest strategy, it might influence the interests of even more individuals who face this same uncertainty – as shown in Figure 5.5(c). It should be noted that unlike those in cell B, these individuals may be susceptible to persuasion by misinformation. Of course a strategy based on misinformation alone would risk exposure in public debate. Yet one based solely on a nationalizing the interest strategy would hinge on the attractiveness of the idea and how credibly it could be linked with a positive externality.

Individuals in cells B and D are key to a nationalizing the interest strategy. Thus far, we have seen that by using ideas, an interest group is able to 'hook' these individuals by either altering the shape of their indifference curves or by positioning their ideal points within areas of uncertainty. That is, the group exaggerates its commitment to the east–west dimension (ideas/ideology) so as to encourage movement of individuals on the north–south dimension (interests). By portraying its policy preference as one that not only yields economic benefits to its members, but also cares about such things as a clean environment, national security, rural values and so on, the group captures the attention of non-group members who care about these things as well. The image and the argumentation of the group acquire an ideas dimension which attracts non-group members – but this is not to say that such individuals naïvely accept the group's message. The 'hook' of ideas has two ends. Because individuals care about the east–west dimension, they can play hard to get with the interest group. They can demand some evidence of the group's stated commitment to ideas (environment, national security and rural values) in return for support for the group's policy objective. These may be in the form of side agreements or concessions of various sorts. The group, in turn, is willing to concede on the east–west dimension, since it cares relatively less about it. (Taking Figure 5.2(b) as the group's preference function, it would be willing to concede far more of X than Y in order to move closer to the individual's ideal point.) Figure 5.5(d) illustrates the east–west movement of the group's preference function, bringing it nearer to the ideal points of individuals b and c. Note, however, that a commitment on ideas made to b and c distances the group further from individual a. Assuming a single ideas dimension (as I have thus far), the group may simply accommodate the majority and cut its losses with a. However, it is more likely that multiple dimensions of ideas exist. For example, a belief in family values and environmentalism might be *two* dimensions of ideas, so that an individual's position on the former would not determine his position on the latter. With multiple dimensions to ideas, a group could appeal to different segments of the population by tailoring its position across the various dimensions. Thus, environmentalism might resonate with some individuals, and preservation of family values with others. The east–west dimension would be replaced by an n-dimensional space, so as to allow the group to move towards b and c on, say, the dimension of environmentalism, but toward a on the dimension of family values. But, as n-dimensions are difficult to graph, Figure 5.6 illustrates the same east–west movement as in Fig. 5.5(d), but in response to individuals who know that their interests conflict with the group (individuals in Table 5.1, cell B – previously graphed in Figure 5.4).

An individual in cell E mistakenly thinks that her economic interests conflict with those of the group, so the group provides her with information on their commonality of interests. No recourse to ideas or ideology is necessary (if the information is successfully conveyed). Finally, the group's strategy with regard to individuals in cell F is ambiguous. It may choose to leave them alone, since they already (mistakenly) believe that their interests coincide with the groups.' Or, the group may attempt to provide these individuals with misinformation that confirms their mistaken understanding of their interests.

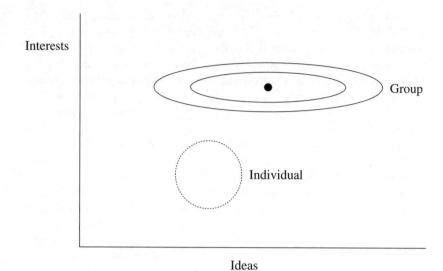

a. Uncertain individual

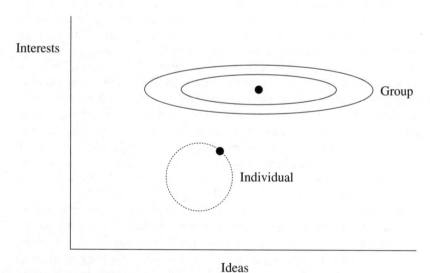

b. Group positions individual's ideal point

Figure 5.5   Group and individual's interest conflict (and group exploits asymmetry of information)

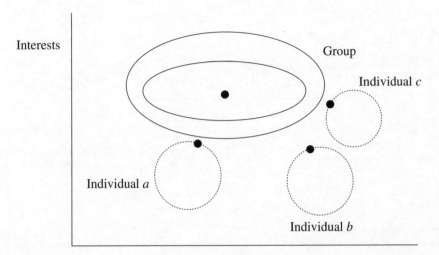

c. Group expands use of ideas to position ideal point

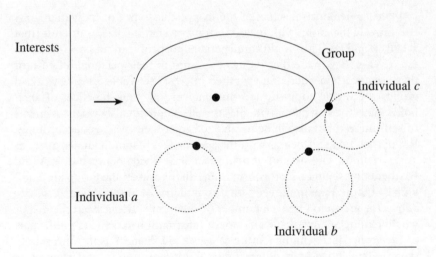

d. Individuals shift group's indifference curves

Figure 5.5 (cont.)

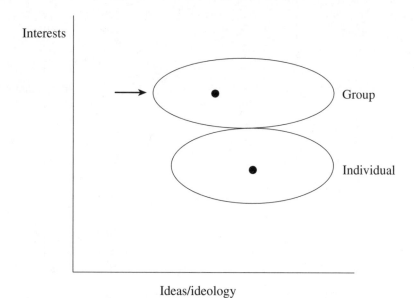

Figure 5.6   Group gains support for interests but concedes on ideas

Table 5.1 demonstrates that of the six possible 'types' of individual, only two provide the group with the opportunity to nationalize its interest (that is, cells B and D). This would entail persuading people to support (or acquiesce to) a policy that either they know is not in their personal interest, or they are uncertain whether it is in their interest. Yet Table 5.1 only works if groups are highly sophisticated not only in knowing the effect of their policy objectives on all individuals, as well as individuals' own assessments of self-interest, but also in being able to target their messages accordingly. Recall that Table 5.1 begins with the assumption that individuals' interests are exogenous. This assumption allows a clear divide between cells A and B, where no asymmetry of information exists between the group and individual. In the remaining cells, the asymmetry of information *in theory* allows the group to pursue a number of different strategies, but *in practice* would require an unrealistic amount of information and ability on the part of the group. The defining feature of cells C, D, E and F is the uncertainty surrounding individuals' interests. It is this uncertainty that suggests a bifurcation in Table 5.1, into Table 5.2, with the interests of individuals in cells A and B defined as exogenous and the interests of individuals in the remaining cells defined as endogenous. Hence, a nationalizing the interest strategy targeted at individuals in cell B would appeal strictly to benefits accruing to the larger societal welfare, and not to the individual's welfare.

Table 5.2 The interplay between the mutuality of individuals' and groups' interests, and individuals' knowledge of self-interest, revised

1. Individual's interests are exogenous (no asymmetry of information between group and individual)

	Individual's and group's interests *coincide*	Individual's and group's interest *conflict*
Individual *knows* her interests	A. *Group provides confirming information* ('You really are one of us')	B. *Group persuades* ('Okay, we know you are not one of us, but X [the positive externality that our goal creates/enhances] benefits us all')

2. Individual's interests are endogenous (asymmetry of information exists between group and individual)

Possible Group Strategies

Individual *is uncertain* about her interests

D. *Manipulate information* (provide objective, subjective, distorted or no information)

E. *Invoke positive externality* Linked with idea or ideology to shape individuals' perception of self-interest

Allowing the remaining individuals' interests to be endogenous gives rise to a far more sweeping use of nationalizing the interest. That is, the group would not only appeal to the effect of the positive externality on the broader societal welfare, but could also point to benefits accruing to individuals' own well-being. For these individuals, the very position of their ideal point would be influenced by the group's use of ideas.

4. Economic Interests and Political Parties

In section 3 I noted that polities with highly ideological parties may constrain interest groups from nationalizing the interest, while polities with ideologically weak parties may produce the opposite effect. This assertion makes sense if we assume that an equilibrium level of 'ideologizing' exists in any polity, and that in the first instance, it is political parties that provide the bulk of the ideological thinking. If parties sacrifice ideology for the economic interests of their members, an 'ideological vacuum' is created. This in turn creates an opportunity for interest groups to fill the vacuum through a strategy of nationalizing the interest.[10]

Some authors tend to think of political parties and interest groups as entirely different entities, with the former driven by ideology and the latter by interests.[11] Or, parties may be distinct because of the political functions that they perform – mobilizing the citizenry, formulating public policy, aggregating diverse interests and recruiting leaders for public office (King, 1969; Mair, 1990). This distinction between parties and interest groups is too confining, since *both* ideology and interests can be found in *both* political organizations. Indeed, even the functions of parties and interest groups are not mutually exclusive. Parties do not monopolize the aggregation of diverse interests and interest groups are not alone in articulating specific interests. Rather, some interest groups can (by nationalizing the interest) aggregate interests better than political parties, 'and some parties rival interest groups in articulation. The narrower the social basis of a party's support, the more likely they are to articulate interests'.[12] Consequently, we might construct a crude typology of political parties – those that emphasize ideology over interests and those that 'articulate' economic interests over ideology.

Party theorists have long debated the ideology versus interests balance within political parties (Bell, 1960; Duverger, 1961; Kirchheimer, 1966; Lijphart, 1990; Lipset and Rokkan, 1990; Mair, 1990; Schonhardt-Bailey, 1998b; Waxman, 1968). Duverger set the context for this debate by arguing that 'new' political parties were inherently more ideological than 'old' parties. For Duverger, leftist ideology coincided with newer political parties that had originated outside the electoral and parliamentary framework.

The extension of the popular suffrage gave rise to leftist parties, which evolved into 'mass parties'. In contrast, 'cadre' parties were older parties that had originated from the union of parliamentary groups and electoral committees, and were supported by a few influential individuals (Duverger, 1961: 63). Because their origins dictated a top-down organizational structure, the newer leftist parties were *more ideologically coherent, more cohesive and centralized* than were the cadre parties (LaPalombara and Weiner, 1990; my italic).

More recently, Hinich and Munger agree with Duverger that age affects the ideological content of parties, but discard the antecedent variable of party origin. According to Hinich and Munger (1994: 83), ideology is much stronger in new parties than in old parties because new parties must define their party 'image' while old parties may to some extent rest on their laurels:

> When parties are first established, and (if successful) are growing, they must appeal to the beliefs and interests of prospective members through an ideology. Once the party is established, the link to a specific ideology may grow more tenuous, and the party becomes a brokering agent among factions in the legislature.

For these authors, 'a coherent and understandable ideology' is the key to political success, and without one new parties face 'a substantial barrier to entry'.[13]

Party theory is right to note that parties vary in their ideology/interests content. Extending this a step further, we can begin to see that such variations have ramifications for interest group activity. That is, if we accept that some political parties (probably, but not necessarily exclusively, new ones) are more ideological than other parties, and we assume that an equilibrium level of 'ideologizing' exists in any polity, it becomes clear that the less the ideological content of political parties, the greater the opportunity for interest groups to nationalize the interest. Specifically, *if interest groups operate in a polity dominated by highly ideological parties, their ability to adopt a strategy of nationalizing the interest is circumscribed. Conversely, where parties represent the interests of their members over ideology, an ideological vacuum may arise which interest groups may exploit* (Hypothesis 2). In this sense, the *party* institutional context constrains or enhances the ability of interest groups to nationalize their interest.

5. CASE STUDIES

The three cases discussed below are not meant to fully test the merits of nationalizing the interest, since to do so would extend well beyond the pages of this chapter.[14] Rather, the cases present preliminary evidence in support of two of the derivative hypotheses.

According to Hypothesis 1, e*conomic interests will be more successful in obtaining their political objective(s) when, as a collectivity, they are able to 'nationalize the interest'.* Interest groups that are able to appeal to non-members with a positive externality linked to an idea or ideology stand a greater chance of achieving policy success. The positive externality is the tool that a group uses to expand the value dimensionality of the public good, thereby persuading individuals to contribute to the provision of the public good (even though their economic interests are not directly enhanced) (Table 5.2, cell B; Figure 5.4). The positive externality also shapes the perception of self-interest of individuals who are uncertain of their interests, thereby convincing them that they will actually benefit economically from the good, in addition to enjoying its other dimensions (Table 5.2, cell E; Figures 5.5(a), (b), (c)). Hence, through the appeal of ideas, the group is able to shift individuals, preferences along the north–south dimension of the interests–ideas graph. But, to gain this support from non-members, the group must demonstrate some evidence of its stated commitment to the ideas dimension(s), and thereby is subjected to movement along the east–west dimension (Figures 5.5(d) and 5.6). While the positive externality involves tailoring the group's stated policy preference to non-group members, the other conditions of nationalizing the interest have more to do with the ability of the group to organize itself in the first place. Effective organization, strong leadership and a conducive institutional environment all enable groups to strengthen their membership. These latter conditions may facilitate an appeal to non-group members, but they are not essential for nationalizing the interest.

One element of the 'conducive institutional environment' condition is examined in this chapter – namely, whether *a polity in which parties are highly ideological limits the opportunity for interest groups to nationalize the interest, while a polity of ideologically weak parties affords interest groups more freedom to exploit ideology* (Hypothesis 2).

In each of the three trade policy cases we find a pro-change and anti-change lobby, each defending their position with some measure of interests and ideas. In Britain's Repeal of the protectionist Corn Laws (1846), the Anti-Corn Law League embodied the economic interests of the Lancashire cotton industrialists but appealed to the electorate with images of morality and ethics. Anti-Leaguers (primarily landowners) never fully launched a nationalizing the interest strategy, but rather hoped that insider access to MPs (80 per cent of whom were landowners themselves) would be sufficient to counter the momentum of the League.[15] In the election of 1906, the interests of the British electorate divided into two camps: (1) protectionists, who tended to be agriculturalists and certain import-competing manufacturers, and (2) free traders, whose livelihood depended on the export market (Irwin, 1994). In parallel, the clash in ideas was between the ideology of free trade (complete with moral and ethical overtones) and the ideology of empire and nationalism. In Germany's marriage of iron and rye, the protectionist interests of large landowners and heavy industrialists confronted free-trade-oriented interests of workers, consumers and small farmers, while the ideology of nationalism easily defeated a muted ideology of free trade.

Table 5.3 provides a summary of key variables in the three cases and will serve as a reference for the subsequent discussions.

a.   The Repeal of the Corn Laws

The single most important event in nineteenth-century British trade policy was its shift towards unilateral free trade, as evidenced by the Repeal of the protectionist Corn Laws in 1846.[16] Economists, political scientists, historians and sociologists have spilled much ink attempting to explain this historic decision to abolish tariff protection for agriculture.[17] The decision is said to have signified the triumph of Manchester School liberal thinking; marked the birth of its international economic hegemony; launched a new form of British imperialism; paved the way for the disintegration of the Conservative Party for a generation; been the catalyst for class conflict between the rising industrial middle class and the politically dominant landed aristocracy; given testimony to the organization, political astuteness and tenacity of the pro-Repeal lobby, the Anti-Corn Law League; been an inevitable outcome of changes in the financial system and industrial structure; and illustrated the dramatic and abrupt change of mind of one absolutely pivotal individual, Prime Minister Sir Robert Peel.[18] While Iain McLean's Chapter 4 in this volume examines this plethora of competing explanations, the focus here is on the role of the Anti-Corn Law League.

Repeal would not have succeeded without the efforts of the Anti-Corn Law League, organized and led by the free-trade apostles, Richard Cobden and John Bright. This well-organized, well-led lobby effectively nationalized the manufacturers' interest in *immediate* Repeal of the Corn Laws.[19] All three conditions favourable to nationalizing the interest were in place for the League: (1) the existence of positive externalities, made even more persuasive by a well-developed body of theory on free trade; (2) good organization and leadership; and (3) a conducive institutional environment – in the form of legislation from the 1832 Reform Act, an ideological vacuum created by the Conservative and Liberal Parties (neither of which had established a clear, consistent or coherent ideological grounding), and support for free trade within the Board of Trade.

Table 5.3   Overview of cases

Case	Lobby seeking to nat. the interest	Lobby that achieved policy success	Positive ext. of winning lobby	Positive ex of losing lobby
Repeal of Corn Laws (Britain, 1838–46)	Anti-Corn Law League	Anti-Corn Law League (free trade)	Economic prosperity; morality of F.T; anti-aristocracy	None
Tariff Reform (Britain, 1903–6)	Free Trade Union and Tariff Reform League	Free Trade Union	Economic prosperity; internationalism; morality of F.T.	Empire; Nationalis
Marriage of iron and rye (Germany, 1890–1900)	Bund der Landwirte	Bund der Landwirte (protectionist)	Extreme nationalism; anti-Semitism; Conservatism	None

1. Positive externalities

Tables 5.1 and 5.2 illustrate the limited potential for nationalizing the interest when individuals' interests are exogenous, but note the possibility of a greater potential when individuals' interests are made endogenous (that is, when uncertainty arises). When individuals' interests are exogenous (Table 5.2(1) and Figure 5.3), the cases in cell (A) can be explained with simple interest group theory – that is, individuals with interests coinciding with those of an interest group will tend to support its goal(s). The League functioned both as an 'ordinary' interest group (in gaining the support of like-interested individuals) and as an 'extra-ordinary' group (in nationalizing its interest by use of a free-trade ideology). In its capacity as an ordinary interest group, the League acquired the support (if not monetary, certainly vocal) of export-oriented interests that had multiplied across the country in the 1830s and early 1840s. I document this growth elsewhere (Schonhardt-Bailey, 1991a). Relevant to this study is its ability to nationalize the manufacturers' interest in free trade by transforming the political economists' qualified support for free trade into an argument for *immediate* Repeal of the Corn Laws, and then persuading farmers and workers alike to support this policy shift.

Political economists were concerned with the effect of free trade on the

Leadership of winning lobby	Leadership of losing lobby	Org. of winning lobby	Org. of losing lobby	Ideolog. content of parties
Excellent (Cobden, Bright)	Poor	Excellent	Poor	Weak
Moderate (+ ghost of Cobden)	Strong (Chamberlain) but divided (Chamberlain vs Balfour)	Moderate	Moderate	Split within Cons. Party; moderate in Liberal Party
Moderate	Very poor	Excellent	Very poor	Initially weak in Cons. Party; mixed in other parties

public purse. Although Peel instituted the first peace-time income tax in 1842, the government still relied on customs duties for 38 per cent of its revenue in 1846. Sensitive to this reliance, Nassau Senior advocated levying duties only for the purposes of revenue, while J. R. McCulloch argued for a moderate, fixed duty to replace the sliding scale. A fixed duty would remedy the problem of speculation and would protect agriculture as a 'business', while also bolstering the government's revenue. The League rejected the revenue defence for maintaining even moderate duties on agriculture. Charles Villiers, League activist and MP, argued that the Corn Laws actually reduced revenue from customs by increasing the domestic cost of production of exportables (presumably by increasing wage costs) and thereby limited foreign trade, including the volume of taxable imports.[20] The Corn Laws also reduced the Government's revenue from excise duties by limiting domestic consumption. Although customs and excise provided 75 per cent of Government revenue, Villiers maintained that Repeal would not lead to a loss of revenue. The League also linked the revenue issue to the importance of expanding British exports, and thereby ensuring the future prosperity of the country. Both of these replies, to concerns of some of the political economists, illustrate a nationalizing the interest strategy. The argument that lower prices would encourage more consumption (which in turn would yield more government revenue in taxes) illustrates how the League sought to shape the economic interests of non-Leaguers (Table 5.2, cell (E); Figure 5.5(c)).

In response to doubts about the impact of Repeal on the Government's revenue, Leaguers sought to define the interests of consumers as free-trade-oriented (that is, position the ideal points of consumers as near to their own free-trade preference as possible) In other words, they sought to endogenize the interests of non-Leaguers by invoking a larger concern over the societal welfare, namely that instead of reducing Government revenue, Repeal would actually increase it, which in turn would (presumably) enable the Government to lower taxes elsewhere. The second argument that expanded British exports would ensure the country's future prosperity may either (a) assume that individuals' interests are exogenous and then introduce a further dimension (the idea of the country's future prosperity) to expand these non-Leaguers' indifference curves (Figure 5.4); or (b) endogenize individuals' interests by persuading non-Leaguers that ultimately, their own and the country's interests are one and the same, in as much as they benefit personally from a prosperous economy (Figure 5.5 (c)).[21]

A further example of Leaguers nationalizing the interest is their frequent appeals to a higher order. Morality and ethics were often woven into their economic arguments in an effort to pitch the battle in terms of good versus evil. Free traders clearly had the advantage over the protectionists in this form of argumentation. Free trade was said to constitute: (1) a 'civil liberty', as it ensured the right to buy in the cheapest market and sell in the dearest; (2) 'political justice', or a justice which shows no favouritism or partisanship; (3) 'peace' in bringing peace between nations and peace between classes; and (4) 'civilization', or the bringing of man near man, for mutual help and solace. Eugenio Biagini argues that Cobden's contribution 'consisted in clothing free trade with a moral cloak, not in elaborating a "philosophy of history"' (Biagini, 1992: 14, 38). He continues:

> The alliance between Christianity and Liberalism was one of the reasons for the latter's success. . . . It was difficult to start any radical popular movement without arguments involving a political interpretation of the Bible: when [free trade agitator] John Buckmaster began his campaign to convert the agricultural labourers and artisans of country villages to the cause of free trade, he focussed on 'the anti-Scriptural character of the Corn-Laws', maintaining that 'if the Corn-Laws had been in existence when Jesus Christ was on earth He would have preached against them'.

The League, moreover, sought and obtained the backing of the religious community, in spite of Chartists' efforts to persuade ministers and clergy to endorse a more sweeping campaign for parliamentary reform.

2. Leadership and organization

The Anti-Corn Law League was formed in 1838 by the Manchester textile manufacturers to push for the Repeal of protection for British agriculture. Historians refer to the League as 'the most impressive of nineteenth-century pressure groups, which exercised a distinct influence on the repeal of the Corn Laws' (Howe, 1984). Its centralized administration and 'formidable propaganda apparatus' has earned it the name, the 'league machine' (McCord, 1958: 187). Across the country the League combined its voter registration campaign with a massive propaganda effort. As League agents distributed propaganda tracts to every elector in 24 county divisions and 187 boroughs, these agents submitted to League headquarters extensive reports on the electorate in their districts. These reports provided a comprehensive picture of the electoral scene throughout England, thereby allowing the League much greater knowledge of, and control over, electoral districts than either the Conservatives or Liberals possessed 'with their more limited and local organization' (McCord, 1958: 147–50). This provided the League with an extensive database from which they could inflict political pressure on MPs seeking re-election.

3. Institutional environment

A key feature of the League's operational strategy was its nationwide propaganda and electoral registration campaign (Schonhardt-Bailey, 1991c: chapters 1 and 5). After electoral losses in 1841–2, the League focused on returning a pro-free trade majority in the anticipated general parliamentary election of 1848. Its strategy included manipulating the voter registers, by adding as many free traders and deleting as many protectionists as possible (through objections at the annual revisions of the registers). The League exploited the 40s. county property qualification for voting, a feature of 1430 that was left intact in the 1832 Reform Act (which effectively enfranchised the middle class). In comparison with the Act's new property qualifications that required yearly values of £10 and £50 for copyholders and leaseholders, respectively, and £50 annual rentals for tenants, the 40s. qualification was a conspicuous anomaly. The League used the 40s. qualification to create several thousand new free-trade voters in county constituencies with large urban electorates, constituencies whose number was increased from 188 to 253 (an increase from roughly 29 per cent to 38 per cent of the total parliamentary seats). John Bright referred to the 40s. qualification as 'the great constitutional weapon which we intend to wield' (Schonhardt-Bailey, 1997a: volume II, article 19). Leaguers went so far as to urge parents, wanting to create a nest egg for a son, to make him a freeholder, for as Cobden argued, 'it is an act of duty, for you make him thereby an independent freeman, and put it in his power to defend himself and his children from political oppression' (Schonhardt-Bailey, 1997a: volume II, article 18).

The 1832 Reform Act thus provided the League with the means to either purchase directly or encourage others to purchase voting rights for free traders in county constituencies. Moreover, the importance of these voting rights was magnified by the increase in the number of county seats. Cobden's statement (and those of other Leaguer's who encouraged individuals to purchase 40s. freehold) employs an idea – that of fighting political oppression – to persuade individuals (whom Leaguers assumed would be in favour of free trade) to acquire voting rights. In terms of Table 5.2, Cobden's message was directed towards individuals in cells (A) and (B). He sought to enlarge the free-trade lobby by making politically active individuals in cell (A) – namely, urban residents whose interests most likely would have coincided with the League (as in Figure 5.3). Yet, because urbanites included workers who may have been drawn to the Anti-Leaguer's argument that the true motive of the industrialists was to obtain lower wages through Repeal, it is likely that Cobden was also addressing individuals who believed that their interests conflicted with the League. Therefore, by highlighting class conflict, Cobden sought to persuade non-Leaguers (particularly those in Table 5.2, cell (B), Figure 5 (C)) that Repeal was not so much an issue of economics (that is, economic self-interest) as it was one of politics – namely, the political oppression of the landowners.

A weak party system is a second institutional feature that bolstered the efforts of the League to nationalize the interest of its members. According to party theorists, the Conservative and Liberal parties of the 1830s/1840s were *cadre* parties, or groupings of notables, and the real impetus for *modern* parties only arose with the extension of the suffrage in 1867 and 1884. Thus, in 1846, the parties were internally created and faced no new (mass) parties in what approximated a two-party system. Both exhibited weak organization and cohesiveness, and neither had a coherent ideological grounding.[22] McLean offers an insightful analysis of the leadership and ideological cohesion of the Whigs and Tories. His conclusion is that party allegiance and survival were low priorities in the minds of both party leaders, Lord John Russell and Sir Robert Peel. For instance, Russell grasped a flimsy excuse to refuse to form a government in late 1845 because he wanted 'to duck the responsibility for repeal, in the knowledge that it was likely to come in any case and it might as well come through Peel as through himself' (Chapter 4, this volume). Peel, on the other hand, caused his party to disintegrate as the result of his decision to push through repeal. McLean notes that 'by June 1846 Peel had lost interest in either his own or his (former) party's electoral survival, while [House of Lords leader] Wellington's heresthetic had required him to state again and again that he stood above party' (Chapter

4, this volume). It is clear, then, that neither party was led by a leader committed to the ideological cohesiveness of his party. McLean is correct that Peel became personally persuaded by the ideology of free trade, but what is more important here is that his ideology was not his party's ideology. Very simply, repeal was not an issue that separated the two parties, first because of the divisions within the Conservatives over Repeal, and second because of the feeble and rather tardy support for Repeal given by the Liberal leadership. In this context, the ideological debate originated from outside Parliament, with the League easily trouncing its poorly funded, poorly organized and 'ideologically challenged' opponent, the Anti-League.[23]

A third role for institutions is that played by the Board of Trade and the Treasury. Both of these government departments are prime examples of how institutions (through memos and briefings) filter the ideas or ideologies that gain political access, and how ideologies acquire added permanency by virtue of becoming the established wisdom of authoritative institutions. Building on Lucy Brown's work (Brown, 1958), McLean notes that '(p)erhaps the best example of an institution which embedded free trade values was the Board of Trade'. Certainly James Deacon Hume's (Joint Secretary to the Board of Trade) testimony before the House of Commons Committee on the Import Duties in 1840 (Schonhardt-Bailey, 1997a: volume II, article 2) is a brilliant argument for Repeal, and was referred to frequently in the parliamentary debates leading up to Repeal.

b. Tariff Reform

In contrast with Repeal of the Corn Laws, the attention given to the tariff reform campaign (especially by political scientists) is meagre.[24] This may be because it is a case where policy did not change, and so an explanation seems unwarranted. Yet with Joseph Chamberlain's tariff reform campaign (1903–6), free trade faced its most serious assault in over 50 years. This raises the question of why, in the face of fierce economic competition and declining relative economic power, did the British electorate firmly endorse the continuation of free trade in the general election of 1906?

Two recent interpretations of the 1906 election (one by an economist and the other by a historian) provide an excellent representation of the interests versus ideas debate. Douglas Irwin finds compelling quantitative evidence of the link between the economic interests of constituencies and their propensity to vote for the 'free trade party' (Liberals) or the 'protectionist party' (Conservatives) (Irwin, 1994). Because free trade was *the key issue* that divided the political parties during this general election, Irwin maintains that tariff reform presents an unusual case of direct democratic voting on trade policy. Workers in export-oriented industries such as coal, engineering, shipbuilding and chemicals, together with consumers, backed the Liberals, while individuals tied to import-competing industries such as agriculture, tool and scientific instruments backed the Conservatives. Irwin concludes that Britain's reliance on exports created more than enough interests in free trade to assure the electoral victory of the Liberals.[25]

Anthony Howe takes issue with Irwin's 'public choice' explanation of tariff reform, arguing that it was not producers' interests that mattered, but rather those of consumers.[26] More broadly, free-trade ideology had been transformed from one driven by a producer's logic to one driven by a consumer's logic. For Howe, the 1906 election was a battle of ideas that were effectively carried to the electorate during the campaign. On the one side was the ideology of free trade, reinterpreted and reapplied to a new era that accepted the need for an active state. New liberalism was able to dissociate free trade from *laissez-faire*, thereby allowing a synthesis of new social policies that allied Liberals, intellectuals and workers. Moreover, free trade exhibited a 'cosmopolitan' flavour that clashed directly with the rhetoric of nationalism invoked by tariff reformers. According to Howe, the idea of nationalism failed because Britain's 'recent history had emphasized free trade as central both to the providential mission of Britain in the nineteenth-century world and as a calculable gain to the welfare of the British people'. Thus, in juxtaposition to nationalism, free trade did not appear anti-British, since 'free trade itself was a vital element in national identity, part of the definition of the people as the nation' (Howe, 1997: 40, 267).

While Irwin and Howe disagree on the relative influences of ideas and interests, they agree that political party dynamics were critical to the case of tariff reform. By the late nineteenth century, British political parties had become organized, relatively cohesive and ideologically coherent. Parties were not weak as they were in the 1840s, and so Hypothesis 2 would suggest less of an opportunity for economic interest groups to nationalize the interest. This is indeed the case – neither the free traders nor the protectionists had an economic interest group to lead their campaigns. Rather, the Free Trade Union (FTU) and the Tariff Reform League were both inspirations of party leaders (Liberal and Conservative, respectively). Both groups were at arm's length from their respective party, but both sought to nationalize the *political* interest of the party – which was, of course, electoral victory. Thus, the trade policy objective became synonymous with victory in the 1906 general election.

1. Positive externalities

If we incorporate Irwin's categorization of economic interests into Table 5.2, free traders faced a large number of voters in cell A. That is, a large portion of the electorate was tied to export-oriented industries. These individuals required no recourse to ideology, since interests alone indicated support for the free-trade Liberals. Conversely, relatively fewer voters had interests that coincided with tariff reformers, and so with recourse to interests alone, the free traders had an advantage. We might conclude that this is the end of the story – the larger group of free-trade interests won out over the smaller group of protectionist interests. However, this ignores the vast majority of voters who produced for the domestic market (shopkeepers, builders and domestic staff) and of course the interests of the average consumer. While Irwin accepts that 'support for free trade is likely to have been buttressed' by producers for the domestic market and consumers (especially since over half of working-class expenditure was spent on food), he attributes the Liberal's success to the economic interests of producers for Britain's export markets (Irwin, 1994: 104). Yet as Irwin notes, his model fails to account for the *over-whelming* support for the Liberals, partly because this support was spread too evenly throughout the country (and so the variation in geographic concentration is insufficient to be captured by regression analysis), and partly because support for the Liberals was so great that only in areas of significant concentrations of protectionists was the correlation between interest and vote significant.

The real problem for Irwin is that his focus on producers fails to provide an explanation for the groundswell of support for free trade among the vast majority of the electorate – domestic producers and consumers. We can assume that these individuals should have supported free trade because of their interest in low food prices, but this ignores other benefits they may have enjoyed from the contribution of tariff revenue to social reforms, compensation to employers (for example, domestic producers) who suffered losses from factory legislation, and so on. Tariff reform was a policy filled with uncertainty as to its ultimate effects on individual, regional and national welfare. This means that most voters fell into cell E of Table 5.2 – that is, they were uncertain about their interests and therefore subject to persuasion by interest groups. It is to these individuals (that is, in cell E) that the battle of ideas was targeted.

The ideas that each side employed to nationalize its political interest were not equally appealing to the electorate. Howe characterizes the Liberal's battle for the electorate's support as a populist one that 're-evoked the Victorian cult of Cobden in Edwardian progressive garb [thereby] reincarnating the "people's" champion of the 1840s' as its leader.[27] Free trade was said to be vital to working-class welfare. Not only did it encapsulate material benefits, but it also reflected the 'justice dearly won from an oppressive aristocracy' (Howe, 1997).[28] The central motif of the FTU was the evocation of the past, coining the phrase the 'hungry forties' to recall the misery from which Cobden and Bright delivered the British people with the Repeal of the Corn Laws. The Union was also forward-looking in its creation of the Women's FTU. Free trade was said to be 'a women's question' in as much as it summoned women to defend their domestic budgets (Howe, 1997: 260).

The tariff reformers' message to the electorate was quite different. E. H. H. Green argues that tariff reform reflected both the empire and property streams of the Conservative Party:

> For the party of Empire the imperial aspect of the tariff programme offered three things. First . . . it held out the prospect of imperial strength through unity in an increasingly hostile world of large-scale States. Second, imperial preference was to reconcile the economic aspirations of Mother country and Colonies, and thereby avoid the necessity for greater Colonial independence. Third, it was to demonstrate the benefits of Empire to broad sections of the electorate and convince them that the Conservatives were still the only true party of Empire. For the party of property the tariff reform programme offered two things. First, the balanced tariff benefits offered to industrial and agricultural interests were to cement town and country in a joint campaign against liberal political economy. Second, tariffs were to demonstrate the unity of capital and labour in defence of national production, provide revenue for social reforms, and compensate employers for any additional input costs that social or factory legislation caused. In other words they were to provide a positive alternative to counter the appeal of Socialism (Green, 1996: 22–3).

The only real positive externality of tariff reform was a vague appeal to nationalism through the preservation of the British Empire. While free traders could tailor their appeals to non-members across several idea dimensions (recall the discussion on Figures 5.5(d) and 5.6), tariff reformers had just the one idea of empire. Hence, free traders could move on the east–west dimension towards individuals b and c – who cared about working-class welfare – without sacrificing support from individual a – who cared about the cosmopolitan element of free trade. The downfall of nationalism as a positive externality was its inability to shape individuals' perceptions of self-interest in such a way that they thought they could benefit personally from tariff reform (that is, the inability to position individuals' ideal points nearest to the tariff reform ideal point). The two planks of tariff reform that reflected the 'party of property' were essentially attempts either to garner the support of agriculturalists and some import-competing producers who would benefit from protection (Table 5.2, individuals in cell A), or to offer economic incentives of unknown value to individuals in the remaining cells. That tariff reform failed to persuade then comes as no surprise.

2.   Organization, leadership and institutions

To say that the tariff reformers failed to persuade is not to say that they did not enjoy significant advantages. The Tariff Reform League well surpassed the FTU in funding and organization. In 1904–5, the Tariff Reform League was spending five to ten times as much as the FTU.[29] The FTU, moreover, never attained a national organizational structure, instead relying on 'the encouragement of spontaneous local free trade bodies' (Howe, 1997: 257).

Whether the free traders or the protectionists enjoyed the benefit of leadership is unclear. For the free traders, no one except the ghost of Cobden offered a focal point around which to gather the masses. For the protectionists, Joseph Chamberlain was both a plus and a minus. In 1903, Chamberlain resigned his ministerial position as Colonial Secretary to have a free hand to convert the British electorate to the need for tariff reform through a series of public speeches.[30] Before leaving the Cabinet, Chamberlain had convinced Prime Minister Arthur Balfour of the need for reform, but not necessarily Chamberlain's three-pronged package. For Chamberlain, tariff reform meant: (1) consolidating the British empire by taxing food for the purpose of giving preference to the colonies, which in turn would give preference to British manufactured exports; (2) pressuring protectionist countries to lower their tariffs on British goods by imposing retaliatory measures; and (3) countering 'dumping' with 'measures of commercial war against those Governments'.[31] In brief, tariff reform meant countering the large US and German markets with a vast imperial market, while also imposing retaliatory tariffs and anti-dumping measures. Balfour, on the other hand, saw the food tax in colonial preference as electorally unacceptable. He was persuaded that retaliatory measures were required, but remained vague on exactly how the Government intended to implement a policy of retaliation.[32] Balfour maintained that he simply sought a mandate to negotiate with other countries to lower their tariffs. Thus, while Chamberlain stomped the country with his message of tariff reform, ministers, backbenchers and other observers were frustrated by Balfour's ambiguous intentions and his lack of firm acceptance or rejection of Chamberlain's package.[33] In addition to Chamberlain, Balfour lost a number of other talented and experienced cabinet ministers.[34] Hence, the message of the Tariff Reform League was that of the Chamberlain wing of the Conservative Party, but the public remained uncertain as to Balfour's precise stance on fiscal policy. In sum, while the free traders suffered the absence of a living dynamic leader, the protectionists were encumbered with strong but divided leadership.

The evidence for the third condition facilitating nationalizing the interest – a conducive institutional environment – is mixed. On the one hand, voter restrictions probably harmed the free traders since (as Irwin notes) this prevented a good number of occupational groups that should have favoured free trade from voting. On the other hand, the ideology of free trade had become embedded in the Treasury and the Board of Trade, as reflected in their memorandums to the Government. The net effect of a restricted franchise and a pro-free trade Treasury and Board of Trade is unclear.

The analysis in this study suggests that both interest groups – the Tariff Reform League and the FTU – engaged in a nationalizing the interest strategy. While some of the conditions for nationalizing the interests did not favour the FTU (namely, organization and leadership), the one factor that weighed heavily in favour of the free traders was their ability to link free trade with positive externalities (ideas of morality, a cosmopolitan Britain, historical images of the victory over the aristocracy, and so on). With these positive externalities, they were able to persuade individuals (Table 5.2, cell E) that free trade was indeed in their own self-interest.

c. The Marriage of Iron and Rye

Germany's 'marriage of iron and rye' refers to a series of trade policies that occurred over several decades (from 1879 through approximately World War I). The 'marriage' was a coalition of diverse interests, in which heavy industry and the large agricultural estate owners of east Elbian Prussia (the Junkers) coalesced around a tariff policy for both industrial and agricultural imports.

In the early 1870s rapid advances in transportation coupled with increased competition in world grain markets meant that German Junkers, who were formerly net exporters of grain, became import-competing producers (Lambi, 1963). At about the same time, the Great Depression squeezed the profitability of industrial firms (Blackbourn, 1984; Kitchen, 1978; Rosenberg, 1967). Because many of these firms were newly created, or had expanded during the previous boom years, the problem of excess capacity in the domestic market was severe – and made worse with the integration into the Zollverein of the Alsace–Lorraine iron, steel and cotton spinning industries. Reductions in iron and steel tariffs (1873) and the complete abolition of the pig iron tariff in 1877 helped to mobilize heavy industry against Germany's free-trade orientation. Grain producers and heavy industrialists, heretofore suspicious adversaries, converged upon a common interest in protection. The tariff of 1879 enacted this policy shift into legislation.

In the 1880s agricultural tariffs were raised twice, while industrial tariffs remained virtually constant. By the early 1890s, real and potential retaliation from Germany's trading partners convinced German industry of the need to regain (and expand) export markets. Between 1891 and 1894, Chancellor Bismarck's successor, Caprivi, negotiated numerous foreign trade agreements that exchanged lower German tariffs on agriculture for reductions in foreign tariffs on German industrial goods. As Caprivi's treaties approached their expiration, Chancellor Bülow introduced the 'general tariff' in 1902, thereby signalling a resumption of high agricultural tariffs (Ashley, 1920: 86).

Most historians of Imperial Germany accept that the 1879 tariff marked a watershed in Imperial German politics. Political party ideology, it is argued, gave way to pressure group politics. Elsewhere I test this proposition and find partial support for the ideology-to-interests thesis (Schonhardt-Bailey, 1998a). For the period 1879 to 1902, roll-call votes in the Reichstag reveal that ideology mattered more for the leftist parties – the Social Democrats and Left Liberals – than for the Conservatives, the National Liberals or the Centre. Yet this interpretation oversimplifies ideology within each party, and particularly within the Conservatives.

Conservatism underwent a distinct ebb and flow in balancing ideology and interests. Whereas 'old' German conservatism was ideological in orientation, new conservatism (organized in 1876 as the *Deutsch-Konservative Partei*) represented the economic interests of the landowning aristocracy (Berdahl, 1972: 20; Puhle, 1978: 698). By the early 1890s, under threat from the Caprivi trade reforms, militant Prussian landowners created an interest group, the *Bund der Landwirte*. Rather than competing with the Conservative Party, the *Bund* strengthened it by broadening the electoral support base for conservatism, particularly among the smaller proprietors and lower middle classes. The *Bund* appealed to smaller farmers with a yet newer ideology of *volkish* nationalism, thereby enveloping the protectionist interests of the Prussian landowners into a more national conservative movement.[35] In this way, the *Bund* successfully nationalized the landowners' economic interest in protection against grain imports.

1. Positive externalities
The *Bund* undoubtedly engaged in a strategy of 'nationalizing the interest' of the large landowners in high grain tariffs. It relied on an effective ideology of extreme nationalism and anti-Semitism to persuade both non-agrarians, and small landowners and peasant farmers of the need for agricultural protection. In appealing to the non-agrarians, it sought to 'mask conflicts of interest with its unclear formulations'. As Puhle (1986: 94) continues, the new ideology 'suited conservatism's increasing need to integrate and recapture anti-aristocratic, "leftist" deviants. Because of expanding industrialization and universal male suffrage, at least in the Reich, the Conservatives realized that they had to address the middle and lower classes'. The *Bund* did precisely that by replacing old conservative concepts like *individuality* and *freedom* with new ones that were based on social Darwinism, social imperialism, militantism and anti-Semitism. The

new ideology highlighted the larger societal 'interest' in maintaining the German race and preserving (and enhancing) Germany's position in world affairs, and thereby sought to integrate both industrialists and workers into a larger conservative movement (Puhle, 1986: 94; Stegmann, 1993; Vascik, 1993; Wehler, 1985: 78–80). Recalling Table 5.2, this strategy exemplifies cell B, where individuals' interests conflict with those of the group, and while these individuals are aware of the conflict, the group introduces other ideological dimensions in order to shift the individuals' indifference curves on the north–south dimension.

To the small landowners and peasant farmers (who, as livestock producers, were interested in low grain prices), the *Bund* added to this ideology the argument that all agrarians shared the large landowners' economic interest in high land prices (which resulted from agricultural protection). While it is clear that all landowners benefited from rising land prices in the later nineteenth and early twentieth century, it is also generally accepted that large landowners reaped the bulk of the rewards.[36] For peasants in southern and south-western areas whose land inheritance patterns were more restrictive and therefore could not really benefit from increasing land values, Puhle maintains that the *Bund* relied exclusively on ideological persuasion and its organizational skills in recruiting supporters (Puhle, 1986: 101).

It is difficult to assess how far conservative ideology *shaped* the interests of the peasant farmers, and this is a much debated issue among historians. At dispute is whether the Junkers benefited from agricultural protection (through the perpetuation of feudalism) at the expense of the peasant farmers, or whether the latter, as producers primarily of livestock (and therefore consumers of grain for feed), obtained some benefit as well (Gerschenkron, 1943; Gerschenkron, 1962; Moore, 1966). The traditional interpretation, focusing on Junker benefits, cannot explain why peasant farmers generally supported agricultural protection, except to lament that they were duped into regarding the large landowners as spokesmen for the whole of agriculture.[37]

Recent studies have given more credit to the rationality of peasant farmers, arguing that they gained from restrictions on the import of livestock, and from grain tariffs themselves (Hunt, 1974; Moeller, 1981; Webb, 1982). It is likely that some farmers benefited and some were harmed. But to say that farmers were duped fails to appreciate how ideas as hooks actually work. The *Bund* invoked themes of nationalism and anti-Semitism to persuade farmers of the value of positive externalities accruing from agricultural protection – that is, convince them that agricultural protection had multiple dimensions beyond simply maintaining income for grain producers. Where economic interests coincided, for instance where small landowners benefited partially from rising land values, this may have been sufficient reason to support the *Bund* (as in Figure 5.3). But, where economic logic failed, nationalistic and racist 'logic' succeeded. Specifically, the benefit that small landowners received from rising land prices would place them in cell A of Table 5.2, meaning that the *Bund* would not have resorted to its ideology to garner support from these individuals. However, to the extent that many small landowners were also livestock producers who preferred low grain prices (the result of lower grain tariffs), any residual opposition may have been subjected to the integrative ideology propagated by the *Bund*. The *Bund's* appeal to these individuals (who would fall into either cell B or E of Table 5.2) would constitute an exercise in nationalizing the interest, as would its appeal to the peasant farmers.

2.   Leadership and organization

In many ways, the *Bund* resembled the Anti-Corn Law League. It, too, has been described as a 'powerful, modern and well-organized machine' (Puhle, 1986: 98) that quickly acquired a mass following and exerted substantial political leverage over members of the Reichstag. The leaders of the *Bund* patterned its organization after the widespread agricultural societies and even were quite successful in acquiring the support of a number of the peasant associations (Tirrell, 1951: 171). The *Bund* was organized as a strict hierarchy and at the top were the large landowners of east Elbia, who comprised just 1 per cent of the membership but who controlled the organizational committees. Like the Anti-Corn Law League, the *Bund* distributed a number of publications and circulated special speakers 'to arouse and draw together "the indolent masses" who had hitherto stayed away from the polls' (Tirrell, 1951: 177). Its following grew from 200000 in 1894 to 330000 in 1913 (Puhle, 1986: 92), in part because its publications were purposely written in a populist style (a tactic that was copied from the Radicals and Social Democrats) (Tirrell, 1951: 182). The *Bund* also benefited from the regional nature of the peasants' own associations, which inhibited them from organizing themselves at the national level, as well as from their general 'apolitical nature' (Puhle, 1986: 91).

While the *Bund* was closely allied with the Conservative Party, it sought to cut across party lines in exerting pressure on Reichstag delegates. Beginning with the election of 1893, the *Bund* announced that it would support only those candidates who would pledge to vote to reject all commercial treaties that lowered tariffs for agriculture. In that election, *Bund* pressure contributed both to the increase in numbers of delegates from the Right, and among these, in returning mostly those who were unconditional agrarians (Tirrell, 1951: 186–90). The influence of the *Bund* on candidates continued through the early 1900s:

Out of a total of 397 Reichstag representatives in 1898, 118 from five different political parties were committed to the League, and 76 of these were actual League members. In 1903 the figure was 89, in 1907, 138, and in 1912, 78. In the Prussian lower house, consistently more than one-third of the representatives were League members, and 1908 they even constituted an absolute majority (Puhle, 1986: 92).

3. Institutional environment

Similar to the Anti-Corn Law League, the *Bund,* as an interest group, enjoyed certain institutional advantages that were not available to, say, peasant associations and workers' unions at that time. First, state intervention into the agrarian sector had become 'institutionalized'.[38] The *Bund* 'strengthened these tendencies' towards state intervention by dominating and then enveloping the traditional representatives of the agrarian interests into a single movement, joined together by an integrating ideology.

Second, the *Bund*, like the Anti-Corn Law League, was able to exploit an ideological vacuum. According to Hypothesis 2, interest groups that face highly ideological parties will find it more difficult to nationalize their interest (inasmuch as the parties dominate the ideological debate), but where parties represent the interests of their members over ideology, an ideological vacuum is created which interest groups may exploit. For instance, the Anti-Corn Law League captured the ideological debate on free trade (and liberalism more generally) because neither political party was able or prepared to develop the ideology of free trade within its party platform. The German case is less straightforward, but still demonstrates how an interest group (the *Bund*) can exploit a political party's ideological vacuum.

Political ideology in nineteenth-century Germany exhibited at least two dimensions – a standard left/right, or socialist/conservative dimension and a religious dimension. In the first dimension, the Social Democrats and Left Liberals fell on the left while the Conservatives and the National Liberals[39] were on the right, with the Catholic Center Party[40] falling somewhere in between.[41] In terms of religion, however, the Centre Party occupied the Catholic end of the spectrum while the Conservatives dominated the Protestant end. It was at the right of the political spectrum that an ideological vacuum opened for the *Bund*. In the early 1890s, the Junkers faced both a growing socialist movement[42] (which not only opposed grain tariffs but also challenged the entire Prussian Conservative hold on the reins of power) and the economic setback of Caprivi's trade treaties. Both events highlighted the weakness of the Conservative Party, which was handicapped by its narrow socio-economic base. What was required was a new form of conservatism that would appeal both to non-agrarians and to small landowners and peasant farmers, and a highly organized propaganda machine that would convince workers and peasants that grain protection and German nationalism went hand in hand. The challenge to the Conservatives was, therefore, both ideological and economic – and the Conservative Party was ill-equipped to meet either challenge. It was the *Bund* that provided the ideological cohesion, the leadership and the organization to (a) shift the ideology/interests balance within the Conservative Party towards a new, more nationalistic ideology, thereby giving conservatism a broader base of support, and (b) re-enact high tariffs for agriculture (Puhle, 1986: 93–4). As Puhle (1978: 702) notes:

> At the beginning of the 1890s, the [Conservative Party] was rent by internal disputes, politically paralysed by desertions and scandals within its ranks. The League affected it organizationally, by creating grassroots associations in rural areas and lending it electoral support and the assistance of its own apparatus, one effect of which was to tighten coordination and discipline within the party. Moreover, it also finally institutionalized the conservative attempt – hitherto largely unsuccessful – to build up a reliable political base among smaller proprietors and the lower middle classes, establishing it as an integral part of Conservative election campaigning and political propaganda.

A third factor that facilitated a nationalizing the interest strategy was perhaps an unforeseen consequence of the social reforms enacted by Bismarck. Though many historians have interpreted Bismarck's social reforms as an effort to placate the demands of the left while denying them any real influence in policy making, one effect was that it introduced a populist element into German politics, albeit one manipulated and controlled by the élite establishment. Puhle argues that an important precondition to the success of the *Bund* was

> the fact that Bismarck's manipulative techniques had already created a 'political mass market', expanding the sphere of public politics and increasing popular political influence over parliaments and government. By the1890s the Reich and Prussian governments could no longer carry out manipulative policies with the same decisiveness, and a power vacuum was created. A modern, well-organized, determined and radical interest group could easily fill this vacuum and exploit the situation to establish itself (Puhle, 1986: 105).

Though it may be a stretch to interpret this 'political mass market' as an ideology encased in an institution, it certainly makes sense to note some element of populism creeping into the German polity, which the *Bund* was able to exploit.

6. CONCLUSION

Traditional interest group theorists like Schattschneider saw interest groups as falling into two types – either they pursued economic objectives or ideological objectives. Rational choice theorists like Olson shifted the analysis of interest group activity towards a more precise specification of the motivations of individuals to join a group (or not), and these motivations were almost always seen in terms of economic self-interest. Both interest group theory and the logic of collective action have provided a firm basis for understanding how and why groups organize. The assumption of these two literatures is that the relevant dialogue is between group leaders and group members. What has been lacking, however, is an understanding of how groups appeal to *non-members;* how they gain the acquiescence if not the support of these individuals for their policy objective. What nationalizing the interest offers is a first step towards understanding the relationship between groups and non-members, and I maintain that at the heart of that relationship is the persuasive use of ideology.

By way of concluding remarks, some interesting linkages and tensions may be noted with the other articles in this co-authored volume. As Pahre himself accepts, a political support-maximizing model that limits politicians to one tool – redistributing income – will invariably underestimate the ability of politicians to increase their political support. Notably, political support may be influenced not only by economic interests, but also by ideas and ideology. As I have argued in this chapter, ideas can be used quite effectively to influence preferences. More to the point, by focusing entirely on producers' interests, Pahre overlooks important features of trade policy that are not derived strictly from economic interests. For instance, Pahre explains that Caprivi's motivation in negotiating German trade treaties was that he was trying to gain the support of labourers (and anyone else with an interest in free trade). With the repeal of the Socialist legislation, the marginal value of labour to national politicians increased.

Pahre argues that the political gains from reciprocal trade agreements were a useful tool for Caprivi as he tried to broaden his political base. Not only would lower grain tariffs (from the trade treaties) gain Caprivi the support of workers, but 'the increased support from capital and labour would outweigh the opposition from the Junkers, a political effect not found in any purely domestic tariff legislation'. This argument clashes directly with my interpretation of the German case. Caprivi's presumed attempt to broaden his political base was pre-empted by agrarians who were engaged in a longer-term strategy to widen their own support base with the use of ideas. But, let us accept for a moment that the marginal political value of labour to national politicians increased with the repeal of the Socialist legislation, and that it increased substantially in the years thereafter as labour organizations expanded their memberships. Surely, then, Chancellor Bülow would have extended the trade treaties, rather than letting them expire and introduce new autonomous tariffs. Pahre's account dismisses out of hand the role of ideas, namely the nationalist ideology used by the *Bund* to expand the agrarian resistance to freer trade. The strength of the protectionist sentiment in the early 1900s stemmed not from interests, but from militant nationalism, racism and anti-socialism.

To be fair, however, Pahre's and McGillivray's Chapters 2 and 3 illustrate the tendency of conventional public choice models to work with a simple conception of actors' goals. Such approaches are therefore limited in their ability to theorize about the dimensionality of the issue space, or speculate on the hierarchical structure of goals and sub-goals. Conventional public choice models are adept at saying something definite about a simplified problem. The introduction of ideas allows one to say something about a larger, more complex problem, but often in only a suggestive way. Each strategy has its strengths and weaknesses. The goal for both strategies is to theorize about complex goal sets in ways that generate determinate and revealing conclusions.

Turning finally to the discussions of institutions offered by the authors of this volume, Pahre's and McGillivray's chapters clearly reflect their bias towards economic interests. Pahre maintains that institutions matter to trade policy since they 'affect the support maximization problem and thus also shape both tariffs and trade agreements'. McGillivray argues that institutions affect trade policy by determining the interests that different groups represent, and by determining which groups succeed and which fail. But McLean points to the limitations of institutions in explaining trade policy: 'the conventional mapping from inputs [namely interests] to outcomes [policies] via a set of institutions is embodied in the theory of endogenous protection, which fails to explain the repeal of the Corn Laws'. Pahre maintains that institutions 'affect' political support, McGillivray that institutions 'determine' interests and their likelihood of success, and McLean that institutions 'frame' political outcomes. I have argued that a key role for institutions is to enhance or constrain the ability of a group to nationalize its interest. For both McLean and myself, institutions shape how interests *and* ideologies affect trade policy outcomes. For Pahre and McGillivray, institutions interact predominantly with interests.

It is worth noting, however, that the focus of all four authors varies considerably – from Pahre's sweeping analysis of many countries over a long time period, to McGillivray's discussion of many states interacting with a foreign nation, to my examination of how interest groups relate to non-group members, to McLean's detailed account of how heresthetic reveals what interests alone cannot. One might conclude that level of detail has afforded the luxury of adding another dimension – that of ideas or ideology. But, as both McLean and I have demonstrated, ideas can be (and indeed should be) conceptualized as interacting with interests within an institutional setting.

Ignoring ideas may allow for greater simplification and clarity of analysis of interests, but by so doing, one risks mis-specifying preferences and utility functions, which of course lie at the heart of an interests model of policy outcomes. While I can offer no remedy to this tension between interests and ideas, a volume such as this takes some steps in the direction of integrating what we all know to be important in any study of policy outcomes (trade or other) – the interaction of institutions, interests and ideas.

NOTES

1. To name but a few in political economy: (Goldstein, 1993; Hall, 1989; Henderson, 1986; Hood, 1994; Jacobsen, 1995; Sikkink, 1991; Woods, 1995)
   The revival of ideology also extends to the foreign policy, electoral choice, legislative voting, public policy and political theory literatures: (Goldstein and Keohane, 1993a; Goodin, 1996; Grier, 1993; Haas, 1992; Hinich and Munger, 1994; Langston, 1992; McCormick and Black, 1983; Risse-Kappen, 1994; Sabatier and Jenkins-Smith, 1993; Silverman, 1985; Yee, 1996).
2. To avoid confusion from the outset, I do not use this term in any reference to the nationalization of industries, or to the debates surrounding private and public industries.
3. The literature on ideology is vast, but some texts that I have found useful include (Manning, 1980; Méxzáros, 1989; Plamenatz, 1970).
4. Functions (1) and (2) raise a 'chicken and egg' problem in that brand names can be based on the past experiences which give rise to expectations embedded in roadmaps, a problem that I unfortunately do not resolve here.
5. A quote from Peter Hall in Yee (1996).
6. To be specific, the goods are enjoyed by non-contributors who actually value the abolition of capital punishment, a clean environment and a nuclear-free world.
7. I set aside here the issue of congestibility.
8. To be sure, members of such groups may be true believers of the ideology. However, the concern here is not whether *members* are true believers, but rather with the use of ideology to obfuscate the public good benefits.
9. I owe this notion of multidimensionality to Kenneth Shepsle.
10. My thanks to Tim McKeown for bringing this to my attention.
11. 'Pressure groups focus on only a few, or even a single, issue. There need be no overarching set of ethical norms or ideas; pressure groups want what they want because they want it. Party ideologies represent a recounting of the shared ideas of a coalition of interests, but pressure groups focus on an interest or idea that may have no relation to any other policy' (Hinich and Munger, 1994: 92).
12. Paraphrasing Richard Jankowski in Janda (1993: 170).
13. The authors qualify this point by noting that 'the party may . . . come into existence with only the simplest of doctrinal commitments, and then its ideology [evolves] into a more complete set of ideas' (Hinich and Munger, 1994: 85–6).
14. In a forthcoming manuscript I test the theory of nationalizing the interest.
15. Some attempt was made by protectionists to launch a nationalizing the interest strategy, but only after Peel had changed his position to support repeal. They hoped at least to delay a parliamentary decision until after the next general election (Stewart, 1971).
16. For a synopsis of British trade policy from 1815 to 1906, see Schonhardt-Bailey (1997b).
17. For a selection of the more recent literature, see Schonhardt-Bailey (1997a: volume 4).
18. For references to and examples of these arguments, see Schonhardt-Bailey (1997a: volumes 1 and 4).
19. Not one of the leading political economists advocated immediate free trade.

20. For articles by Senior, McCulloch and Villiers, see Schonhardt-Bailey (1997a: volume 2).
21. Illustrations of the two-ended hook of ideas (Figures 5(d) and 5.6) are given in my forth-coming manuscript.
22. For instance, Ian Newbould (1985: 139) argues that because the Liberal Party was frag-mented in its composition (that is, consisting of Whigs, Radicals, Liberals and so on), it was deliberately disorganized. In other words, the Whigs eschewed party organization because it would only enable and encourage the Radical faction to push for further reform measures – measures which undermined the Whig position. He also argues that MPs touted their independent position on issues, resulting in a government which 'was never sure of its support'. In fact, Newbould quotes Melbourne as saying, 'No one knows beforehand what parliament or members of parliament will do or how they will vote'.
    Norman Gash (1982) argues that the Conservative Party similarly lacked organiza-tion. There existed: (1) 'no regular practice of calling party meetings before the start of the parliamentary session' (p. 140); (2) little or no discipline among Conservative peers in the House of Lords; and (3) no real collaboration between Peel (the Conservative leader in the House of Commons) and Wellington (the Conservative leader in the House of Lords). On this last point, Gash quotes Wellington as having said in 1837, 'I do not like to interfere in the affairs of the House of Commons, first because I have nothing to say to them; and next, because I really do not understand them' (ibid., p. 143). Fourth, Gash notes a growing loss of contact between Peel and his followers between 1841 and 1846, as evidenced by fewer and less satisfying party meetings, and as evidenced by Peel's deliberate avoidance of the party process for gaining support for Repeal of the Corn Laws. Gash writes, '(i)n 1846 . . . , over the repeal of the Corn Laws, the breach had become so great that Peel seems not even to have considered summoning a party meeting to explain his policy.
    When Brougham subsequently suggested that the disruption of the party could have been avoided if Peel had taken leading members into his confidence and called a general meeting, Peel merely observed to Aberdeen that if he had done so, he would have failed in his object of carrying the repeal of the Corn Laws – and 'I was resolved not to fail'. No stronger proof is needed of his realization that repeal could not be carried by the ordinary processes of party government' (Gash, 1982: 143–4). Finally, Gash concurs with Newbould that MPs enjoyed and preferred to maintain their status as independent thinkers. MPs 'spoke of 'the gentlemen with whom I usually act' or more informally of 'our friends'. But they did not as a rule talk of being members of a party; and they strove to give the appearance of being independent and unfettered in their parliamentary conduct' (ibid., p. 156).
    Consequently, I have argued elsewhere that British political parties of the 1840s are best thought of – and modelled – as intervening, rather than independent variables (Schonhardt-Bailey, 1994). The model in this study works backwards from my earlier work to develop a better understanding of the antecedent variables of party affiliation.
23. In 1844, as the League's success – particularly that of its registration campaign in the counties – became more conspicuous, a defensive Anti-League (or, Agricultural Protection Society) emerged (see Schonhardt-Bailey, 1997a: volume 2, articles 21 and 22). This group of protectionist landowners and farmers did not, however, obtain the momentum or backing of the League. According to Chaloner (1970), the Anti-League 'failed to make an impression on British agricultural policy because Conservative poli-ticians were reluctant to speak or vote against Sir Robert Peel until 1846, and it cannot be said that its literary contribution was as solid or as logical as that of the Free Traders'. In financial terms, while the League grew from a £5000 annual fund in 1839 to one of £250000 in 1845, the latter year saw the core of the Anti-League (the Essex Agricultural Protection Society) scraping together the paltry sum of £2000 to fund its campaign (Crosby, 1976; McCord, 1958)
24. An important recent exception is Friedberg (1988).
25. Indeed Irwin maintains that their victory would have been greater had there been fewer voter restrictions.
26. Conversation with author (16 July, 1998), based on his argument in Howe (1997).

27. (Howe, 1997: 263). The legacy of Cobden continued to influence British trade policy throughout the nineteenth century. The Cobden Club, set up in 1866 with the support of the Liberal Party, 'developed as an important propaganda branch of Liberalism sustaining a vast range of publications devoted to the ideas of its eponymous hero'. As Howe explains: 'This was an educational role comparable in some ways to that played by the League in the 1840s. But the Club also acquired a sensible political appeal as threats to free trade emerged in the late 1860s, late 1870s and early 1880s. At this point the Club sought to work through forging working-class alliances, such as with the TUC and Arch's Agricultural Labourer's Union in order to counter incipient attacks on free trade. Here the Club importantly sustained popular loyalties to free trade. . . . The Club also complemented well the emergence of a wider cult of Cobden expressed in mid-Victorian England, for example, in several public busts and statues and numerous popular biographies . . . This was of vital long-term importance in inoculating the late Victorian electorate against both Fair Trade and Tariff Reform (Howe, 1998).

28. Howe (1997: 265).

29. Irwin (1994), citing A. K. Russell (1973: 41).

30. Some reprinted in Schonhardt-Bailey, (1997a: volume 3, articles 17 and 18).

31. A nice summary of tariff reform is given by Charles Thompson Ritchie, Chancellor of the Exchequer (Schonhardt-Bailey, 1997a, volume 3, article 16).

32. Schonhardt-Bailey (1997a: volume 3, articles 19 and 21).

33. Schonhardt-Bailey (1997a: volume 3, articles 20, 23, 25, 26 and 27).

34. Charles Thompson Ritchie (Chancellor of the Exchequer), Lord Balfour of Burleigh (Secretary of State for Scotland), Duke of Devonshire (President of Council) and Lord George Hamilton (Secretary for India).

35. Geoff Eley (1993) takes issue with Puhle's interpretation of the new conservatism of the League. He contests Puhle's contention that the League 'was called into existence as a nationally based agrarian movement by intelligent Junker politicians, both to secure their economic demands and to legitimize their social and political privileges through a general agrarian ideology [where] the BdL claimed to speak for rural society as a whole, but in reality it was concerned with preserving the social and political power of aristocratic estate owners in a special region of the country' (p. 189). He argues that this interpretation exaggerates the leadership capabilities of the Junkers. Moreover, Eley argues that the contribution of the Agrarian League to the evolution of the German Right was actually greater in the west than it was in the east, since the League had to overcome a deep hostility to the Prussian aristocracy among western farmers.

36. 'Prussian land prices climbed an average of 17 per cent between 1895–7 and 1901–3 for all property sizes. From 1907–9 the prices climbed 33 per cent, almost twice as high as in the preceding period. This time, however, large landholdings took the lion's share. Land prices for estates with 100 to 500 hectares rose 49 per cent in Prussia, and prices for estates over 500 rose 53 per cent. Even middle and large peasant holdings experienced an above-average increase of 37 per cent' (Puhle, 1986: 101).

37. For a more nuanced interpretation, see Abraham (1981: 65); Puhle, (1986: 99).

38. There were many deep roots for this – the tradition of the Prussian state, east Elbian colonization policies and the protective laws for peasants and property, something which most German states had in common. The state also managed large agricultural holdings. Since the beginning of the nineteenth century, it encouraged the formation of scientific agricultural societies and agricultural associations (*landwirtschaftliche Vereine*). From the mid-century onwards, these associations began to combine into central organizations at the regional level, which worked together closely with state authorities. With the state's aid, by the end of the century these bodies transformed themselves into legal, public, corporatist professional organizations called Agricultural Chambers (*Landwirtschaftskammern*). . . . By interlocking public and private organizational types, these interest groups and Agricultural Chambers had become privileged partners of the government by the turn of the century. . . . The protectionist agitation of the 1870s and the comprehensive demands of the Agrarian League for state intervention in the 1890s only strengthened these tendencies (Puhle, 1986: 88).

39. The National Liberal Party, which was permanently weakened in the late 1870s after losing its position as the 'government party', split on the question of tariffs as a result of the internal divide between light and heavy industries (Lambi, 1963: 209–11). Its leaders subsequently refused to include tariff policy as a party matter. Many authors have noted that the National Liberals (and to some extent all liberal parties) lacked both a distinctive social profile and a regional identity (Langewiesche, 1990; Ritter, 1990; Sheehan, 1978: 160–241). This coincided with the National Liberals' claim to speak for the nation rather than for any particular group, but it also meant that the liberals were unable to consolidate any electoral strongholds (in contrast to, say, the Centre Party that controlled the Catholic rural districts and the Conservatives that held the agricultural regions east of the Elbe). Socio-economic and regional diversity thereby weakened the political party 'focus' of liberalism (Tipton, 1976: 141).

40. The Centre was a Catholic Party, but since farmers were over-represented in the Catholic population, the Party tended to favour the interests of agriculture (Ritter, 1990: 35).

41. While the Zentrum called itself a Centre Party, its orientation was unmistakably Conservative. However, because the Liberal Parties (and the SPD) were anticlerical and the Conservatives were closely tied to the Protestant faith, the denominational character of the Centre Party meant that it could not be situated on a normal left–right political spectrum. Evans (1981: 33) notes that the problem of naming the party 'reflected the problem of the nature and purpose of the party, which was never fully resolved throughout its history. . . . If the party was to be Catholic, it could not be exclusively conservative, and if it was to be "Christian" and concerned with a variety of social and political issues it could not be exclusively Catholic. The old, noncommittal name of *Zentrum*, the Center, was consequently chosen . . .'.

   Moreover, the heterogenous socio-economic base of the Party (including workers, farmers, shop keepers, civil servants, industrialists and aristocrats) lends to the difficulty in situating the interests of its members on a left–right spectrum. (On its socio-economic base, see Ritter, 1990) . To say that the Zentrum fell in the middle of the political spectrum is clearly a misnomer, but it certainly did not fall at either of the extremes. One might reasonably conclude that its socio-economic base moderated its conservatism while its denominational character distanced it from both the anticlerical Social Democrats and the Protestant Conservatives.

42. The end of the Anti-Socialist Legislation in 1890 gave further momentum to the socialist movement.

6. A unifying theory of interests, institutions and ideas? Concluding remarks

Cheryl Schonhardt-Bailey

Few, if any, political scientists would disagree with the basic premise of this book – namely, that interests, institutions and ideas or ideology all matter for understanding political outcomes. A fundamental source of disagreement, however, lies in the weights assigned to these factors and the linkages that are said to exist between them. Without question, interests-based explanations have prevailed as the dominant paradigm in political science since the 1960s. Yet in the past few decades, scholars have become increasingly dissatisfied with the simple rationality assumption that underpins most interests-based explanations of political outcomes. It is not that rationality fails to provide a useful premise upon which to theorize – it certainly does – but that exceptions to and deviations from rational behaviour have encouraged political scientists to explore the conditions under which preferences are formed and the mechanisms (both formal and informal) by which these preferences evolve into observable political outcomes.[1]

Institutions thus become attractive for understanding both how preferences form and the context in which these preferences are channelled into political behaviour. In the words of one author, '(s)tanding at the intersection of political inputs and outputs, political institutions represent the "black box" of politics through which societal interests are translated into policies and political outcomes' (Remmer, 1997: 60). And so, by unpacking the institutional 'black box' we may better understand why some interests prevail and others do not. Similarly, ideas and ideology are useful for understanding how preferences deviate from what a simple interests-based model may predict, and in particular, they help us to understand why some coalitions of interests succeed while others fail (Bawn, 1999). In sum, as scholars question the centrality of interests-based explanations for political outcomes, institutions and/or ideology have become increasingly attractive as explanatory variables.

Yet, to say that interests, institutions and ideology (the three 'I's') all matter is not very helpful for theory building. It provides multiple arrows

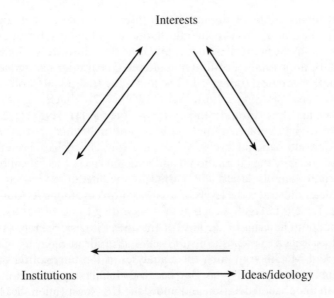

Interests

Institutions   Ideas/ideology

Figure 6.1   The causality of interests, ideas and institutions

of causality, as can be illustrated by Figure 6.1, but ultimately fails to answer several key questions. For instance, how does each 'I' intersect with each other? What conditions the influence of each 'I'? Why do interests matter more in one context and ideas (or institutions) more in another? When and why do particular ideas or ideologies matter and why do they make a difference? (Garrett and Weingast, 1993: 203; Hall, 1989; Keohane, 2000). How do we define, let alone measure, such imprecise concepts as institutions and ideas? While the introduction to this volume provides definitions to these concepts, it does so with each concept standing alone, rather than interacting with the remaining 'I's'. To build theory more work is required to establish 'the reciprocal influence of institutional constraints and political strategies and, more broadly, on the interaction of ideas, interests, and institutions' (Thelen and Steinmo, 1992). That is, the causal arrows depicted in Figure 6.1 must be dissected more finely and methods of accurately measuring and testing each factor must be established.

1.   INTERESTS, INSTITUTIONS AND IDEAS ACROSS LEVELS OF ANALYSIS

While the introduction to this volume situates the three I's into the larger endogenous tariff theory literature, this concluding chapter considers the empirical ramifications of discussing the three I's within a single framework. It is the aim of this concluding chapter to outline two fundamental divisions within the political economy literature that illustrate the difficulty, and perhaps impossibility, of unifying interests, institutions and ideology into a single theoretical framework. The first is the traditional 'problem' of the levels of analysis (Singer, 1961; Waltz, 1959, 1979) – that is, the problem of whether and how to unify theory across the various levels of causal forces (for example, international, national and individual, but also, the regional and sub-national levels). While numerous efforts have been made to bridge especially the international and national levels, theoretical biases towards autonomous levels still permeate the literature. Indeed, this volume nicely illustrates the levels of analysis problem among its four contributors. Table 6.1 classifies each author according to his or her focus of discussion, both in terms of the level of the underlying causal force(s) and the emphasis given to interests, institutions and/or ideas.

Pahre and McGillivray pitch their analyses at the intersection of the international and national levels. But, because McGillivray explores the US states both under confederation and under the US Constitution, her focus can also be said to include sub-national (that is, state) actors. Schonhardt-Bailey aims her discussion at both the sub-national (party, group) and individual levels, while McLean focuses exclusively on the individual level. Taken together, the authors span most of the levels of analysis, but individually they gravitate towards one or two levels. In a parallel vein, Pahre and McGillivray offer analyses of the intersection of interests and institutions but give scant attention to the role of ideas or ideology. Schonhardt-Bailey explores all three I's at the sub-national level, and the interplay between interests and ideology at the individual level. McLean is unique in gauging his discussion of all three I's entirely at the individual level.

The bias of Pahre and McGillivray towards 'higher' levels of analysis and away from ideology, and conversely the bias of Schonhardt-Bailey and McLean towards 'lower' levels of analysis and towards ideational factors, seems to suggest (as I noted in chapter 5) that the level of detail might afford the luxury of adding a third 'I' to the explanatory framework. Yet, there is no reason why ideas cannot have causal force at the national level, as various studies of foreign economic policy have shown (for example, (Goldstein, 1993; Goldstein and Keohane, 1993a; Rohrlich, 1987), or even at the international level, as Hall and his colleagues have well demonstrated (Hall, 1989). Hence, two possible criticisms of this volume are that (a) only half of the authors include all three I's in their analysis, and (b) the four authors, taken together, form a cleavage between the international/national levels of analysis (Pahre and McGillivray) and the sub-national/individual levels of analysis (McLean and Schonhardt-Bailey). Yet, given the current

Table 6.1   *The intersection of levels and interests, institutions and ideas/ideology*

	Interests	Institutions	Ideas/ideology
International/global	Pahre, McGillivray	Pahre, McGillivray	
Regional			
National / domestic	Pahre, McGillivray	Pahre, McGillivray	
Sub-national (parties, groups, states)	McGillivray, Schonhardt-Bailey	McGillivray, Schonhardt-Bailey	Schonhardt-Bailey
Individual	McLean, Schonhardt-Bailey	McLean	McLean, Schonhardt-Bailey

state of theory of the intersection of interests, institutions and ideology, and the unresolved levels of analysis problem, these criticisms in fact help us to appreciate the difficulty of juggling the three 'I's' simultaneously. Rare is the author who manages to tackle all three 'I's' while bridging all levels of analysis.[2]

A recent edited volume on 'strategic choice' in international relations (Lake and Powell, 1999a) serves to clarify the theoretical hurdles that scholars face as they attempt to build a theory of interests, institutions and ideology across levels of analysis. Lake and Powell introduce strategic choice as a new approach that promises to 'transcend the levels-of-analysis distinction' (Lake and Powell, 1999b: 26) by making strategic interactions between actors, rather than actors themselves, the units of analysis. These interactions consist of (1) *actors* (who possess preferences and beliefs about the preferences of others), and (2) the *environment* in which they interact (which in turn decomposes into a set of actions and an informational structure). The approach is very much dependent on a rational choice framework in which actors' preferences are ideally deduced from existing theory, or alternatively, are assumed or are revealed by observed behaviour (Frieden, 1999). From strategic interaction to strategic interaction, preferences may vary (that is, they may be endogenized), but importantly, actors' preferences are said to be fixed over the course of any particular interaction. Lake and Powell describe the approach with a 'boxes within boxes' metaphor, which I present as a graphic in Figure 6.2.

Actors are said to be aggregates of more basic actors so that the approach as a whole is characterized as a collection of boxes within boxes (Lake and Powell, 1999b: 15), ranging from the individual, to the subnational level (for example, groups, parties, states, firms and so on), to the nation, the region (for example, the European Union, trading blocs and so on), and finally to the international or systemic level. Within each box or level, four key attributes define the strategic setting in question: the *preferences* and *beliefs* of actors, and the set of *actions* and *informational structure* available to actors. These four attributes recur at all levels, with each level (or box) feeding into higher levels of aggregation 'seamlessly' and in a 'well-defined way' (Lake and Powell, 1999b: 17). Hence, aggregation and disaggregation implies that models of causality may endogenize or exogenize the attributes from one box to another (illustrated by the upward and downward causal arrows in Figure 6.2), but within a given box actors' preferences, for example, are taken as exogenous so as to examine their effects on choices and outcomes.

The strategic choice approach offers a way to bridge the levels of analysis, but it relies on just two of our three I's, as it discounts entirely the role of ideas or ideology. Lake and Powell fault approaches that rely on ideas

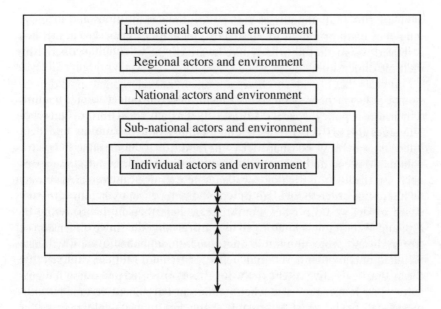

Figure 6.2   The 'boxes within boxes' of strategic choice

and ideology ('cognitive approaches') for their lack of parsimony. A strategic choice approach which focuses on informational asymmetries between actors is said to be inherently preferable to one that examines how individuals process information (Lake and Powell, 1999b: 31) – although the reasons for this preference are left unstated. Rogowski rejects the ideological dimension on the basis of McKelvey's chaos theorem (McKelvey, 1976; Schofield, 1976; Shepsle and Weingast, 1984). He notes that political outcomes that rely on a single dimension of policy on which individuals hold single-peaked preferences guarantee stable outcomes. 'When voters divide independently over more than one dimension (e.g., over both left-right redistributional issues *and* religion), a majority can often be mustered against any particular outcome and results can wander unpredictably throughout the entire policy space' (Rogowski, 1999: 128). If ideas and ideology can represent a second (and even third) dimension to the single dimension of interests (especially interests based on redistributive issues such as trade policy), then the intersection of ideas and interests makes political outcomes difficult, if not impossible, to predict. Yet this skepticism is unwarranted. If a policy issue is inherently two- (or multi-) dimensional, it is both theoretically and empirically appropriate to consider it as such. Many issues are multi-dimensional, and institutions are purposely designed to prevent circularity of policy outcomes (Shepsle, 1979). Heresthetical manoeuvring that emphasizes new policy dimensions in order to change the policy equilibrium (as illustrated in McLean's Chapter 4, this volume) is indeed a sign that politicians are aware of the possibilities offered by multiple dimensions.'

It is clear that a strategic choice approach that relies on a single dimension of policy is theoretically more elegant than one that allows for a multidimensional policy space. Multiple dimensions give rise to unstable outcomes in part because preferences (which previously were based on interests) can now be shaped by the additional dimension(s). In this volume, McLean and Schonhardt-Bailey both introduce multidimensionality – in the form of ideology or ideas – to examine how preferences may be altered in order to yield an outcome different from what an interests-based model would predict. For McLean, heresthetical manoeuvring by Peel and Wellington is interpreted as transforming the single dimension of free trade and protection into a multidimensional policy space which also included public order and famine relief for Ireland. McLean explains that the median legislative voter (who would have supported protection for agriculture) no longer prevailed when opinion in Parliament became multidimensional. In the midst of possible chaos and majority rule cycling over the issue space (which would yield an unstable outcome), Peel and Wellington – as herestheticians – were able to induce front- and backbenchers to support Repeal by using arguments only tangentially related to Repeal to gain their support. For Schonhardt-Bailey, ideas intersect with interests to give rise to a nationalizing the interest strategy by lobbying groups. An interest group may exaggerate its commitment to a particularly appealing idea or ideology (that is, one with an identifiable positive externality) in order to capture support from non-group members – and, where an asymmetry of information exists between group and individual, groups may even be able to shape how individuals define their self-interests. But, these individuals may also condition their support on some evidence of the groups' commitment to the idea or ideology, and thereby shape the ideas dimension at the level of the group.

More generally, by introducing another dimension (namely some form of idea or ideology), individuals or groups can destabilize the existing (interests-based) majority outcome. Without a model of ideas to explain the transformation of interests, policy outcomes can indeed become unpredictable. However, as McLean and Schonhardt-Bailey illustrate, an appreciation of how an individual politician may structure the situation in such a way that pertinent actors will naturally fall into line with his preferred objective, and interest groups may invoke ideas to shape the preferences of non-group members, helps to make outcomes more understandable, if not predictable. Undoubtedly, the richer is the theory of how ideas intersect with interests and institutions, the better we are able to predict outcomes. McLean's heresthetic and Schonhardt-Bailey's nationalizing the interest both offer beginnings of a theory of ideas, but it remains to be seen whether either of these explanatory frameworks can be extended to higher levels of analysis. Indeed, it is highly questionable whether such a theory of ideas can be developed. Yet, to deny any role for the effect of ideas in shaping preferences is automatically to bias the explanation for political outcomes in favour of interests (and even institutions) and away from ideas and ideology. To sacrifice the insights that may be gained from ideas and ideology is a price too high to pay for the sake of theoretical parsimony.

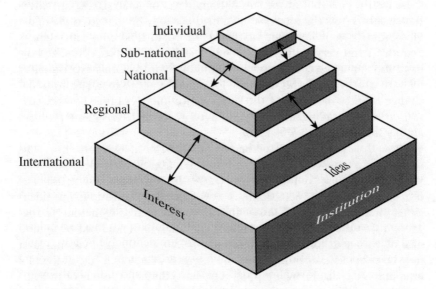

Figure 6.3   The 'boxes within boxes' of interests, institutions and ideas?

How, then, might we adapt the boxes within boxes of strategic choice to include ideas and ideology? Figure 6.3 illustrates the goal that is aspired to by this volume – namely the inclusion of the ideas or ideology in each of the boxes, or levels. It also, unfortunately, illustrates the theoretical difficulties that plague this aspiration. Let us take, for example, the intersection of interests, institutions and ideas/ideology at the individual level. Following Lake and Powell's (1999b; 11–12) 'conceptual experiments' analysis, we may assume that the effects of interests, institutions and ideas are analytically separable at the level of the individual. Using the strategic choice approach, Lake and Powell suggest as a first experiment to vary the properties of actors while holding constant their environment, and as a second

experiment to vary the environment while holding constant actors' properties. We could suggest at a minimum three similar conceptual experiments.
Using our Figure 6.3, we might wish to first, hold constant (that is, define
as exogenous) interests and institutions, while varying (endogenizing) ideas.

In McLean's Chapter 4 to this volume, the interests of parliamentarians
and the parliamentary institutions are taken as given, while he varies ideas
by introducing the multiple dimensions of public order and Irish famine
relief. That is, he equates new ideas to new dimensions.[3] Second, we could
hold constant institutions and ideas, and vary interests. By introducing the
institutions of groups and political parties, along with the ideas infused in
these institutions (but at the sub-national level of analysis), Schonhardt-
Bailey shows how the interests of individuals may be shaped in the midst
of asymmetries of information. Third, we could hold constant interests
and ideas, and vary institutions. While it is difficult to conceptualize how
institutions may be endogenous at the individual level, this experiment is
relevant to other levels. McGillivray, for example, allows for an institutional
change with the inception of the US Constitution to examine how the centralization of trading authority resolved the collective action problem
among the separate 13 US states.

These three conceptual experiments demonstrate at least three problems
that plague a theory of interests, institutions and ideas across levels of analysis. First, because we retain actors (rather than strategic interactions) as
our unit of analysis, and examine how interests, institutions and ideas
either affect actors (that is, exogenous I's) or are shaped by actors (endogenous I's) at each level or in each box, our analysis is muddied by a good
deal of variance. For instance, interests of actors at the sub-national level
may be taken as exogenous while the interests of actors at the individual
level may vary – as interest groups may shape the self-interests of individuals by employing a nationalizing the interest strategy. Because this strategy includes the manipulation of ideas, the precise weights of the effects of
interests versus ideas on individuals' assessment of self-interest may be
difficult to establish. Moreover, if institutions are said to affect a group's
ability to nationalize the interest, it becomes even more difficult to separate
out the independent effects of interests, institutions and ideas on individuals' self-interest. This leads to a second but highly related problem – namely,
the interactive effects of the three I's (especially those between interests and
ideas) within each box. One may envisage an experiment that aims to test
the effects of, say, the national interest on group or individual preferences.
However, if one accepts that preferences are the product of both economic
interests and ideologies, there is no way to know whether the national interests resonated more with the interests or the ideologies of groups and individuals. And because it is likely that the interactive effects of interests and

ideology may differ at each level, sorting out a clear causal link between interests and ideology both across and within boxes becomes highly complex, if not downright impossible.

A third problem points to the added value – but also added complexity – of including institutions as constraints on interests and ideas, particularly in constraining how preferences are aggregated. Returning for a moment to strategic choice, the authors appear to diverge somewhat in how 'seamless' is the aggregation process. Rogowski offers a number of hypotheses for how domestic institutional features – namely, the nature of the franchise, the mechanisms of political representation, and the decision rules that bind political representatives – can constrain foreign policy outcomes. For instance, a franchise that privileges one group's preferences will bias the policy outcome: 'If only landowners can vote, and if agriculture is threatened by imports, agricultural protection becomes a near certainty' (Rogowski, 1999: 122). Or, if decision rules allow for multiple bodies and veto points, the policy outcome will be biased towards the status quo, whereas if authority over the agenda (that is, few veto points and greater 'gatekeeper' power) is more concentrated, the holder(s) of that authority will be advantaged (ibid., p. 124). Hence, Lake and Powell's 'seamless' aggregation of preferences is subject to important institutional constraints which must be understood and specified in advance. Without this specification of institutional constraints, preferences cannot at all be said to aggregate in a 'well-defined way'.

McGillivray aptly demonstrates in Chapter 3 (this volume) that under the Articles of Confederation, property restrictions in the franchise and the holding of public office led to the over-representation of landowners. This bias in representation translated into a policy bias towards the interests of farmers. Moreover, a decentralized political structure gave rise to a collective action problem among the US states that frustrated their attempts to retaliate against British trading practices – in other words, the preferences of the states could not be aggregated. A fundamental institutional change – the ratification of the US Constitution, which among other things concentrated the authority to formulate and enforce trade policy within a single legislative body – resolved the collective action problem and thereby provided a mechanism to aggregate states' preferences. This institutional change did not, however, reverse the policy bias in favour of farmers as the franchise and officeholding requirements favoured landholding adult white males for some time to come. Pahre also provides examples of how franchise restrictions biased the representativeness of some groups over others, and thereby affected national tariff levels. Changes in institutions that privileged the political access of import-competing interests over export interests (and vice versa) helped to explain shifting balances of power among domestic interests. McLean, on the other hand, explains how a policy bias in favour of agricultural protection (the product of an electoral system that still favoured landowners and a Parliament still governed primarily by land-owning aristocrats) can be negated if agenda-setting power is sufficiently concentrated and ideology is given its due weight. In sum, while institutions can certainly constrain how preferences are aggregated, if one accepts that preferences are the product of both interests and ideas, an institutional con-straint upon the aggregation of interests may be mitigated by an ideology that reshapes preferences.

Clearly the levels of analysis problem complicates the development of a unifying theory of interests, institutions and ideas. But this is not to say that an overarching concept – such as strategic interaction – could not emerge to bridge the levels and solve the endogeneity and exogeneity problems among the three I's. Or, it may be that not all three causal variables are rel-evant at every level of analysis, and so to resign one or two of the I's to the residual would be entirely appropriate. Ultimately, these are empirical issues that require investigation at every level of analysis, and a conceptual open mind as to the possible influence of each 'I'. Parsimony is, of course, a valuable goal in theory building, but the simplification that is required to achieve parsimony needs to be weighed against the possible distortion of results which stems from omitting key explanatory factors.

2.   MEASURING AND TESTING INTERESTS, INSTITUTIONS AND IDEAS

The methodological cleavage between quantitative and qualitative research constitutes a second fundamental division within political economy, and political science more generally. Nowhere is this more evident than in the lively reaction to King, Keohane and Verba's (commonly referred to as 'KKV') call for infusing qualitative research with the basic tenet of statis-tics – that is, inference.[4] KKV maintain 'that the differences between the quantitative and qualitative traditions are only stylistic and are methodo-logically and substantively unimportant' (King, Keohane and Verba, 1994: 4). The goal of all scientific research – quantitative or qualitative – is to make inferences from what we can discover through empirical investigation to a larger population whose properties must remain unknown: 'The facts we do not know are the subjects of our research questions, theories, and hypotheses. The facts we do know form our (quantitative or qualitative) data or observations' (ibid., p. 46). KKV delineate key aspects of building good theory, including research design, explaining as much as possible with as little as possible (or, 'maximizing leverage'), how to collect data properly, establishing causality and avoiding various methodological pitfalls (like endogeneity,[5] measurement error, biased results, inappropriate case selection). But their underlying goal is to provide a way of *evaluating theory* – or to use empirical data to achieve 'scientific opinions' about theories and hypotheses: 'Our social scientist uses theory to generate *observable implications*, then systematically applies publicly known procedures to infer from evidence whether what the theory implied is correct' (King, Keohane and Verba in Laitin et al., 1995: 476).

Many of the complaints levelled against KKV's book reveal underlying disagreements about how theory should develop in political science, what constitutes 'good' and 'bad' theory, and how to strike a balance between simplification and preserving contextual integrity. While I do not attempt to delve into the details of this debate here, some aspects are relevant to this book since they reflect the methodological cleavage between interests-based approaches and ones that highlight institutions or ideas. Because interests are inherently easier to measure, interests-based approaches are typically conducive to quantitative testing while approaches that highlight institutions or ideas/ideology tend to be more qualitative. Moreover, the quantifiable nature of interests often allows for the introduction of greater number of cases (because economic variables are easier to measure and aggregate) and thereby gives rise to statistical methods of analysis (which in turn makes the application of the rules of inference straightforward). Institutions and ideas/ideology are inherently more difficult to measure and the context richer in detail and complexity, and so often give rise to single case studies or analyses with small numbers of cases. Defenders of studies with few cases (for example, Rogowski in Laitin et al., 1995, and McKeown, 1999) maintain that the road to good theory is founded not just (or even primarily) on theory evaluation but on how to achieve powerful and internally consistent theory in the first place. A single case of recognized importance may reveal more depth and insight into underlying causal forces (and thereby contribute more to the development of theory) than scores of observations that, individually and as a whole, are less well understood.

A unifying theory of interests, institutions and ideas must inevitably confront the difficulties inherent in measuring and testing institutions and ideas/ideology. The contributions to this book illustrate some ways in which these difficulties may be managed. Pahre, for example, comes closest to the ideal KKV approach by presenting a formal theory of trade treaties in the nineteenth century, deriving observable implications of the theory and subjecting these to quantitative testing. By selecting a large number of country cases he is able to employ measures of association and regression analysis to test the before and after effects of changes in domestic institutions on trade treaties. Moreover, he balances this with intertemporal descriptive statistics for individual countries in order better to gauge the effects of domestic institutional change on trade treaties. McLean, on the other hand, adopts a single case study approach to understanding the policy shift from protection to free trade in mid-nineteenth-century Britain. In order to get a handle on the interplay between interests and ideology, he first analyses the private papers and letters of the key decision-makers, and then supplements this with quantitative analysis of the interests and ideologies of the larger coalitions in Parliament.

But these are only a few ways in which studies using large and small numbers of cases[6] can subject ideology and institutions (especially *vis-à-vis* interests) to empirical testing. The basic point is that while ideology and institutions may be difficult to measure and test, political scientists have made great strides in overcoming these difficulties. A particularly good example of empirical testing of ideology versus interests can be found in the legislative studies literature, where various statistical methods have been used to tease out the relative weights of constituency interests and ideology, party affiliation, and representative's own interests and ideology on roll-call votes (to name just a few, Hill, 1998; Hird, 1993; Irwin and Kroszner, 1999; Kalt and Zupan, 1990; McCormick and Black, 1983; Peltzman, 1984; Schonhardt-Bailey, 1998a; Uslaner, 1999). Poole and Rosenthal's (1991, 1997) NOMINATE approach is arguably the most technologically sophisticated approach to studying the ideological content of Congressional voting behaviour although it is not without its critics (for example, Groseclose, Levitt and Snyder, 1999; Heckman and Snyder, 1997; Koford, 1989; Snyder, 1992; Wilcox and Clausen, 1991). And finally, new computer software and hardware give rise to even further avenues for measuring and testing the causes and effects of ideology on political actors.[7]

While theory on institutions has developed in several directions – with rational choice institutionalism (Alston and North, 1996; Dowding and King, 1995; Goodin, 1995) and historical institutionalism (Hall, 1992; Steinmo and Longstroth, 1992; Thelen and Steinmo, 1992) probably constituting the two dominant strands – it is difficult to locate a parallel groundswell of statistical applications.[8] Yet, as Rogowski notes in his critique of KKV (Laitin et al., 1995), rigorous hypothesis testing constitutes just one of three pillars of scientific inquiry. Two other pillars – elaborating precise models and deducing their logical implications – may in some cases advance theorizing more effectively. Recent developments in formal and game theory applications to institutions take precisely this approach (Cox and McCubbins, 1993; Krehbiel, 1991; Shepsle and Weingast, 1995), and thus can be said to be extending two of the three pillars of scientific inquiry. In brief, while a methodological cleavage certainly continues to separate interests-based approaches from institutions- and ideology-based approaches, (1) political scientists are increasingly willing and able to employ quantitative/statistical methods to ideology and institutions, and (2) rigorous empiricism is not the only (or even the best) route to building theories of institutions and ideology. Thus, the methodological divide is whittling away with the construction of empirical bridges and development of other avenues to theory building.

3.   CONCLUDING REMARKS

While the levels of analysis problem and the methodological cleavage between interests-based approaches and ones that rely on institutions and ideas both complicate a grand theory of interests, institutions and ideas, this is not to say that there is no room for optimism. First, if a unifying concept like strategic interaction can be found to overcome the levels of analysis problem (and sort out the direction of causality problem among the three I's), then it is possible to conceive of a theory of the three I's across levels of analysis. Or, it may be that such an aspiration is wasted effort and that theory is better developed by accepting different causal forces for different levels, or a single dominant explanatory variable across all levels. Empirical investigation will ultimately be the judge.

Second, while political scientists may lament difficulties and conflicts arising from methodological biases, the reality is that many bridges are already in place that quantify the effects of institutions and ideas on political outcomes. And, where quantification is not achieved, theory is developing with the assistance of other analytical tools like game theory and mathematical deduction. So, while KKV's recommendation for inference in qualitative studies is welcome and is being heeded, scientific inquiry into the combined effects of interests, institutions and ideas on political outcomes is progressing along non-empirical routes as well.

NOTES

1. It should, of course, be noted that much work has been done in refining the concept of rationality (the literature is far too vast to cite here, but as examples see Czada and Windhoff-Heritier, 1991; Friedman, 1996; Mitchell, 1993; Nicholson, 1992). For example, some rational choice scholars delineate between thin and thick rationality. Thin rationality takes as given the beliefs and desires that underpin rational behaviour. Yee (1997) explores various remedies to thin rationality (for example, 'equilibrium refinements', Bayesian updating, appeals to external constraints and assumptions of excessive epistemic capacities) but finds these plagued with difficulties. Thick rationality, on the other hand, adopts a rational choice framework but also provides some description of actors' preferences and beliefs, and in so doing introduces ideas and persuasion into the notion of rationality (see also Elster, 1983).

2. An important exception is Milner (1997), who constructs a model of the interaction between domestic and international politics, using a slightly different set of I's (interests, institutions and *information*). As noted in Schonhardt-Bailey's Chapter 5 on nationalizing the interest, a fine line exists between ideas and information. From a rational choice perspective, information is a more manageable concept than ideas. Information is easier to identify and quantify, while ideas are plagued with a good deal of subjectivity. This volume does not attempt to tackle the role of information *vis-à-vis* interests, institutions and ideology.

   It should also be noted that some authors have indeed focused on the role of ideas at the international level, and how these ideas intersect with interests (Finnemore, 1996a; Finnemore, 1996b).

3. It might be possible to introduce new ideas along a single dimension, thereby altering the interpretation of this dimension. One difficulty in discussing ideas in the contest of dimensions is the lack of clarity in deciding whether new ideas (if and when they arise) require a revised interpretation of the original dimension, or the introduction of an entirely new dimension. In Chapter 5 by Schonhardt-Bailey, all ideas were collapsed onto a single dimension so as to juxtapose an ideas dimension with an interests dimension. While the possibility of three or more dimensions is raised, she notes that higher dimension models are not only theoretically challenging, they are also difficult to graph.

4. See King, Keohane and Verba (1994). References to the text are too numerous to cite here, but see in particular Laitin et al. (1995) and more recently McKeown (1999).

5. Endogeneity refers to instances in which the values of the independent variables are a consequence, rather than a cause, of the dependent variable. This is precisely the sort of problem illustrated by the arrows in Figures 6.2 and 6.3. KKV note that endogeneity is often a problem in work on the effect of ideas and ideology on policy: 'Insofar as the ideas *reflect the conditions* under which political actors operate – for instance, their material circumstances, which generate their material interests – analysis of the ideas' impact on policy is subject to omitted variable bias: actors' ideas are correlated with a causally prior omitted variable – material interests – which affects the dependent variable – political strategy. And insofar as ideas serve as *rationalizations* of policies pursued on other grounds, the ideas can be mere *consequences* rather than causes of policy. Under these circumstances, ideas are endogenous: they may appear to explain actors' strategies, but in fact they result from these strategies' (King, Keohane and Verba, 1994: 191). KKV offer a number of ways to avoid this endogeneity problem – but particularly illuminating is the suggestion to transform the problem into one of omitted variable bias, which then allows the researcher to compare alternative explanatory hypotheses (King, Keohane and Verba, 1994: 191–6).

6. I use 'large' and 'small' in a loose sense here to depict the basic difference between a multiple case study and a single case study. Realistically speaking, the numbers in Pahre's multiple country case may be deemed by some as small (certainly relatively to studies with thousands of cases), while the number of individual MPs in McLean's regression analysis is large although he is essentially working within a single case framework.

7. Recent improvements in optical scanning, for instance, provide opportunities to put large amounts of textual material (for example, parliamentary debates) into electronic form, and improvements in computer-assisted qualitative software allow more sophisticated analysis of this material. I aim to demonstrate this capacity in a forthcoming project which uses a CD-ROM of British parliamentary debates on trade policy from 1816–46 (Schonhardt-Bailey, 1999).

8. This is not to say that good empirical work has not been done on institutions – a few recent examples include Hall and Franzese (1998); Irwin and Kroszner (1999); Iversen (1998); Leblang (1999); Reynolds (1999).

References

Abraham, David (1981), *The Collapse of the Weimar Republic: Political Economy and Crisis*, Princeton: Princeton University Press.

Alston, Lee J., T. Eggertsson and D.C. North (1996), *Empirical Studies in Institutional Change*, Cambridge: Cambridge University Press.

Anderson, Kym (1992a), 'Analytical issues in the Uruguay Round negotiations on agriculture", *European Economic Review*, **35** (2): 519–26.

Anderson, Kym (1992b), 'Agricultural trade liberalization and the environment: a global perspective', *The World Economy* **15** (1): 153–72 (January).

Anderson, Kym and Yujiro Hayami (eds) (1986), *The Political Economy of Agricultural Protection: East Asia in International Perspective*, London: Allen and Unwin.

Anderson, Kym and Robert Baldwin (1987), 'The political market for protection in industrialized countries', in A.M. El-Agraa (ed.), *Protection, Cooperation, Integration and Development*, London: Macmillan Press, pp. 20–36.

Anon. (1998a), Farmer Franz Fischler digs in, *The Economist*, 4 April, p. 52.

Anon. (1998b), Not all as cosseted as consumers say, *The Economist*, 19 December, p. 59.

Anon. (1999), The EU's coming wrangle for reforms and spoils. *The Economist*, 2 January, p. 33.

Arrow, Kenneth J. (1951), *Social Choice and Individual Values*, New York: John Wiley and Sons.

Ashley, Percy (1920), *Modern Tariff History: Germany–United States–France*, London: John Murray. (US edn, 1926, New York: E.P. Dutton & Company.)

Atack, Jeremy and Peter Passell (1979), *A New Economic View of American History*, New York: W.W. Norton & Company Ltd.

Austen-Smith, David (1981), 'Voluntary pressure groups,' *Economica*, **48**, 143–53.

Austen-Smith, David (1991), 'Rational consumers and irrational voters: a review essay on black hole tariffs and endogenous policy theory by MBY', *Economics and Politics*, **1**, 73–92 (March).

Axelrod, Robert (1984a), *The Evolution of Cooperation*, New York: Basic Books.

Axelrod, Robert (1984b), 'The emergence of cooperation among egotists', *American Political Science Review*, **75**, 306–18.

Axelrod, Robert and Robert O. Keohane (1986), 'Achieving cooperation under anarchy: strategies and institutions', in Kenneth A. Oye, (ed.) *Cooperation Under Anarchy*, Princeton: Princeton University Press, pp. 226–54.

Aydelotte, W. O. (1970), *Study 521 (Codebook) 'British House of Commons 1841–1847'*, Iowa City, IA: Regional Social Science Data Archive of Iowa.

Bagwell, Kyle and Robert W. Staiger (1990), 'A theory of managed trade', *American Economic Review* **80** (4), 779–95 (September).

Bagwell, Kyle and Robert W. Staiger (1999), 'Multilateral Trade Negotiations, Bilateral Opportunism and the Rules of GATT', Cambridge, Mass.: National Bureau of Economic Research Working Paper 7071.

Bailey, Michael A., Judith Goldstein and Barry R. Weingast (1997), 'The institutional roots of American trade policy. Politics, Coalitions, and International Trade', *World Politics*, **49**, 309–38 (April).

Baldwin, Robert (1985), *The Political Economy of U.S. Import Policy*, Cambridge, Mass: MIT Press.

Barnett, Michael (1990), 'High politics is low politics: the domestic and systemic sources of Israeli security policy 1967–1977', *World Politics*, **42**, 529–62.

Bates, Robert H. and Anne O. Krueger (1993), 'Generalizations arising from the country studies', in Robert H. Bates and Anne O. Krueger (eds), *Political and Economic Interactions in Economic Policy Reform: Evidence from Eight Countries*, Oxford: Basil Blackwell Ltd., pp. 444–72.

Bates, Robert H. et al. (1998), *Analytic Narratives*, Princeton: Princeton University Press.

Bates, Robert H. Philip Brock and Jill Tiefenthaler (1991), 'Risk and trade regimes: another exploration', *International Organization*, **45**, 1–18.

Bawn, Kathleen (1999), 'Constructing "Us": Ideology, coalition politics, and false consciousness', *American Journal of Political Science*, **43** (2), 303–4.

Beard, Charles (1935), *An Economic Interpretation of the Constitution of the United States*, New York: The Macmillan Company.

Becker, Gary S. (1983), 'A theory of competition among pressure groups for political influence', *Quarterly Journal of Economics*, **98**, 371–400.

Becker, Gary S. (1985), 'Public policies, pressure groups, and dead weight costs', *Journal of Public Economics*, **28**, 329–47.

Beer, Samuel H. (1966), *British Politics in the Collectivist Age*, New York: Alfred A. Knopf.

Bell, Daniel (1960), *The End of Ideology*, New York: Free Press.

Berdahl, R. M. (1972), 'Conservative politics and aristocratic landholders in Bismarckian Germany', *Journal of Modern History*, **44**, 1–20.

Biagini, Eugenio F. (1992), *Liberty, Retrenchment and Reform: Popular Liberalism in the Age of Gladstone, 1860–1880*, Cambridge: Cambridge University Press.

Blackbourn, David (1984), 'The discrete charm of the bourgeoisie: reappraising German history in the nineteenth century', in David Blackbourn and Geoff Eley (eds), *The Peculiarities of German History*, Oxford: Oxford University Press, pp. 159–292.

Blake, R. (1970), *The Conservative Party from Peel to Churchill*, London: Eyre & Spottiswoode.

Bliss, C. (1998), 'The Corn Laws and the CAP', in G. Cook (ed.), *The Economics and Politics of International Trade* (2 volumes, London: Routledge), vol. 2., pp. 148–65.

Bohara, Alok K. and William H. Kaempfer (1991), A test of tariff endogeneity in the United States', *American Economic Review* **81**, 952–60 (September).

Brown, L. (1958), *The Board of Trade and the Free Trade Movement*, Oxford: Clarendon Press.

Browne, William P. et al. (1992), *Sacred Cows and Hot Potatoes: Agrarian Myths in Agricultural Policy*, Boulder: Westview Press, pp. 11–15.

Bueno de Mesquita, Bruce and David Lalman (1992), *War and Reason*, New Haven: Yale University Press.

Butler, D. E. and D. Stokes (1969), *Political Change in Britain*, London: Macmillan.

Cain, P. J. and A. G. Hopkins (1980), 'The political economy of British expansion overseas, 1750–1914'. *Economic History Review* 2d series **33**, 463–90. Reprinted in Cheryl Schonhardt-Bailey (ed.) (1997), *The Rise of Free Trade*, vol. 4, London: Routledge, pp. 3–37.

Calvert, Randall L. (1995), 'The rational choice theory of social institutions: cooperation, coordination and communication', in Jeffrey S. Banks and Eric A. Hanusheck (eds), *Modern Political Economy: Old Topics, New Directions*, Cambridge: Cambridge University Press, pp. 60–95.

Cameron, David (1978), 'The expansion of the public economy: a comparative analysis', *American Political Science Review*, **72**, 1243–61.

Cassing, James H., Timothy J. McKeown and Jack Ochs (1985), 'The political economy of the tariff cycle', *American Political Science Review*, **80**, 843–62.

Caves, Richard E. (1976), 'Economic models of political choice: Canada's tariff structure,' *Canadian Journal of Economics*, **9**, 279–300.

Chaloner, W. H. (1970), 'The agitation against the Corn Laws,' in J. T. Ward (ed.), *Popular Movements, c. 1830–1850*, London: Macmillan, pp. 135–51.

Church, Clive H. (1983), *Europe in 1830: Revolution and Political Change*, London: George Allen & Unwin.

Cobden, Richard (1870), *Speeches on Questions of Public Policy*, 2 vols., London: Macmillan.

Cohen, G. A. (1978), Karl Marx's Theory of History: A Defence, Princeton: Princeton University Press.

Conybeare, John A. C. (1983), 'Tariff protection in developed and developing countries', *International Organization*, **37**, 441–65.

Conybeare, John A. C. (1984), 'Politicians and protection: tariffs and elections in Australia', *Public Choice*, **43**, 203–9.

Conybeare, John A. C. (1987), *Trade Wars: The Theory and Practice of International Commercial Rivalry*, New York: Columbia University Press.

Coppa, Frank J. (1970), 'The Italian tariff and the conflict between agriculture and industry: the commercial policy of liberal Italy, 1860–1922', *Journal of Economic History*, **30** (4): 742–69 (December).

Cowhey, Peter F. and Matthew D. McCubbins (1995), *Structure and Policy in Japan and the United States*, Cambridge: Cambridge University Press.

Cox, Gary and Matthew McCubbins (1993), *Legislative Leviathan: Party Government in the House*, Berkeley: University of California Press.

Cox, Robert W. (1981), 'Social forces, states and world orders: beyond international relations theory', *Milennium, Journal of International Studies*, **19** (2), 126–55. Reprinted in Robert O. Keohane, ed., *Neorealism and Its Critics* (1986), New York: Columbia University Press, 204–54.

Cox, Robert W. (1986), Social forces, states and world orders: beyond international relations theory', in Robert O. Keohane (ed.), Neorealism and Its Critics, New York: Columbia University Press, 204–254.

Crafts, N. (1985), *British Economic Growth during the Industrial Revolution*, Oxford: Clarendon Press.

Crosby, Travis L. (1976), *Sir Robert Peel's Administration, 1841–1846*, Newton Abbot: David & Charles.

Czada, R. M. and A. Windhoff-Heritier (eds) (1991), *Political Choice: Institutions, Rules, and the Limits of Rationality*, Boulder: Westview Press.

Davis, John R. (1997), *Britain and the German* Zollverein, *1848–66*, Houndmills, Basingstoke: Macmillan Press Ltd. and New York: St. Martin's Press, Inc.

Dawson, William Harbutt (1904), *Protection in Germany: A History of German Fiscal Policy during the Nineteenth Century*, London: P. S. King & Son.

Deardorff, Alan and Robert Stern (1983), 'The economic effects of complete elimination of post-Tokyo Round tariffs,' in W. Cline (ed.), *Trade Policy in the 1980s*. Cambridge: MIT Press, pp. 673–710.

Denzau, A. and R. Mackay (1981), 'Structure induced equilibrium and perfect foresight expectations', *American Journal of Political Science*, **25**, 762–79.

Denzau, A. and M. Munger (1986), 'Legislators and interest groups: how unorganized groups get represented', *American Political Science Review*, **80**, 89–106.

Destler, I. M. (1985), *American Trade Politics* 3rd edn., Washington, DC: Institute for International Economics.

Diermeier, Daniel and Tim Fedderson (1996), 'Voting cohesion in parliamentary and presidential legislatures', unpublished manuscript.

Dion, Doug (1998), 'Evidence and inference and the comparative case study', *Comparative Politics*, **30** (2), 127–45 (January).

D'Lugo, David and Ronald Rogowski (1993), 'The Anglo-German naval race and comparative constitutional "Fitness"', in Richard Rosecrance and Arthur A. Stein (eds), *The Domestic Bases of Grand Strategy*, Ithaca: Cornell University Press, pp. 65–95.

Dougherty, K. L. and M. Cain (1997), 'Marginal cost sharing and the articles of confederation', *Public Choice*, **90**, 201–13.

Douglass, Elisha P. (1955), *Rebels and Democrats: The Struggle for Equal Political Rights and Majority Rule During the American Revolution*, Chapel Hill, NC: The University of North Carolina Press.

Dowding, K. and D. King (1995) (eds), *Preferences, Institutions and Rational Choice*, Oxford: Clarendon Press.

Downs, Anthony (1957), *An Economic Theory of Democracy*, New York: Harper and Row.

Downs, George W., David M. Rocke and Peter N. Barsoom (1998), 'Managing the evolution of multilateralism', *International Organization*, **52** (2), 397–419 (Spring).

Dunham, Arthur Louis (1930), *The Anglo-French Treaty of Commerce of 1860 and the Progress of the Industrial Revolution in France*, Ann Arbor: University of Michigan Press.

Duverger, Maurice (1961), *Political Parties: Their Organization and Activity in the Modern State*, 2nd edn., London: Methuen & Co. Ltd.

Eley, Geoff (1993), 'Anti-Semitism, agrarian mobilization, and the Conservative Party: Radicalism and containment in the founding of the Agrarian League, 1887–94', in Larry Eugene Jones and James Retallack (eds), *Between Reform, Reaction, and Resistance: Studies in the History of German Conservatism from 1789–1945*, Oxford: Berg Publishers, pp. 187–227.

Elster, Jon (1983), *Sour Grapes: Studies in the Subversion of Rationality*, Cambridge: Cambridge University Press.

Epstein, Lee and Thomas G. Walker (1995), *Constitutional Law for a Changing America: Institutional Power and Constraints*, 2nd edn., Washington, DC: Congressional Quarterly Inc.

Evans, Ellen Lovell (1981), *The German Center Party 1870–1933*, Carbondale and Edwardsville: Southern Illinois University Press.

Farrand, Max (1913), *The Records of the Federal Convention of 1787*, III, New Haven, US and London, UK: Yale University Press.

Fay, H. Van V. (1927), 'Commercial policy in post-war Europe: reciprocity versus most-favored nation treatment', *Quarterly Journal of Economics*, **41** (3), 441–70 (May).

Finger, J. M., H. Keith Hall and Douglas R. Nelson (1982), 'The political economy of administered protection', *American Economic Review*, **72** (3), 452–66 (June).

Finnemore, M. (1996a), *National Interests in International Society*, Ithaca: Cornell University Press.

Finnemore, M. (1996b), 'Norms, culture, and world politics: insights from sociology's institutionalism', *International Organization*, **50**, 325–47.

Fiske, Joseph (1892), *The Critical Period of American History 1783–1789*, Boston: Houghton, Mifflin.

Foot, M. R. D. and H. C. G. Matthew (1974), *The Gladstone Diaries*, vol. 3, Oxford: Clarendon Press.

Freeman, John (1989), *Democracy and Markets: The Politics of Mixed Economies*, Ithaca: Cornell University Press.

Frey, Bruno S. (1984), 'The public choice view of international political economy', *International Organization*, **38**, 199–223.

Friedberg, Aaron L. (1988), *The Weary Titan: Britain and the Experience of Relative Decline, 1895–1905*, Princeton: Princeton University Press.

Frieden, Jeffry A. (1991), 'Invested interests: the politics of national economic policies in a world of global finance', *International Organization*, **45**, 425–51.

Frieden, Jeffry A. (1999), 'Actors and preferences in international relations', *Strategic Choice and International Relations*, David A. Lake and Robert Powell (eds), Princeton: Princeton University Press, pp. 39–76.

Frieden, Jeffry, A. and Ronald Rogowski (1996), 'The impact of the international economy on national policies: an analytical overview', in Robert O. Keohane and Helen V. Milner (eds), *Internationalization and Domestic Politics*, Cambridge: Cambridge University Press, pp. 25–47.

Friedman, J. (ed.) (1996), *The Rational Choice Controversy: Economic Models of Politics Reconsidered*, New Haven: Yale University Press.

Fudenberg, Drew and Eric Maskin (1986), 'The folk theorem in repeated games with discounting or with incomplete information', *Econometrica*, **54** (3), 533–54.

Gabel, Matthew J. (1998), *Interests and Integration: Market Liberalization, Public Opinion and European Union*, Ann Arbor: University of Michigan Press.

Garrett, Geoffrey M. (1992), 'International cooperation and institutional choice: the EC's internal market.' *International Organization*, **46**, 533–60.

Garrett, Geoffrey and Barry Weingast (1993), 'Ideas, interests and institutions: constructing the European Community's internal market', in Judith Goldstein and Robert Keohane (eds), *Ideas and Foreign Policy: Beliefs, Institutions, and Political Change*, Ithaca: Cornell University Press, pp. 173–206.

Gash, Norman (1972), *Sir Robert Peel: the Life of Sir Robert Peel after 1830*, London: Longman.

Gash, Norman (1982), 'The organization of the Conservative Party, 1832–1846, part 1: the parliamentary organization', *Parliamentary History*, 1, 137–59.

Gerschenkron, Alexander (1943), *Bread and Democracy in Germany*, Ithaca: Cornell University Press.

Gerschenkron, Alexander (1962), *Economic Backwardness in Historical Perspective*, Cambridge, Mass.: Harvard University Press.

Gibbard, Allan (1969), 'Social choice and the Arrow conditions', unpublished manuscript.

Gilligan, Michael J. (1997), *Empowering Exporters: Reciprocity, Delegation, and Collective Action in American Trade Policy*, Ann Arbor: University of Michigan Press.

Gleig, G. R. (1864), *The Life of Arthur, First Duke of Wellington*, London: People's Edition.

Golden, Miriam (1993), 'The dynamics of trade unionism and national economic performance', *American Political Science Review*, **87**, 439–54.

Goldstein, Judith (1989), 'The impact of ideas on trade policy: the origins of U.S. agricultural and manufacturing policies', *International Organization*, **43**, 31–71.

Goldstein, Judith (1993), *Ideas, Interests, and American Trade Policy*, Ithaca: Cornell University Press.

Goldstein, Judith and R. O. Keohane (eds) (1993a), *Ideas and Foreign Policy: Beliefs, Institutions, and Political Change*, Ithaca: Cornell University Press.

Goldstein, Judith and Robert O. Keohane (1993b), 'Ideas and foreign policy: an analytical framework', in Judith Goldstein and Robert O. Keohane (eds), *Ideas and Foreign Policy: Beliefs, Institutions, and Political Change*, Ithaca: Cornell University Press, pp. 3–30.

Goodin, Robert E. (ed.) (1995), *The Theory of Institutional Design*, Cambridge: Cambridge University Press.

Goodin, Robert E. (1996), 'Institutionalizing the public interest: the defense of deadlock and beyond', *American Political Science Review*, **90** (2), 331–43 (June).

Gorlin, Jacques J. (1990), 'Foreign trade and the constitution', *Foreign Policy and the Constitution*, Washington, DC: The AEI Press.

Gourevitch, Peter A. (1986), *Politics in Hard Times: Comparative Responses to International Economic Crisis*, Ithaca: Cornell University Press.

Gowa, Joanne (1994), *Allies, Adversaries, and International Trade*, Princeton: Princeton University Press.

Gray, P. (1999), *Famine, Land and Politics: British Government and Irish Society 1843–1850*, Dublin: Irish Academic Press.

Green, D. P. and I. Shapiro (1994), *Pathologies of Rational Choice Theory: A Critique of Applications in Political Science*, New Haven: Yale University Press.

Green, E. H. H. (1996), *The Crisis of Conservatism: The Politics, Economics and Ideology of the British Conservative Party, 1880–1914*, London: Routledge.

Grieco, Joseph (1988), 'Realist theory and the problems of international cooperation', *Journal of Politics*, **50**, 600–24.

Grieco, Joseph M. (1990), *Cooperation among Nations: Europe, America, and Non-Tariff Barriers to Trade*, Ithaca: Cornell University Press.

Grier, Kevin B. (ed.) (1993), Empirical studies of ideology and representation in American politics, *Public Choice*, **76** (Special Issue), 1–2 (June).

Groseclose, T., S. D. Levitt and Snyder (1999), 'Comparing interest group scores across time and chambers: adjusted ADA scores for the U.S. Congress', *American Political Science Review*, **93** (1), 33–50.

Grossman, Gene M. and Elhanan Helpman (1995), 'Trade wars and trade talks', *Journal of Political Economy*, **103** (4), 675–707.

Grossman, Herschel I. and Tae-joo Han (1993), 'A theory of war finance', *Defence Economics*, **4** (1), 33–44.

Haas, Peter (1992), *Knowledge, power, and international policy coordination*, *International Organization*, **46** *(Special Issue)*, (Winter) 1–36.

Haggard, Stephan and Beth A. Simmons (1987), Theories of international regimes', *International Organization* **41** (3), 491–517 (Summer).

Haggard, Stephan (1990), Pathways from the Periphery: The Politics of Growth in the Newly Industrializing Countries, Ithaca: Cornell University Press.

Halévy, E. (1961), *A History of the English People in the Nineteenth Century*, 6 vols. paperback edn. London: Ernest Benn. Originally published in French in 1923.

Hall, Peter A. (ed.) (1989), *The Political Power of Economic Ideas: Keynesianism across Nations*, Princeton: Princeton University Press.

Hall, Peter A. (1992), 'The movement from Keynesianism to monetarism: institutional analysis and British economic policy in the 1970s', in S. Steinmo, K. Thelen and F. Longstreth (eds), *Structuring Politics: Historical Institutionalism in Comparative Analysis*, Cambridge: Cambridge University Press, pp. 90–113.

Hall, Peter A. and Robert J. Franzese (1998), 'Mixed signals: central bank independence, coordinated wage-bargaining, and European Monetary Union', *International Organization*, **52** (3), 505–74.

Hallerberg, Mark (1996), 'Tax competition in Wilhelmine Germany and its implications for the European Union', *World Politics*, **48** (3): 324–57 (April).

Hamilton, Alexander, James Madison and John Jay (1787), *The Federalist*, edited by Jacob E. Cooke, Middletown, Conn: Wesleyan University Press, 1961.

Hansen, Wendy L. (1990), 'The International Trade Commission and the politics of protectionism', *American Political Science Review*, **84**, 21–46.

Heckman, J. J. and James M. Snyder (1997), 'Linear probability models of the demand for attributes with an empirical application to estimating the preferences of legislators', *RAND Journal of Economics*, **28** (0): S142–S189.

Heesom, A. (1973), '"Two perennial groups labelled Whig and Tory"; parties and party leaders in Early Victorian England', *Durham University Journal*, new series, **25**, 81–92.

Henderson, David (1986), *Innocence and Design: The Influence of Economic Ideas on Policy*, Oxford: Basil Blackwell.

Henderson, William O. (1939), *The Zollverein*, Cambridge: Cambridge University Press.

Herrigel, Gary (1993), 'Identity and institutions: the social construction of trade unions in nineteenth-century Germany and the United States', *Studies in American Political Development*, **7**, 371–93.

Hill, K. Q. (1998), 'Multiple-method Measurement of Legislators' Ideology', American Political Science Association Annual Meeting, Boston.

Hillman, Arye L. (1982), 'Declining industries and political-support protectionist motives', *American Economic Review*, **72**, 1180–7.

Hillman, Arye L., Ngo Van Long and Peter Moser (1995), 'Modelling reciprocal trade liberalization: the political-economy and national-welfare perspectives', *Swiss Journal of Economics and Statistics*, **131** (3), 503–15.

Hilton, B. (1988), *The Age of Atonement*, Oxford: Clarendon Press.

Hinich, Melvin J. and Michael C. Munger (1994), *Ideology and the Theory of Political Choice*, Ann Arbor: University of Michigan Press.

Hird, J. A. (1993), 'Congressional voting on superfund: self-interest or ideology?' *Public Choice*, **77**, 333–57.

Hood, Christopher (1994), *Explaining Economic Policy Reversals*, Buckingham, England: Open University Press.

Howe, Anthony (1984), *The Cotton Masters, 1830–1860*, Oxford: Oxford University Press.

Howe, Anthony (1997), *Free Trade and Liberal England, 1846–1946*, Oxford: Clarendon Press.

Howe, Anthony (1998), 'Free trade and the Victorians: free trade and its reception 1815–1960', in A. Marrison (ed.), *Freedom and Trade*, vol. 1; *Free Trade and its Reception, 1815–1960*, London: Routledge, pp. 164–83.

Huber, John D. (1996), *Rationalizing Parliament: Legislative Institutions and Party Politics in France*, Cambridge: Cambridge University Press.

Hunt, James C. (1974), 'Peasants, grain tariffs, and meat quotas: Imperial German protectionism reexamined', *Central European History*, **7**, 311–31.

Husted S. and M. Melvin (1993), *International Economics*, New York: Harper.

Imlah, Albert H. (1958), *Economic Elements in the Pax Britannica: Studies in British Foreign Trade in the Nineteenth Century*, Cambridge: Harvard University Press.

Inglis, B. (1966), *The Story of Ireland*, 2nd edn. London: Faber & Faber.

Irwin, Douglas A. (1988), 'Welfare effects of British free trade: debate and evidence from the 1840s', *Journal of Political Economy*, **96** (6), 1142–64.

Irwin, Douglas A. (1989), 'Political economy and Peel's Repeal of the Corn Laws', *Economics and Politics*, **1**, 41–59. Reprinted in Cheryl Schonhardt-Bailey, ed. (1997), *The Rise of Free Trade*, vol. 4, London: Routledge, pp. 287–308.

Irwin, Douglas A. (1991), Mercantilism as strategic trade policy: the Anglo-Dutch rivalry for the East India trade', *Journal of Political Economy* **99** (6), 1296–1314 (December).

Irwin, Douglas A. (1994), 'The political economy of free trade: voting in the British general election of 1906', *Journal of Law and Economics*, **37**, 75–108 (April).

Irwin, Douglas A. (1996), *Against the Tide: An Intellectual History of Free Trade*, Princeton: Princeton University Press.

Irwin, Douglas A. and R. S. Kroszner (1999), 'Interests, institutions, and ideology in securing policy change: the Republican conversion to trade liberalization after Smoot-Hawley', *Journal of Law and Economics*, **42**, 643–73 (October).

Iversen, Torben (1998), 'Wage bargaining, central bank independence, and the real effects of money', *International Organization*, **52** (3), 469–504.

Jacobsen, John Kurt (1995), 'Much ado about ideas: the cognitive factor in economic policy', *World Politics*, **47** (2), 283–310 (January).

Janda, Kenneth (1993), 'Comparative political parties: research and theory', in Ada W. Finifter (ed.), *Political Science: The State of the Discipline II*, Washington, DC: American Political Science Association pp. 163–92.

Jennings, L. J. (ed.) (1884), *The Correspondence and Diaries of the Late Right Honourable John Wilson Croker, LL.D., FRS, Secretary to the Admiralty from 1809 to 1830*, 3 vols., London: John Murray.

Jensen, Merrill (1950), *The New Nation: A History of the United States During the Confederation 1781–1789*, New York: Vintage Books.

Jones, Kent (1984), The political economy of voluntary export restraints', Kyklos 37, 82–101.

Kalt, J. P. and M. A. Zupan (1990), 'The apparent ideological behavior of legislators: testing for principal–agent slack in political institutions', *Journal of Law and Economics*, **33**, 103–31 (April).

Kennan, John and Raymond Riezman (1990), Optimal tariff equilibria with customs unions', *Canadian Journal of Economics* **23** (1), 70–83 (February).

Kennedy, Paul M. (1980), *The Rise of the Anglo-German Antagonism 1860–1914*, London: The Ashfield Press.

Keohane, Robert O. (1984), *After Hegemony: Discord in the World Political Economy*, Princeton: Princeton University Press.

Keohane, Robert O. (2000), 'Ideas part-way down (forum on [Alexander Wendt's] social theory of international politics)', *Review of International Studies*, **26**, 123–4.

Keohane, Robert O. and Helen V. Milner (1996), *Internationalization and Domestic Politics*, Cambridge: Cambridge University Press.

Kindleberger, Charles P. (1973), *The World in Depression 1929–1939*, Chicago: University of Chicago Press.

Kindleberger, Charles P. (1975), 'The rise of free trade in Western Europe, 1820–1875', *Journal of Economic History*, **35** (1), 20–55.

King, Anthony (1969), 'Political parties in Western democracies: some sceptical reflections', *Polity*, **2** (2), 111–41.

King, Gary, Robert O. Keohane and Sidney Verba (1994), *Designing Social Inquiry: Scientific Inference in Qualitative Research*, Princeton: Princeton University Press.

Kirchheimer, Otto (1966), 'The catch-all party'. Reprinted in Peter Mair, ed. (1990), *The West European Party System*, Oxford: Oxford University Press, pp. 50–60.

Kitch, Edmund W. (1981), 'Regulation and the American common market', in D. Tarlock (ed.), *Regulation, Federalism, and Interstate Commerce*. Mass: Oelgeschlager, Gunn and Hain, pp. 7–59.

Kitchen, Martin (1978), *The Political Economy of Germany 1815–1914*, London: Croom Helm Ltd.

Kiyono, Kazuharu, Masahiro Okuno-Fujiwara and Kaoru Ueda (1991), 'Industry specific interests and trade protection: a game theoretic analysis', *Economic Studies Quarterly*, **42** (4), 347–59 (December).

Koford, K. (1989), 'Dimensions in congressional voting', *American Political Science Review*, **83** (3), 949–62.

Krasner, Stephen D. (1976), 'State power and the structure of international trade', *World Politics*, **28** (3), 317–413 (April).

Krasner, Stephen D. (ed.) (1977), *International Regimes*, Princeton: Princeton University Press.

Krasner, Stephen D. (1994), 'Rules, regimes and the rise of Asia', Stanford University, manuscript.

Krasner, Stephen D. (1978), *Defending the National Interest*, Princeton: Princeton University Press.

Krehbiel, Keith (1991), *Information and Legislative Organization*, Ann Arbor: University of Michigan Press.

Krugman, Paul R. (1986), *Strategic Trade Policy and the New International Economics*, Cambridge: MIT Press.

Laitin, David D. et al. (1995), 'The qualitative–quantitative disputation: Gary King, Robert O. Keohane, and Sidney Verba's "Designing Social Inquiry: Scientific Inference in Qualitative Research"', *American Political Science Review*, **89** (2), 454–81.

Lake, David A. (1988), *Power, Protection, and Free Trade: International Sources of U.S. Commercial Strategy, 1887–1939*, Ithaca: Cornell University Press.

Lake, David A. and Robert Powell (eds) (1999a), *Strategic Choice and International Relations*, Princeton: Princeton University Press.

Lake, David A. and Robert Powell (1999b), 'International relations: a strategic-choice approach', in David A. Lake and Robert Powell (eds), *Strategic Choice and International Relations*, Princeton: Princeton University Press, pp. 3–38.

Lambi, Ivo Nikolai (1963), *Free Trade and Protection in Germany 1868–1879*, Wiesbaden: Franz Steiner Verlag GMBH.

Láng, Ludwig (1906), *Hundert Jahre Zollpolitik*, Alexander Rosen, trans. Wien und Leipzig: Kaiserliche und königliche Hof-Buchdruckerei und Hof-Verlags-Buchhandlung Carl Fromme.

Langewiesche, Dieter (1990), 'German liberalism in the Second Empire, 1871–1914', in Konrad H. Jarausch and Larry Eugene Jones (eds), *In Search of a Liberal Germany*, Oxford: Berg Publishers, pp. 217–36.

Langston, Thomas S. (1992), *Ideologues and Presidents*, Baltimore, MD: Johns Hopkins University Press.

LaPalombara, Joseph and Myron Weiner (1990), 'The origin of political parties', in Peter Mair, (ed.), *The West European Party System*, Oxford: Oxford University Press, pp. 25–30.

Lavergne, R. P. (1983), *The Political Economy of Tariffs: An Empirical Analysis*, Ontario: Academic Press Canada.

Le May, G. H. L. (1979), *The Victorian Constitution: Conventions, Usages and Contingencies*, New York: St. Martin's Press.

Leamer, Edward (1984), *Sources of International Comparative Advantage: Theory and Evidence*, Cambridge, Mass.: MIT Press.

Leblang, D. A. (1999), 'Domestic political institutions and exchange rate commitments in the developing world', *International Studies Quarterly*, **43** (4), 599–620.

Legro, Jeffrey W. (1996), 'Culture and preferences in the international cooperation two-step', *American Political Science Review*, **90** (1), 118–37 (March).

Lijphart, Arend (1990), 'Dimensions of ideology in European party systems', in Peter Mair (ed.), *The West European Party System*, Oxford: Oxford University Press, pp. 253–65.

Lindgren, Raymond E. (1959), *Norway–Sweden: Union, Disunion, and Scandinavian Integration*, Princeton: Princeton University Press.

Lipset, Seymour Martin and Stein Rokkan (1990), 'Cleavage structures, party systems, and voter alignments', in Peter Mair (ed.), *The West European Party System*, Oxford: Oxford University Press, abridged from pp. 1–64 *Party Systems and Voter Alignments: Cross-national Perspectives* (The Free Press, 1967).

Lipson, Charles (1984), 'International cooperation in economic and security affairs.' *World Politics*, **37**, 1–23 (October).

Lipson, Charles (1985), 'Bankers' dilemmas: private cooperation in rescheduling sovereign debts', *World Politics*, **38**, 200–25 (October).

Lohmann, Susanne (1992), 'Electoral cycles and international policy cooperation', *European Economic Review*, **36**, 1–19.

Lohmann, Susanne (1997), 'Linkage politics', *Journal of Conflict Resolution*, **41** (1), 38–68 (February).

Lohmann, Susanne and Sharyn O'Halloran (1994), 'Divided government and U.S. trade policy: theory and evidence', *International Organization*, **48**, 595–632.

Long, Ngo Van and Neil Vousden (1991), 'Protectionist responses and declining industries', *Journal of International Economics*, **30**, 87–103.

Lupia, Arthur and Matthew McCubbins (1998), *The Democratic Dilemma:*

Can Citizens Learn what they Need to Know? Cambridge: Cambridge University Press.

Lusztig, M. (1996), *Risking Free Trade: The Politics of Trade in Britain, Canada, Mexico, and the United States*, Pittsburgh, PA: University of Pittsburgh Press.

Magee, Stephen P. (1972), 'The welfare effects of restrictions on US trade', *Brookings Papers on Economic Activity*, 3, 645–701.

Magee, Stephen P. (1997), 'Endogenous protection: the empirical evidence', in Dennis C. Mueller (ed.), *Perspectives on Public Choice: A Handbook* , Cambridge: Cambridge University Press, pp. 526–61.

Magee, Stephen P., William A. Brock and Leslie Young (1989), *Black Hole Tariffs and Endogenous Policy Theory*, Cambridge: Cambridge University Press.

Mair, Peter (ed.) (1990), 'Introduction', *The West European Party System*, Oxford: Oxford University Press.

Manning, D. J. (ed.) (1980), *The Form of Ideology*, London: George Allen & Unwin Ltd.

Marsh, Peter T. (1999), *Bargaining on Europe: Britain and the First Common Market, 1860–1892*, New Haven: Yale University Press.

Martin, Lisa L. (1993), 'Credibility, costs, and institutions, cooperation on economic sanctions', *World Politics*, 45, 406–30.

Marvel, Howard P. and Edward J. Ray (1985), 'The Kennedy Round: evidence on the regulation of international trade in the USA', *American Economic Review*, 75, 190–7.

Marvel, Howard P. and Edward J. Ray (1987), 'Intraindustry trade: sources and effects on protection', *Journal of Political Economy*, 95, 1278–91.

Marx, Karl (1895/1964), *Class Struggles in France*, New York: International Publishers.

Mayer, Wolfgang (1984), 'Endogenous tariff formation', *American Economic Review*, 74, 970–85.

Mayer, Wolfgang and Jun Li (1994), 'Interest groups, electoral competition, and probabilistic voting for trade policies', *Economics and Politics*, 6 (1), 59–77 (March).

Mayer, Wolfgang and Raymond Riezman (1987), Endogenous choice of trade policy instruments', Journal of International Economics 23, 377–381.

McCloskey, Donald N. (1980), 'Magnanimous Albion: free trade and British national income, 1841–81', *Explorations in Economic History*, 17, 303–20.

McCord, Norman (1958), *The Anti-Corn Law League, 1838–1846*, London: George Allen & Unwin.

McCormick, James M. and Michael Black (1983), 'Ideology and senate voting on the Panama Canal treaties', *Legislative Studies Quarterly*, **8** (1), 45–63 (February).

McCusker, John M. and Russell Menard (1991), *The Economy of British America 1607–1789*, Chapel Hill, US and London, UK: The University of North Carolina Press.

McGillivray, Fiona (1997), 'Party discipline as a determinant of the endogenous formation of tariffs', *American Journal of Political Science*, **41**, 584–607.

McGillivray, Fiona and Alastair Smith (1997), 'Institutional determinants of trade policy', *International Interactions*, **23**, 119–43.

McKelvey, Richard, D. (1976), 'Intransitivities in multidimensional voting models and some implications for agenda control', *Journal of Economic Theory*, **12**, 472–82.

McKelvey, Richard, D. (1979), 'General conditions for global intransitivities in formal voting models', *Econometrica*, **47**, 1085–112.

McKeown, Timothy J. (1983), 'Hegemonic stability theory and 19th century tariff levels in Europe', *International Organization*, **37** (1), 73–92 (Winter).

McKeown, Timothy J. (1989), The politics of corn law repeal and theories of commercial policy', *British Journal of Political Science* **19**, 353–380.

McKeown, Timothy J. (1999). 'Case studies and the statistical worldview: review of King, Keohane, and Verba's "Designing Social Inquiry: Scientific Inference in Quantitative Research"', *International Organization*, **53** (1), 161–90.

McLean, Iain (1992), 'Rational choice and the Victorian voter', *Political Studies*, **40**, 496–515.

McLean, Iain (1995), 'Railway regulation as a test-bed of rational choice', in K. Dowding and D. King (eds), *Preferences, Institutions, and Rational Choice*, Oxford: Clarendon Press, pp. 134–61.

McLean, Iain (1998), 'Irish potatoes, Indian corn, and British politics: interests, ideology, heresthetics and the Repeal of the Corn Laws', in A. Dobson and J. Stanyer (eds), *Contemporary Political Studies 1998* (2 volumes, Nottingham: PSA) vol. 1, pp. 124–41.

McLean, Iain (2001), *Rational Choice in British Politics: An Analysis of Rhetoric and Manipulation from Peel to Blair*, Oxford: Oxford University Press.

McLean, Iain and Camilla Bustani (1999), 'Irish potatoes and British politics: interests, ideology, heresthetic and the Repeal of the Corn Laws', *Political Studies*, **47**, 817–36

McLean, Iain and C. Foster (1992), 'The political economy of regulation: interests, ideology, voters and the U.K. Regulation of Railways Act 1844', *Public Administration*, **70**, 313–31.

Menard, S. (1995), *Applied Logistic Regression Analysis*, Thousand Oaks, CA: Sage Publications.

Mészáros, István (1989), *The Power of Ideology*, Hemel Hempstead: Harvester Wheatsheaf.

Milner, Helen V. (1988), *Resisting Protectionism: Global Industries and the Politics of International Trade*, Princeton: Princeton University Press.

Milner, Helen V. (1997), *Interests, Institutions, and Information: Domestic Politics and International Relations*, Princeton: Princeton University Press.

Milner, Helen V. and B. Peter Rosendorff (1997), 'Democratic politics and international trade negotiations: elections and divided government as constraints on trade liberalization', *Journal of Conflict Resolution*, **41** (1), 117–46 (February).

Mitchell, W. C. (1993), 'The shape of public choice to come: some predictions and advice', *Public Choice* **77**, 133–44 (September).

Moe, Terry M. (1989), 'The politics of bureaucratic structure', in John E. Chubb and Paul E. Peterson (eds), *Can the Government Govern?* Washington, DC: The Brookings Institution.

Moeller, Robert G. (1981), 'Peasants and tariffs in the *Kaiserreich*: how backward were the *Bauern*?' *Agricultural History*, **55**, 370–84.

Mokyr, J. (1983), *Why Ireland Starved: A Quantitative and Analytical History of the Irish Economy, 1800–1850*, London: Allen & Unwin.

Monaghan, Frank (1935), *John Jay*, New York: Bobbs-Merrill.

Moore, Barrington (1966), *Social Origins of Dictatorship and Democracy*, Boston: Beacon Press.

Moore, Dennis C. (1965), 'The Corn Laws and high farming', *Economic History Review*, new series, **18**, 544–61.

Morley, J. (1903), *The Life of Richard Cobden*, London: T. Fisher Unwin.

Morley, J. (1908), *The Life of William Ewart Gladstone*, 2 vols., London: Edward Lloyd.

Mueller, Dennis C. (1989), *Public Choice II: A Revised Edition of Public Choice*, Cambridge: Cambridge University Press.

Nelson, Douglas (1988), 'Endogenous tariff theory: a critical survey', *American Journal of Political Science*, **21**, 285–300.

Nettels, Curtis P. (1962), *The Emergence of a National Economy 1775–1815*, New York: Holt, Weinhart and Winston.

Nevins, Allan (1927), *The American States During and After the Revolution: 1775–1815*, New York: Macmillan.

Newbould, Ian (1985), 'Whiggery and the growth of Party 1830–1841: organization and the challenge of reform', *Parliamentary History*, **4**, 137–56.

Nicholson, Michael (1992), *Rationality and the Analysis of International Conflict*, Cambridge: Cambridge University Press.

North, Douglass C. (1966), *The Economic Growth of the United States 1790–1860*, New York: W.W. Norton and Company.

North, Douglass C. (1981), *Structure and Change in Economic History*, New York: Norton.

North, Douglass C. (1990), *Institutions, Institutional Change and Economic Performance*, Cambridge: Cambridge University Press.

North, Douglass C. (1994), 'Economic performance through time', *American Economic Review*, **84** (3), 359–68 (June).

Nye, John Vincent (1990), 'Revisionist tariff history and the theory of hegemonic stability', St. Louis: Washington University Political Economy Working Paper, April.

Nye, John Vincent (1991), 'Changing French trade conditions, national welfare, and the 1860 Anglo-French Treaty of Commerce', *Explorations in Economic History*, **28** (4), 460–77.

O'Donnell, Guillermo (1978), 'State and alliances in Argentina, 1956–1976', *Journal of Development Studies*, **15** (1), 3–32 (October).

O'Halloran, Sharyn (1994), *Politics, Process and American Trade Policy*, Ann Arbor: University of Michigan Press.

Olson, Mancur (1965), *The Logic of Collective Action*, Cambridge, Mass.: Harvard University Press.

Olson, Mancur (1982), *The Rise and Decline of Nations*, New Haven: Yale University Press.

O'Rourke, Kevin H. and Jeffrey G. Williamson (1999), *Globalization and History: The Evolution of a Nineteenth-century Atlantic Economy*, Cambridge: The MIT Press.

Ostrom, Elinor (1990), *Governing the Commons: The Evolution of Institutions for Collective Action*, Cambridge: Cambridge University Press.

Oye, Kenneth (ed.) (1986), *Cooperation Under Anarchy*, Princeton: Princeton University Press.

Oye, Kenneth (1992), *Economic Discrimination and Political Exchange*, Princeton: Princeton University Press.

Pahre, Robert (1994), 'Multilateral cooperation in an iterated prisoners' dilemma', *Journal of Conflict Resolution*, **38** (2), 326–52 (June).

Pahre, Robert (1995), 'Wider and deeper: the links between expansion and integration in the European Union', in Thomas Bernauer, Gerald Schneider and Patricia A. Weitsman (eds), *Towards a New Europe: Stops and Starts in European Integration*, Boulder: Praeger/Greenwood Press, pp. 111–36.

Pahre, Robert (1997a), 'Endogenous domestic institutions in two-level games and parliamentary oversight of the European Union', *Journal of Conflict Resolution*, **41** (1), 147–74 (February).

Pahre, Robert (1997b), 'The rise of free trade in Britain', in Cheryl

Schonhardt-Bailey (ed.) (1997b), *The Rise of Free Trade*, vol. 4, London: Routledge, pp. 570–96.

Pahre, Robert (1998), 'Reactions and reciprocity: tariffs and trade liberalization in 1815–1914', *Journal of Conflict Resolution*, **42** (4), 467–92 (August).

Pahre, Robert (1999), *Leading Questions: How Hegemony Affects the International Political Economy*, Ann Arbor: University of Michigan Press.

Pahre, Robert (2001a), 'Divided government and international cooperation in Austria-Hungary, Sweden-Norway, the *Zollverein*, and the European Union', *European Union Politics* **2**(2), 131–62.

Pahre, Robert (2001b), 'Most-favored-nation clauses, domestic politics, and clustered negotiations, *International Organization*, forthcoming.

Pahre, Robert and P. Papayoanou (1997), 'Using formal theory to link international and domestic politics', *Journal of Conflict Resolution*, **41** (1), 4–11 (February).

Palairet, Michael (1997), *The Balkan Economies c. 1800–1914: Evolution without Development*, Cambridge: Cambridge University Press.

Papayoanou, Paul (1999), *Power Ties*, Ann Arbor: University of Michigan Press.

Peel, Sir Robert (1856–7), *Memoirs*, Earl of Stanhope and E. Cardwell (eds) (2 volumes), London: John Murray.

Peltzman, Sam (1976), 'Toward a more general theory of regulation', *Journal of Law and Economics*, **19**: 211–39.

Peltzman, Sam (1984), 'Constituent interest and congressional voting', *Journal of Law and Economics*, **27**, 181–210.

Pincus, J. J. (1975), 'Pressure groups and the pattern of tariffs', *Journal of Political Economy*, **53**, 757–78.

Pincus, Jonathan J. (1977), *Pressure Groups and Politics in Antebellum Tariffs*, New York: Columbia University Press.

Plamenatz, John (1970), *Ideology*, London: Pall Mall Press Ltd.

Pollins, Brian M. (1989), 'Does trade still follow the flag?' *American Political Science Review*, **83** (2), 465–80 (June).

Poole, K. T. and H. Rosenthal (1991), 'Patterns of congressional voting', *American Journal of Political Science*, **35** (1), 228–78.

Poole, K. T. and H. Rosenthal (1997), *Congress: A Political-economic History of Roll Call Voting*, New York: Oxford University Press.

Powell, Robert (1991), Absolute and relative gains in international relations theory', *American Political Science Review* **85** (4), 1303–1320.

Prest, J. (1972), *Lord John Russell*, London: Macmillan.

Puhle, Hans-Jürgen (1978), 'Conservatism in modern German history', *Journal of Contemporary History*, **13**, 689–720.

Puhle, Hans-Jürgen (1986), 'Lords and peasants in the Kaiserreich', in Robert G. Moeller (ed.), *Peasants and Lords in Modern Germany: Recent Studies in Agricultural History*, Winchester: Allen and Unwin, pp. 81–109.

Quirk, Paul (1988), 'In defense of the politics of ideas', *The Journal of Politics*, **50** (1), 31–41.

Rakove, Jack N. (1990), 'Making foreign policy – the view from 1787', *Foreign Policy and the Constitution*, Washington, DC: The AEI Press.

Rakove, Jack N. (1996), *Original Meanings: Politics and Ideas in the Making of the Constitution*, New York: Alfred A. Knopf.

Ratcliffe, Barry M. (1978), 'The tariff reform campaign in France, 1831–1836', *Journal of European Economic History*, **7** (1), 61–138 (Spring).

Ray, Edward J. (1974), 'The optimum commodity tariff and tariff rates in developed and less developed countries', *Review of Economics and Statistics*, **56**, 369–77.

Ray, Edward J. and Howard P. Marvel (1984), 'The pattern of protection in the industrialized world', *Review of Economics and Statistics*, **66**, 452–58.

Remmer, K. L. (1997), 'Theoretical decay and theoretical development: the resurgence of institutional analysis', *World Politics*, **50** (1), 34–61.

Reynolds, A. (1999), 'Women in the legislatures and executives of the world: knocking at the highest glass ceiling', *World Politics*, **51** (4), 547–72.

Richardson, Martin (1993), 'Endogenous protection and trade diversion', *Journal of International Economics*, **34**, 309–24.

Riker, William H. (1962), *The Theory of Political Coalitions*, New Haven: Yale University Press.

Riker, William H. (1980), 'Implications from the disequilibrium of majority rule for the study of institutions', *American Political Science Review*, **74**, 432–46.

Riker, William H. (1982), *Liberalism against Populism*, San Francisco: W. H. Freeman.

Riker, William H. (1986), *The Art of Political Manipulation*, New Haven: Yale University Press.

Risse-Kappen, Thomas (1994), 'Ideas do not float freely: transnational coalitions, domestic structures, and the end of the Cold War', *International Organization*, **48** (2), 185–214 (Spring).

Ritter, Gerhard A. (1990), 'The social bases of the German political parties, 1867–1920', in Karl Rohe (ed.), *Elections, Parties and Political Traditions: Social Foundations of German Parties and Party Systems, 1867–1987*, Oxford: Berg Publishers, pp. 27–52.

Rogowski, Ronald (1987), 'Trade and the variety of democratic institutions', *International Organization*, **41**, 203–24.

Rogowski, Ronald (1989), *Commerce and Coalitions: How Trade Affects Domestic Political Alignments*, Princeton: Princeton University Press.

Rogowski, Ronald (1997), 'Pork, patronage, and protection in democracies: how differences in electoral systems govern the extraction of rents', unpublished manuscript.

Rogowski, Ronald (1999), 'Institutions as constraints on strategic choice', in David A. Lake and Robert Powell (eds), *Strategic Choice and International Relations*, Princeton: Princeton University Press, pp. 115–36.

Rohrlich, P. E. (1987), 'Economic culture and policy making: the cognitive analysis of economic policy making', *International Organization*, **41** (1), 61–92.

Rosenberg, Hans (1967), *Grosse Depression und Bismarckzeit*, Berlin: W. de Gruyter.

Ruggie, John Gerard (1983), 'International negotiations, transactions and change: embedded liberalism in the postwar economic order', in S. D. Krasner (ed.) (1983), *International Regimes*, Ithaca: Cornell University Press, 195–231.

Ruggie, John Gerard (ed.) (1993), Multilateralism Matters: The Theory and Practice of an Institutional Form, New York: Columbia University Press.

Ruppel, Fred J. and Earl D. Kellogg (eds) (1991), *National and Regional Self-sufficiency Goals*, London: Lynne Rienner Publishers.

Russell, A. K. (1973), *Liberal Landslide: The General Election of 1906*, Hamden, Conn.: Archon Books.

Sabatier, Paul A. and Hank C. Jenkins-Smith (eds) (1993), *Policy Change and Learning: An Advocacy Coalition Approach*, Boulder: Westview Press.

Sartori, G. (1990), 'The sociology of parties: a critical review', in Peter Mair (ed.) (1990), *The West European Party System*, Oxford: Oxford University Press, 150–184.

Satterthwaite, Mark A. (1975), 'Strategy-proofness and Arrow's conditions: existence and correspondence theorems for voting procedures and social welfare functions', *Journal of Economic Theory*, **10**, 187–217.

Schattschneider, E. E. (1960), *The Semisovereign People: A Realist's View of Democracy*, New York: Holt, Rinehart & Winston.

Schofield, N. (1976), 'Instability of simple dynamic games', *Review of Economic Studies*, **45**, 575–94.

Schonhardt-Bailey, Cheryl (1991a), ' Lessons in lobbying for free trade in 19th century Britain: to concentrate or not', *American Political Science Review*, **85** (1), 37–58.

Schonhardt-Bailey, Cheryl (1991b), 'Specific factors, capital markets, port-folio diversification, and free trade: domestic determinants of the Repeal of the Corn Laws', *World Politics*, **43** (4), 545–69.

Schonhardt-Bailey, Cheryl (1991c), 'A model of trade policy liberalization: looking inside the British "hegemon" of the nineteenth century', University of California, Los Angeles: Ph.D. dissertation.

Schonhardt-Bailey, Cheryl (1994), 'Linking constituency interests to legis-lative voting behavior: the role of district economic and electoral com-position in the Repeal of the Corn Laws', *Parliamentary History*, **13**, 86–118. Reprinted in Cheryl Schonhardt-Bailey (ed) (1997), vol. 4, *The Rise of Free Trade*, London: Routledge, pp. 135–71.

Schonhardt-Bailey, Cheryl (1997a), 'Introduction', *Rise of Free Trade*, vol. 1, London: Routledge.

Schonhardt-Bailey, Cheryl (ed.) (1997b), *The Rise of Free Trade*, 4 vol., London: Routledge.

Schonhardt-Bailey, Cheryl (1998a), 'Parties and interests in the "Marriage of iron and rye"', *British Journal of Political Science*, **28**, 291–330.

Schonhardt-Bailey, Cheryl (1998b), 'Interests, ideology and politics: agri-cultural trade policy in nineteenth-century Britain and Germany' in Andrew Marrison (ed), *Free Trade and Its Reception, 1815–1960, Freedom and Trade*, London: Routledge, pp. 63–81.

Schonhardt-Bailey, Cheryl (1999), *Ideas and Interests in Parliamentary Debates on Trade Policy, 1814–1846*. A CD-ROM (400 Mb) of selected British Parliamentary Debates, with an introduction and table of contents with links to specific debates (Bell & Howell Multimedia). Project funded by the Nuffield Foundation.

Schonhardt-Bailey, Cheryl (2000), 'Ideology, party and interests in the British Parliament of 1841–1847', paper prepared for delivery at the Annual Meeting of the American Political Science Association, Washington, DC.

Sebenius, James K. (1983), 'Negotiation arithmetic: adding and subtracting issues and parties', *International Organization*, **37** (2), 281–316 (Spring).

Sen, A. K. (1981), *Poverty and Famines: An Essay on Entitlement and Deprivation*, Oxford: Clarendon Press.

Senior, Nassau (1843), 'Free trade and retaliation', *Edinburgh Review*, **78**. Reprinted in Cheryl Schonhardt-Bailey (ed.) (1996), *Free Trade: the Repeal of the Corn Laws*, Bristol: Thoemmes Press, pp. 272–85.

Sheehan, James J. (1978), *German Liberalism in the Nineteenth Century*, Chicago: University of Chicago Press.

Shepherd, James and Gary W. Walton (1972), *Shipping, Maritime Trade, and the Economic Development of Colonial North Americas*. New York: Cambridge University Press.

Shepsle, Kenneth A. (1979), 'Institutional arrangements and equilibrium in multidimensional voting models', *American Journal of Political Science*, **23**, 27–59.

Shepsle, Kenneth A. (1985), 'Comment', in Roger Noll (ed.), *Regulatory Policy and the Social Sciences*, Berkeley: University of California Press, pp. 231–9.

Shepsle, Kenneth, A. (1989), 'Studying institutions: some lessons from the rational choice approach', *Journal of Theoretical Politics*, **1**, 131–49.

Shepsle, Kenneth, A. and Barry R. Weingast (1984), 'Uncovered sets and sophisticated voting outcomes with implications for agenda control', *American Journal of Political Science*, **28**, 49–74.

Shepsle, Kenneth A. and Barry R. Weingast (eds) (1995), *Positive Theories of Congressional Institutions*, Ann Arbor: University of Michigan.

Shugart, Matthew S. and John M. Carey (1992), *Presidents and Assemblies: Constitutional Design and Electoral Dynamics*, Cambridge: Cambridge University Press.

Sikkink, Kathryn (1991), *Ideas and Institutions: Developmentalism in Brazil and Argentina*, Ithaca: Cornell University Press.

Silverman, Lawrence (1985), 'The ideological mediation of party-political responses to social change', *European Journal of Political Research*, **13**, 69–93.

Simmons, Beth A. (1994), *Who Adjusts?* Princeton: Princeton University Press.

Singer, J. David (1961), 'The level-of-analysis problem in international relations', in Klaus Knorr and Sidney Verba (eds), *The International System: Theoretical Essays*, Princeton: Princeton University Press, pp. 77–92.

Siverson, Randolph M., (ed.) (1997), *Strategic Politicians, Institutions, and Foreign Policy*, Ann Arbor: Michigan University Press.

Skocpol, Theda and Kenneth Finegold (1982), 'State capacity and economic intervention in the early new deal', *Political Science Quarterly*, **97** (2), 255–78.

Skocpol, Theda (1985), 'Bringing the state back in: strategies of analysis in current research', in Peter B. Evans et al. (eds), *Bringing the State Back In*, New York: Cambridge University Press, pp. 3–37.

Smith, Alastair and David R. Hayes (1997), 'The shadow of the polls: electoral effects on international agreements', *International Interactions* **23** (1), 27–108.

Smith, Michael Stephen (1980), *Tariff Reform in France 1860–1900: The Politics of Economic Interest*, Ithaca: Cornell University Press.

Snidal, Duncan (1986), 'The game *theory* of international politics', in

Kenneth Oye (ed.), *Corporation Under Anarchy*, Princeton: Princeton University Press, pp. 25–57.

Snidal, Duncan (1991), Relative Gains and the Pattern of International Cooperation', *American Political Science Review* **85** (3), 701–726 (September).

Snyder, James M. (1992), 'Committee power, structure-induced equilibria, and roll call votes', *American Journal of Political Science*, **36** (1), 1–30.

Stegmann, Dirk (1993), 'Between economic interests and radical nationalism: attempts to found a new right-wing party in Imperial Germany, 1887–94', in L. E. Jones and J. Retallack (eds), *Between Reform, Reaction, and Resistance: Studies in the History of German Conservatism from 1789–1945*, Oxford: Berg Publishers, pp. 157–85.

Stein, Arthur A. (1984), 'The hegemon's dilemma: Great Britain, the United States, and the international economic order', *International Organization*, **38** (2), 355–86 (Spring).

Steinmo, Sven, K. A. Thelen and F. Longstreth (1992), *Structuring Politics: Historical Institutionalism in Comparative Analysis*, Cambridge Studies in Comparative Politics, Cambridge: Cambridge University Press.

Stevenson, J. and Quinault, R. (eds) (1974), *Popular Protest and Public Order: Six Studies in British History, 1790–1920*, London: Allen & Unwin.

Stewart, Robert (1971), *The Politics of Protection: Lord Derby and the Protectionist Party, 1841–1852*, Cambridge: Cambridge University Press.

Stigler, George J. (1971), 'The theory of economic regulation', *Bell Journal of Economic and Management Science*, **3** (2), 3–21.

Stolper, Wolfgang F. and Samuelson, Paul A. (1941), 'Protection and real wages', *Review of Economic Studies*, **9**, 58–73.

Strachey, L and Fulford, R. (eds) (1938), *The Greville Diaries*, 7 vols., London: Macmillan.

Sykes, Alan (1979), *Tariff Reform in British Politics 1903–1913*, Oxford: Clarendon Press.

Takacs, Wendy E. (1981), 'Pressures for protectionism: an empirical analysis', *Economic Inquiry*, **19**, 687–93.

Taussig, Frank (1892), *Tariff History of the United States*, New York, US and London, UK: The Knickerbocker Press.

Thelen, Kathleen and Sven Steinmo (1992), 'Historical institutionalism in comparative politics', in Sven Steinmo, K. A. Thelen and F. Longstreth (eds), *Structuring Politics: Historical Institutionalism in Comparative Analysis*, Cambridge: Cambridge University Press, pp. 1–32.

Thompson, J. M. (1983), *Louis Napoleon and the Second Empire*, New York: Columbia University Press.

Thompson, N. (1986), *Wellington after Waterloo*, London: Routledge.

Tipton, Frank B. (1976), *Regional Variations in the Economic Development of Germany During the Nineteenth Century*, Middletown: Wesleyan University Press.

Tirrell, Sarah Rebecca (1951), *German Agrarian Politics After Bismarck's Fall: The Formation of the Farmers' League*, New York: Columbia University Press.

Tollison, Robert D. and Thomas D. Willett (1979), 'An economic theory of mutually advantageous issue linkages in international negotiations', *International Organization*, **33**, 425–49 (Autumn).

Torrens, Robert (1844), 'Letter to Nassau William Senior, Esq., in reply to the article "*Free Trade and Retaliation*"', from *The Budget on Commercial and Colonial Policy*, reprinted in Cheryl Schonhardt-Bailey (ed.) (1996), *Free Trade: the Repeal of the Corn Laws*, Bristol: Thoemmes Press, pp. 321–30.

Trebilcock, Clive (1981), *The Industrialization of the Continental Powers, 1780–1914*, London, UK and New York, US: Longman.

Trefler, Daniel (1993), 'Trade liberalization and the theory of endogenous protection: an econometric study of U.S. import policy', *Journal of Political Economy*, **101** (1), 138–60.

Tsebelis, George (1990), *Nested Games: Rational Choice in Comparative Politics*, Berkeley: University of California Press.

Tsebelis, George (1995), 'Decision making in political systems: veto players in presidentialism, parliamentarism, multicameralism, and multiparty-ism', *British Journal of Political Science*, **25**, 289–326.

Tsebelis, George and Jeanette Money (1997), *Bicameralism*, Cambridge: Cambridge University Press.

Urofsky, Melvin I. (1988), *A March of Liberty: A Constitutional History of the United States*, New York: Knopf.

Uslaner, E. M. (1999), *The Movers and the Shirkers: Representatives and Ideologues in the Senate*, Ann Arbor: University of Michigan Press.

Vascik, George (1993), 'Agrarian conservatism in Wilhelmine Germany: Diederich Hahn and the Agrarian League', in L. E. Jones and J. Retallack (eds), *Between Reform, Reaction, and Resistance: Studies in the History of German Conservatism from 1789–1945*, Oxford: Berg Publishers, pp. 229–60.

Vasquez, John A. (1997), 'The realist paradigm and degenerative versus progressive research programs: an appraisal of neotraditional research on Waltz's balancing proposition', *American Political Science Review*, **91** (4), 899–912 (December).

Verdier, Daniel (1994), *Democracy and International Trade: Britain, France, and the United States, 1860–1990*, Princeton: Princeton University Press.

Vomáková, Vera (1963), 'Österreich und der Deutsche Zollverein', *Historica*, **5**, 109–46.

von Bazant, Johann (1894), *Die Handelspolitik Österreich-Ungarns 1875 bis 1892 in ihrem Verhältnis zum Deutschem Reiche und zu dem westlichen Europa*, Leipzig: Verlag von Duncker & Humblot.

von Mettenheim, Kurt (1997), *Presidential Institutions and Democratic Politics: Comparing Regional and National Contexts*, Baltimore, MD and London, UK: Johns Hopkins University Press.

Wallerstein, Immanuel (1983), *Historical Capitalism*, London: Verso.

Wallerstein, Immanuel (1994), 'Crises, the world-economy, the movements, and the ideologies', I. Wallerstein (ed.), *Unthinking Social Science*, Cambridge: Polity, pp. 23–37.

Wallerstein, Michael (1987), 'Unemployment, collective bargaining and the demand for protection', *American Journal of Political Science*, **31**, 729–52 (November).

Walton, Gary M. and James F. Shepherd (1979), *The Economic Rise of Early America*, New York: Cambridge University Press.

Waltz, Kenneth N. (1959), *Man, the State and War: A Theoretical Analysis*, New York: Columbia University Press.

Waltz, Kenneth N. (1979), *Theory of International Politics*, Reading, Mass: Addison-Wesley.

Waxman, Chaim I. (ed.) (1968), *The End of Ideology Debate*, New York: Funk and Wagnalls.

Webb, Steven B. (1982), 'Agricultural protection in Wilhelminian Germany: forging an empire with pork and rye', *Journal of Economic History*, **42**, 309–26.

Weck-Hannemann, Hannelore (1990), 'Protectionism in direct democracy', *Journal of Institutional and Theoretical Economics/Zeitschrift für die gesamte Staatswissenschaft*, **146**, 389–418.

Wehler, Hans-Ulrich (1985), *The German Empire, 1871–1918*, Oxford: Berg Publishers.

Weitowitz, Rolf (1978), *Deutsche Politik und Handelspolitik unter Reichskanzler Leo von Caprivi 1890–1894*, Düsseldorf: Droste Verlag.

Werner, Yvonne Maria (1989), Svensk-tyska fvrbindelser kring sekelskiftet 1900. Politik och ekonomi vid tillkomsten av 1906 ers svensk-tyska handels- och sjvfartstraktat. Lund: Lund University Press.

Wilcox, C. and A. Clausen (1991), 'The dimensionality of roll-call voting reconsidered', *Legislative Studies Quarterly*, **16** (3), 393–406.

Williams, Judith Blow (1972), *British Commercial Policy and Trade Expansion 1750–1850*, Oxford: Clarendon Press.

Winters, L. Alan (1990), 'Digging for victory: agricultural policy and national security', *The World Economy*, **13** (2), 170–90 (June).

Woodham-Smith, C. (1991), *The Great Hunger: Ireland 1845–1849*, Harmondsworth: Penguin. Originally published in 1962.

Woods, Ngaire (1995), 'Economic ideas and international relations: beyond rational neglect', *International Studies Quarterly*, **39** (2), 161–80 (June).

Yarbrough, Beth V. and Robert M. Yarbrough (1986), Reciprocity, bilateralism, and economic 'hostages': self-enforcing agreements in international trade', *International Studies Quarterly* **30**, 7–21.

Yee, Albert S. (1996), 'The causal effects of ideas on policies', *International Organization*, **50** (1), 69–108 (Winter).

Yee, Albert S. (1997), 'Thick rationality and the missing "Brute Fact": the limits of rationalist incorporations of norms and ideas', *Journal of Politics* **59** (4), 1001–39.

Zornow, William F. (1954a), 'Massachusetts tariff policies 1775–1789', *Essex Institute Historical Collections*, **90**, 194–215.

Zornow, William F. (1954b), 'The tariff policies of Virginia 1775–1789', *Virginia Magazine of History*, **62**, 306–19.

Zornow, William F. (1955), 'Tariff policies in South Carolina 1775–1789', *The South Carolina Historical Magazine*, **55**, 31–45.

Zornow, William F. (1956), 'New York tariff policies 1775–1789', *Proceedings of the New York State Historical Association*, **37**, 40–61.

Index